SWAGGER

Super Bowls, Brass Balls, and Footballs—
A Memoir

Jimmy Johnson
and Dave Hyde

SCRIBNER

New York   London   Toronto   Sydney   New Delhi

Scribner
An Imprint of Simon & Schuster, Inc.
1230 Avenue of the Americas
New York, NY 10020

First Scribner hardcover edition November 2022

SCRIBNER and design are registered trademarks of The Gale Group, Inc., used under license by Simon & Schuster, Inc., the publisher of this work.

For information about special discounts for bulk purchases, please contact Simon & Schuster Special Sales at 1-866-506-1949 or business@simonandschuster.com.

The Simon & Schuster Speakers Bureau can bring authors to your live event. For more information or to book an event, contact the Simon & Schuster Speakers Bureau at 1-866-248-3049 or visit our website at www.simonspeakers.com.

Interior design by Jaime Putorti

Insert photograph credits: 1: University of Arkansas; 2–3, 5–7, 10, 14: Associated Press; 4: David Loo/*The Dallas Morning News*; 8–9, 13, 15, 17–22: courtesy of the author; 11–12: copyright of Miami Dolphins Ltd. All rights reserved. Reproduced with the permission of Miami Dolphins, Ltd.; 16: FOX Sports

Manufactured in the United States of America

1 3 5 7 9 10 8 6 4 2

Library of Congress Cataloging-in-Publication Data

Names: Johnson, Jimmy, 1943– author. | Hyde, Dave, 1961– author.
Title: Swagger : Super Bowls, brass balls, and footballs : a memoir / Jimmy Johnson and Dave Hyde.
Description: First Scribner hardcover edition. | New York, N.Y.: Scribner, 2022. | Includes index.
Identifiers: LCCN 2022032323 (print) | LCCN 2022032324 (ebook) | ISBN 9781668008621 (hardcover) | ISBN 9781668008645 (ebook)
Subjects: LCSH: Johnson, Jimmy, 1943– | Football coaches—United States—Biography.
Classification: LCC GV939.J613 A3 2022 (print) | LCC GV939.J613 (ebook) | DDC 796.332092—dc23/eng/20220720
LC record available at https://lccn.loc.gov/2022032323
LC ebook record available at https://lccn.loc.gov/2022032324

ISBN 978-1-6680-0862-1
ISBN 978-1-6680-0864-5 (ebook)

To Brent, Chad, and Rhonda —
you made my life complete

CONTENTS

SWAGGER

1

WELCOME TO MY WORLD

The only road into the Florida Keys runs south out of Miami, the mainland releasing its grip over an unremarkable, twenty-mile stretch through the Everglades. The road is lined first by Australian pines, as tacky an outsider as some incoming tourists. Concrete telephone poles soon accompany the drive, mile after mile, dotted on occasion by an oversized osprey or eagle nest on top.

Wet landmarks like Jewfish Creek and Lake Surprise offer only a hint of the rare world ahead, the one I've made home, the one coaches, team executives, and franchise owners come to visit under the influence of ambition and obsession like I once had.

A bridge announces the entrance to Key Largo, the largest in the necklace of coral-floored islands. It's here, just a few miles south, where I often meet a visitor at my restaurant, Jimmy Johnson's Big Chill. Maybe it's for lunch. Maybe a drink. There's always a cold Heineken Light waiting there for me, ready to be poured over ice, just the way I like one.

If the conversation is good, if a coach or general manager has more questions, if I'm still in a mood for company, we'll drive fifteen minutes down U.S. 1 to Islamorada and my six acres of paradise tucked against the Atlantic Ocean. It's here that I've created the life I want in retirement—a boating and fishing playground where the ocean view ensures I'll never miss the sight of a locker room. It's also here, while throwing a pre-training-camp party for my Miami Dolphins years back, that Rhonda and I snuck upstairs and got married, both of us in bathing suits, the ceremony performed in the kitchen by the team's director of security, Stu Weinstein. Rhonda and I wrestle with whether the date was July 17 or 19, though it hardly matters. We don't celebrate the anniversary, just as I don't celebrate birthdays, holidays, or just about any other calendar event. When we returned to the team party that day, I announced, "By the way, Rhonda and I just got married . . . Let's party!"

These days, my home parties are quieter, more private affairs. Bill Belichick has visited most off-seasons for decades. It's here at my home, sometimes in the cabana, sometimes in the boat, typically with a cold drink, that Bill and I have discussed the inner wiring of a football team. Drafts. Contracts. Handling success—and even more success, in his case. We once discussed how pushing assistant coaches to be better was a necessary step after a Super Bowl win. Another time we talked about drafting players with little chance of making his championship roster—a similar problem to one I had at the end of my coaching time in Dallas. Those players often made other teams' rosters.

"You don't want to draft players for other teams," I said. "Those picks are like money. Save them if you don't need them. Trade them into the next year."

Bill continues to be a master at that.

Me? I enjoy life on the other side of the finish line. I'm out of the arena. I have no agenda. I don't even have a schedule most days. Often, my big decision after I get up around 5 a.m. and check my computer bridge game is if the weather is good for fishing.

Maybe my having no dog in the fight is what brings these visitors to the Keys—that and the fact I once built what they're trying to build now. I recognize the look, remember the chase, see in their eyes the cold clarity of a consumed life. That's what brings them here. They're hunting for a thought, an idea, anything new to take back home to help a decision in April win a fourth quarter in December.

Football is weekend fun for much of America, but for these visitors it's blood. They arrive with the questions that once got me out of bed, full of energy, around four in the morning without an alarm clock. Each off-season brings new faces. Through the years, nearly a dozen team owners, from New Orleans's Tom Benson to the Los Angeles Chargers' Dean Spanos, have visited the Keys to discuss what to look for in a coach or general manager, how to structure an organization— how to essentially be as successful with their football teams as they are in business.

The Carolina Panthers' Scott Fitterer and the Miami Dolphins' Mike Tannenbaum were the most recent general managers to discuss building teams and analyzing talent. Countless college coaches have come. Sometimes I talked with a college coach on the way up to the NFL, like Chip Kelly, when he went from the University of Oregon to the Philadelphia Eagles, or Kliff Kingsbury at Texas Tech, before he went to the Arizona Cardinals. There was a regular list of subjects. Hiring a staff. Leading a team of men. The difference of college football versus the NFL.

In the days before the 2021 season, Carolina coach Matt Rhule and his son spent the day fishing on my thirty-nine-foot SeaVee boat, *Three Rings*, discussing the five characteristics that mattered to me in evaluating talent—a guideline, really, because judging players is more art form than measuring numbers.

After Carolina, Jacksonville coach Urban Meyer sent a plane to Marathon and flew me in before the 2021 season to talk with his new staff. This was before all the trouble to come for Urban that season. I've rarely left the Keys the past two decades except for my *FOX*

NFL Sunday show in Los Angeles or some corporate speech—and then only grudgingly. Urban and I knew each other from working at FOX, with him first visiting me years ago as the Ohio State coach. Back then, we discussed balancing football and family, a subject we both struggled over with our addictive football DNA. I failed with that struggle at times. It contributed to some dark times. It's also led to the happiest time of my life, this retirement in the Keys with Rhonda and my relationships with my sons, Brent and Chad, and their families.

Often my talks with these visiting coaches or sports executives cross over from football to any sport or business. New York Knicks coach Tom Thibodeau kept my ideas for evaluating talent on a whiteboard in his office for quick reference under the heading "Can He Play?" San Antonio Spurs general manager R. C. Buford visited Islamorada one year to hear how I created the Draft Value Chart, which helped us build our team in Dallas and has been used the past few decades by NFL front offices. R.C. wanted to create a similar chart for the NBA. It didn't work in the NBA's two-round draft, with exaggerated value in the first few picks and the league's smaller team size. But we talked of building teams and managing personalities, and he returned in 2015 when his great Spurs team was aging. We discussed succession throughout an organization. It wasn't just about the players. He wanted to be prepared, if needed, for when legendary coach Gregg Popovich retired. He asked about the issues surrounding my following NFL greats Tom Landry in Dallas and Don Shula in Miami.

I mentioned my three qualities for hiring coaches: intelligence, passion for the game, and a willingness to work beyond good reason at times. Simple concepts, right? The best answers often are. But apply those concepts to the assorted candidates. Hold fast to them when you're criticized by fans, questioned by the media, or just tempted by someone different. Trust me. It's not always so simple.

My door has been open for years to any coach or executive wanting to talk and willing to find their way to my world—well, almost
anyone. Florida and Florida State people know better than to call.
The University of Miami is the only stop on my career that was more
than a stop. It was home. It still is in many ways. I've hosted the coaching staffs at my house. One of my players, Mario Cristobal, is now
Miami's coach. I recruited Mario and his older brother, Luis. I sat
in their home. I talked with their parents. This spring, I talked with
Mario's players just as I once did him.

The visitors don't migrate to the Keys for small talk or social gestures. It's about nuts-and-bolts leadership, some tangible issue before
them, or just to hear how I climbed the mountain—about the Pygmalion Theory and not playing with scared money, about *good* being the
enemy of *great*, and why I ignored the "traditional coach's handbook"
on practices like using humble-speak in public.

I coached with a big attitude. I wanted it to rub off on my teams.
That was my way. It's not for everyone. I made mistakes, too. Maybe
these visitors can learn from those as well. I don't have secret short-
cuts or a special formula for winning. No one comes looking for that
anyway. They come instead for ideas formed over four decades that
were mixed with the hard work and perseverance that built champions in Miami and Dallas.

These visitors don't fly into Miami, drive through the Everglades,
and visit the Keys just to see me.

They come to hear what I learned.

2

SWAGGER

We talked loud. We laughed hard. We danced across the end zone most Saturdays right into America's living rooms, Michael Irvin punching both arms high in the air in his self-anointed "Playmaker" pose or defensive tackle Jerome Brown high-stepping out of a scrum after sacking a quarterback.

Old, frumpy college football never met anything like my University of Miami team in 1986. I hadn't, either, to be honest. All the coaching philosophies that I developed over the previous two decades finally came together in a breakout crescendo.

The full coming-out party was one of the season's first home games at Miami's Orange Bowl stadium, with all the proper dressings: No. 1 Oklahoma versus No. 2 Miami; me versus my old coach and colleague-turned-rival, Barry Switzer; a nationally televised event with the top broadcast team of Brent Musburger and Ara Parseghian; and poor-little-ol'-us cast as six-point underdogs to the defending national champions.

"We're the better team," I told my players that week. "We're going to kick the shit out of them."

That's who I was, how I talked, and how I wanted my team to play, too. The first sign of our new style came during the pregame coin toss. The marketed rebel of college football, Oklahoma linebacker Brian Bosworth, with his trademark Mohawk haircut, stood at midfield opposite our raw and real rebels, Jerome Brown, Winston Moss, and Alonzo Highsmith. Our guys were upset that Bosworth's mug had been splashed across our hometown paper, the *Miami Herald*, the previous day. It was disrespectful, they thought. But if it hadn't been that picture irritating them, something else would get them going.

There they stood at midfield, angry and arms defiantly folded, sweat pouring off their scowls in the subtropical heat, as they stared flat-eyed at Bosworth.

"Don't be afraid, motherfucker," Moss said to him.

When Bosworth said something back, Highsmith said, "I ain't scared of you, bitch." National television picked up the sound enough that it's a GIF all these years later. I see it on social media and chuckle.

Oklahoma won the coin toss, and Brown said to everyone standing there, "Fuck 'em. Give 'em the ball at the fifty-yard line. I don't care. We'll kick their ass."

The ceremonial, have-a-good-game handshake between captains? Sorry, not here. Not as we rewrote college football's unwritten rules. That midfield scene was the public sequel to a private episode that morning. Several of our offensive players called Bosworth's hotel room and woke him up. Normally, you couldn't find the room where a player stayed, much less call through to it. But this was my players' town. Running back Melvin Bratton knew someone working the reception desk at the hotel Oklahoma was staying at. Bratton, Highsmith, and some other offensive players called Bosworth, woke him up, and shouted, "We're going to kick your ass!" and other good-morning greetings.

When our defensive players heard about the offense's wake-up call, they wanted in, too. They called Oklahoma quarterback Jamelle Holieway's room. He picked up the phone to hear several players deliver a mocking rendition of a singsong line from *The Warriors*, a popular gang movie at the time.

"Jam-e-l-l-e, come out to pla-a-ay!" they said in the character's falsetto voice.

When I walked into the team breakfast, these players came up to me, laughing and telling the story of the phone calls. "We got 'em this morning, coach!" they said. "We told 'em we were going to kick their ass."

My reaction?

"Okay, let's go do it," I said.

My way wasn't the old and ordered college way of coaches like Knute Rockne or Bud Wilkinson. Their quaint game grew out of small college towns on lush campuses and regimented behavior. The game I coached at Miami came right off the streets. Many of our players grew up in tough neighborhoods close to the Orange Bowl. We kept the game on those mean streets, too, with a style and substance much of America couldn't grasp or didn't bother to try. That loud style was evident in my nationally televised interview immediately after we dragged Oklahoma up and down the field to an easy, 28–16 win.

"I made no bones about it before the game," I said to CBS's Pat O'Brien on the field. "I said we were the better team. And we were."

Yep, that was my kind of performance, saying you're going to kick someone's ass, doing it thoroughly, and then gloating about it afterward. What's the point of winning if you can't gloat a little? Or sometimes a lot. My style was never to act humbly in victory the way the old unspoken rules read. Nor were my players going to go quietly into the night. We changed the look and feel of college football right then like Muhammad Ali changed boxing with his fast mouth and faster fists.

It wasn't always popular, being bold and brash and so damned dominant that we won 40 of our final 44 games at Miami. That afternoon against Oklahoma cemented the national narrative that began a few games earlier, at the end of the previous season, when we hammered Notre Dame coach Gerry Faust in his final game, 58–7. That was a day. Michael Irvin shouted on the sideline to me, "Pour it on! Pour it on!" Parseghian, the former Notre Dame coach who poured it on opponents for years, tut-tutted from the broadcast booth how we should "show some compassion" after our reserve quarterback threw a touchdown to a reserve receiver to make it 50–7. When we had ten men on the field and still blocked a Notre Dame punt, Musburger sermonized about why I'd "humiliate" another coach. Humiliation wasn't my idea. But let's be clear: I sure wasn't apologizing then or now for that score. It was fun kicking their ass. It's fun thinking about it now.

The funny thing is, I grew up a Notre Dame fan, admiring how they won stomping lesser teams like we crushed Notre Dame that day. Who knows? Maybe that's where I learned that pour-it-on style.

It always interested me how the big-school bully changed the subject once he got punched in the mouth. Bosworth, who lost to us a second time that day in the Orange Bowl, told *Sports Illustrated* we were the "University of San Quentin," referring to the infamous California prison. Notre Dame's great receiver Tim Brown lost all three games against us and fumed, "If they can taunt you and talk about your mama, well, that's the way they play. They play with no class, definitely no class."

So some hated the manner my Miami teams played. So what? Some loved it, too. We were that type of new idea to college football—just as my Dallas Cowboys were on deck to be in the NFL. When *Sports Illustrated* ranked the twenty-five most hated teams in history, our 1986 Miami team was No. 1 and our 1992 Dallas Cowboys team was No. 3. I'm not sure how the 1988–89 Detroit Pistons slipped in there at No. 2. All I know is it takes rare achievement and a different style to be disliked as much as my teams were.

Michael Irvin came into my office one day during that 1986 season when the outside noise about our program was especially loud and asked if I was okay.

"You just keep winning and I'll be fine," I said.

I didn't mind us being branded as villains. It was disappointing and disparaging, the manner it was done at times. But I knew what kind of people we had. I also knew that in every great story there's a good guy and a bad guy. The only thing I demanded in our story was for the bad guy to win. And keep winning.

Something being said did bother me, though, especially as we became a national conversation. It was a developing story line around this team—around me, actually. It accused me of allowing players to act like the uncontrolled renegades the Parseghians, Bosworths, and Browns claimed we were. The story line said I just sat there, doing nothing, as all these on-field celebrations and loud proclamations changed the look of college football.

That's not how it worked at all.

I didn't sit there passively, looking the other way, as players danced and pointed to the skies.

I encouraged them to act that way.

I wanted them to play to their personalities.

That's the same mind-set I had as a coach, too. Why follow someone else's rules? Why not unleash who you really are, and by doing so, become the best version of yourself? Step over a player? Talk some trash? Redefine how college football was going to be played?

I coached everyone to play freely under my rules.

That's not a contradiction. I thought if players talked loud and celebrated, they'd have to back it up. Their energy would run like an electric current through the team if you had similar-minded players, too. But my players were also coached that there's a line out there, even as they played freely, and that line stopped at taunting the opponent, or committing dumb penalties.

That meant we needed a certain kind of player on my team. South Florida was full of them, too. We just had to find the right ones. Later, with the Dallas Cowboys, I'd ask a shorthanded question about draft prospects that my longtime assistants understood: "Is he a *Miami* guy?"

Did he have that open attitude to accompany his talent? Would he work hard, think big, and behave with the discipline our teams needed? Yes, discipline. That was a crucial component to our success. People looked at Irvin throwing his hands in the air after scoring, or Brown cursing at Bosworth, who claimed we had no discipline. What is discipline? Just winning "the right way"? Forever following an old-school ideal of "acting like you'd been there" when scoring a touchdown?

Listen: Discipline is your mind demanding you run that final 110-yard sprint in practice when your body refuses. Discipline is getting up for that early class to keep grades in line for football. Discipline, as Michael Irvin put it about my teams, was when the Orange Bowl sits on you like a blowtorch—no breeze, humidity off the charts, the crowd going crazy—and it's fourth-and-one with two minutes left, everyone exhausted, and the opponent's quarterback comes to the line and gives our defense a hard count. Hut-HUT!

And we don't jump offsides.

And we stop them on fourth down.

That's discipline: mental, physical, emotional discipline. It's needed to compete year after year for championships like we did at Miami. There's a fine line, too, from what can happen if you lose control while coaching this way. A few years after I left for Dallas, Miami beat Texas in the Cotton Bowl, 46–3. The score wasn't memorable. Miami's ridiculous behavior was. That's the word for it, too: *Ridicu-*

lous. Taunting. Flaunting. Making a spectacle at midfield. Miami broke the Cotton Bowl's ninety-year record for penalties—in the first half. A good coach, Dennis Erickson, lost control of his team that day. That was never my way.

At Dallas, too, some of the crazier antics like "The White House," a party house bought by players, came after my time. That wasn't my way, either. Discipline, you see, was the everyday guardrail of any team I ran, even if it wasn't the traditional yes-sir-no-sir brand people recognized. I never felt the need to follow convention. That went for hiring coaches, building game plans, and especially the substance of my coaching strategies, which was sometimes overshadowed by our playing style.

That substance can be reduced to one idea that no one quickly grasped in college or later, in the pros: speed beats size. We took slower safeties at Miami and converted them to fast linebackers, slower linebackers and made them into fast defensive ends, and bigger defensive ends and made them quick tackles.

That made for tired conversations the week before we whipped Oklahoma in our 1986 coming-out party. Their offensive line averaged 280 pounds. Our two defensive ends, Bill Hawkins and Dan Stubbs, weighed 241 and 245 pounds, respectively, but were quick and strong.

"How will they hold up against Oklahoma's power game?" a reporter asked before that game.

"You'll have to watch," I said.

I started answering that question at Oklahoma, of all places, as defensive line coach in 1970. The conventional college defense waited at the line back then and reacted to the offense. I wanted my linemen to *attack.* Shoot the gap. Cause havoc. Make the offense react to *us.* It's how I succeeded enough as a 195-pound nose guard at Arkansas to be named all-conference and, later, to the school's All-1960s Team.

"Upfield pressure," I called this style.

It's how I built teams all the way to winning a national champion-ship and two Super Bowls, meeting conventional resistance all along the way.

"Committing kamikaze," Oklahoma defensive coordinator Larry Lacewell called it my first summer there.

The previous year's defense surrendered the most points in school history. Now, as he saw it, this kid coach whose five whole years of experience were at Iowa State, Wichita State, Louisiana Tech, and Picayune High School wanted to . . . *what? Change how defense was played?* We didn't win a game at Picayune High that 1966 season, either.

Larry let me try it my way and, as he said, it saved that staff's jobs. By 1972, our defense held nine of twelve opponents to a touchdown or less and Oklahoma was ranked No. 2 in the country.

It helped advance me to Arkansas's defensive coordinator, then to Pitt's assistant head coach, Oklahoma State's head coach, and then to the big time at Miami. I collected ideas all along the way. Schemes. Strategies. Philosophies. I tucked big and small thoughts in my pocket—literally in my pocket sometimes. I kept an index card there about the referees. That came from how my boss at Pitt, Jackie Sherrill, interacted with the officials during games.

"Hey, motherfucker, come here!" he would yell at one. Or, for variety: "Hey, asshole, get over here!"

I went a more diplomatic way. My secretary put the names of the referees and their pictures on a card with their children's names, where they went to school, and any other relevant personal detail.

"Hey, Clemson played pretty good yesterday," I might say to an official who attended there before the game. Or simply, "Jim, watch the holding on that play."

So, by that 1986 Oklahoma game, all my ideas were on display, whether college football was ready for them or not. Everything mattered. Nothing was too small. That day against Oklahoma, for instance, just before kickoff, Miami's public address announcer gave the day's temperature and made up the humidity at something over 90 percent—just like I had him announce every game. That planted a seed in the opponent. Some said a few shoulders on the other sideline sagged at that announcement.

My plans were meticulous that way. I also had our band director play an inspirational song linked to the trendy television series *Miami Vice* at the time, "In the Air Tonight," by Phil Collins, just as I'd go around to players with a word of encouragement during pregame stretches. It created a motivational moment, I had hoped. That song was part of an electric time in a changing Miami. We were part of that changed profile, too.

After we laid out Oklahoma that game, we moved to No. 1 and were on our way. We trailed Florida State at half that October, playing tight and tense, and I had everyone hold hands at halftime to make a chain of energy.

"Let's go have fun," I said.

That's what it was always about for me, coaching these teams, playing on this platform. Fun. It was fun playing top opponents, fun being on a nationally televised stage—fun leading players I enjoyed coaching in a city I came to love.

We drubbed Florida State that second half to win, 41–23. We went undefeated in the regular season and advanced to the national title game in the 1987 Fiesta Bowl, where one final lesson awaited me. But my brand became set that 1986 season. All my ideas, all my years working in Ames, Iowa, and Stillwater, Oklahoma, bore that team. I never had more fun in coaching and never was happier on the sideline than watching all my ideas come to life over those years at Miami.

"Go out, play hard, play fast, but play the way *you* know how to play!" I'd tell my Miami teams in the pregame locker room.

Talk. Strut. Celebrate. Dance across the end zone. Tell the opposing captain at the coin toss, "I ain't scared of you, bitch." But be smart, strong, and disciplined at the same time. We introduced college football to a new style right off America's streets. I coached in a way some moralizers and sermonizers weren't ready to accept.

"Showboating," some called it then. "Hotdogging," said others. Those were all words from some previous era of college football in America. The truth is our style was so out on the edge, the word to describe it hadn't been used.

It came later.

We had swagger.

3

WES AND ME

Before talking image and perception, before addressing St. Joe Paterno or *Catholics vs. Convicts*—before even mentioning my University of Miami teams and race in America of the 1980s—there's a scene you need to see: I'm sitting in a gym outside Camden, New Jersey, to watch a Pennsauken High School basketball game. I'm here with my Miami assistant, Art Kehoe, to recruit a talented player named David Griggs.

This was the age before Google and Twitter, so we had a small issue.

"Which one's Griggs?" Art asked a young man seated next to him.

"Griggs is over there," he told us, pointing to a player. "But the best player on the floor is the white kid who will be jumping center."

There were nine Black players on the court and the one white kid jumping center. He stood out as the night went on for more than his color. He dunked. He defended hard. He ran the fast break. He was the best player in the game that night, his 6'4" frame and obvious athleticism piquing the interest of a football coach.

We talked during the game, the three of us in the bleachers—us two middle-aged white men and our new friend, Wes, who was Black. Wes said this white kid was a talented football player, too. It turned out Wes was his neighbor and surrogate big brother. He drove the kid around Camden to get into pickup basketball games where he was the only white player.

"You're going to want this kid for football," Wes said. "And when he goes down to Miami, I'm coming down to watch, too. I want good seats."

Griggs, it turned out, had no interest in talking much to us that night—even if he was the talent we thought. He went to Virginia and had a good NFL career before tragically dying in a car accident at age twenty-eight. But, at the time, with him spurning us . . .

"Let's get that other kid," I told Art.

That's how Greg Mark attended Miami and became an All-American defensive end, the school's all-time sacks leader, and a third-round pick by the New York Giants.

Greg, as good as he became, isn't the point of this story. The kid in the bleachers, William Wesley, is. We struck up a friendship that night. He was smart, aggressive, ambitious—all qualities I'm drawn to in people. Wes had recently graduated from high school. He sold sneakers at an upscale store. We stayed in touch after that night. Wes even called to say we had to take another recruit, a good friend of Mark's named Jason Hicks. We had a scholarship open and signed Hicks, who became a defensive end and earned his degree.

The season following our bleacher conversation, I left a pass for Wes to stand along the sidelines of our game at Maryland. He was walking by the locker room just as I opened the door to lead the team out on the field to start the game. I hadn't seen him since that night in Camden.

"Hey, Wes, you get your pass?" I said.

"Yeah, coach," he said.

"Let's go!" I hollered.

I started down the tunnel and looked back at the team following behind me. Wes didn't realize I was talking to him, too.

"Wes, come on, we've got a football game to play!" I said.

Greg Mark redshirted that freshman year. But before the next season, Wes popped up on campus to help him. He knew Greg was a white player on a predominately Black team. He asked a few players who the team leaders were. He then knocked on the dorm room of Jerome Browne, Alonzo Highsmith, and Melvin Bratton. As Wes recollected: "There's the biggest Black guy I've seen in my life at the door." That was Jerome. Wes introduced himself, told them about his friend, and asked if they'd watch out for him. Wes promised he'd get them good sneakers if they did.

With his good smarts and personality, Wes soon became friends with several players and coaches. He got some players Nike shoes to wear in games that hadn't been released to the public (an orange version of the red-and-black Air Jordan high-tops). He'd run beside me to midfield at game's end when I shook the opposing coach's hand. He helped me manage some players in subtle but significant ways, too. For instance, I asked him to help keep Michael Irvin in at night. Michael liked to run around town. Wes played the card game Tonk in Michael's dorm room. The winner got Air Jordans. Years later, Michael told people how he'd won the shoes from Wes. That made Wes let Michael in on our secret: he let Michael win to keep him home at night for me.

Through the years, Wes and I remained friends. There he is, for instance, in the picture as I'm getting doused with Gatorade after our first Super Bowl win for Dallas. After the following season's NFC Championship Game, he came with a buddy to the after-party in the Dallas stadium for coaches and families. I mentioned wanting to get my Corvette to my home in the Keys. First, though, came the Super Bowl in Atlanta.

"Give me the keys," Wes said.

Wes convinced his friend, who was Jewish, to drive with him to Atlanta.

"Can you imagine a Black guy driving through the South alone?" he said.

His friend answered, "Can you imagine a Black guy and a Jew driving through the South alone?"

Once, when the NFL restricted sideline personnel to only football people, it sent a memo noting people on our sideline not officially with our team. One was my lawyer, Nick Christin. One was our team chaplain, Father Leo Armbrust.

"The third man is someone named Wes," the NFL memo said.

If Wes was a mystery then, he remains one in a different manner today. He's known around the sports world as "World Wide Wes," and the relationship he developed with Nike's Phil Knight helped broker shoe deals for college teams like Miami and NBA stars from Allen Iverson to LeBron James. He became a confidant and business partner to players and executives alike.

"Is This the Most Powerful Man in Sport?" the cover of a GQ magazine read with a long story about him—a story he didn't talk for, by the way, just as he doesn't for other media stories. He branched out to the music world, too. I found myself standing for photos through the years with Wes and rappers like Drake and Jay-Z. He also comes on the yacht of another friend, Michael Jordan, to my fishing tournament most years.

Wes never stopped rising. He's now executive vice president of the New York Knicks. And the president of the Knicks? His Jewish driving buddy of my Corvette to Atlanta, Leon Rose.

Let's return to that first scene. A couple of middle-aged white men whom no one knew came to a high school gym to recruit a Black player. A young Black man, who was friends with a white player, sat beside them. We began talking. And listening. We saw color, of course, but like age and background, it didn't matter. I saw Wes as a fun go-getter whose smarts and energy I admired—and have kept admiring through the years.

And Wes? He saw something beyond my coaching jobs and championship rings as we became friends. He has told people that college basketball coach John Calipari and I are the two most color-blind white guys he knows.

I grew up fortunate that way. I was granted the freedom from racial hang-ups as a kid in Port Arthur, Texas. That might sound odd considering my youth was in a segregated state of the 1940s and 1950s. Schools. Restaurants. Restrooms. Everything had a Black side and a white side. The Black community in Port Arthur was a couple of miles away from my home at the corner of DeQueen Boulevard and Procter Street.

That was the racially divided world around me—but it wasn't my world. I played football starting at age seven or eight on empty lots with Black and white friends. I was called "Scarhead" because of the notches in my scalp from being tackled on the ground by white friends named Wayne and Jimmy and Black friends named Baby Joe and I.E. We didn't always know last names. They didn't matter. My dad always said I saw no difference between my Black and white friends. And why would I? They didn't have any money, same as me. We talked the same, laughed and ran and bled the same in our afternoon football games. No one mentioned race. I never thought about it.

After fourth grade, I took a job at the dairy where my dad worked. Black and Mexican women worked there. I helped on a delivery route with a Cajun named Blackie. There, too, no one mentioned race. We just did the same job, side by side every day.

Looking back, it probably was this foundation that allowed me to avoid making assumptions based on race. When I first heard a racial epithet in my segregated grade school, I spoke up because that's not how I knew the world. When I first played against Black players in sports, I didn't think anything about it like some whites. Throughout my career—from player to coach, from high school to college to the pros—I never felt burdened by prejudice in ways others did. I never pretended to understand what Black people went through. I didn't go through it myself, after all. But I've always accepted people for who they are and had compassion for the journey some made due to the color of their skin.

I noticed some of that segregated Port Arthur in the Miami I arrived to in 1984. "Miam-*uh*," as some said, southern accent intact. I love the school, love the city—but let's be honest about how it was. One practice in my first season there I talked with Walter Highsmith, Alonzo's father and a longtime high school coach. That was a difficult year for many reasons. The previous coaching staff stayed in place when I took over as head coach, and a few were angry at not getting the job themselves. Some media missed my predecessor, Howard Schnellenberger. Maybe there was something more to the uncomfortable undercurrent around me, too.

"Well, coach, one of the biggest reasons you got a cool reception is that people are concerned you're going to recruit too many Black players," Walter Highsmith said.

I was stunned.

"That's kind of your reputation," he added. "And I think some people probably don't want that."

I laughed and guaranteed there would be no head count on whites or Blacks—only on good football players. They weren't hard to find, either. South Florida's backyard offered the most fertile recruiting ground in the country. Our winning fed our recruiting, too. The sales pitch of our offensive coordinator, Gary Stevens, consisted of dropping a championship ring on the table and saying to a prospect,

"You want one of these?" Plenty of these local players played for us, too. Their complexion never entered the discussion. I was a coach. I'd recruit Beverly Hills 90210 if it helped win games. But that wasn't the zip code of our backyard.

I had to reach, not just recruit, these players. The message was the same talking to inner-city Black kids and suburban white kids. But the delivery was different. Years later, I gave an R-rated talk to my Dallas team, bringing the high energy of a church revival. On the way out of the room I walked by two white players, Troy Aikman and Daryl Johnston.

"That wasn't for you," I said.

"We know, coach," one of them said. "We were onto you a while ago."

I learned that at Miami. Maybe it's why, when my career was condensed to A *Football Life* by NFL Films, former ESPN and current radio host Dan Le Batard said, "Jimmy was the first Black coach at the University of Miami."

If that was the perception, it was fine with me — as long as we won. We had the kind of talent NFL scouts drooled over. They'd later tell Alonzo, who became an NFL personnel executive, that they didn't need to attend games to measure our players. They just went to practices. They'd watch a future pro there compete against another future pro. We practiced hard and scrimmaged every day, too, so they saw the toughness and work ethic of our players.

As we rose as a program, the public perception took a turn. We went from "talented" to "thugs." Admittedly, we had some misdemeanor arrests — a fight, an accidental shoplifting, an incident where our players and other students used someone's phone card (this was the age before cell phones, kids). We had issues like college-aged kids had everywhere. But should I have kicked kids out of the program for misdemeanors, as some media and fans wanted? Where else would you want a kid to be other than in a structured program with a chance for a college degree? It was easy to lob a one-liner like *Sports Illustrated's* Rick Reilly, who wrote, "Miami may be the only squad in America that has its team picture taken from the front and the side."

Was there a layer of racism to our perception? There certainly was a layer of ignorance. But, looking back, I suspect many of the people judging our team didn't have intimate relationships with Black people, which would have allowed them to view our players with a fairer perspective.

More media could have gotten to know our players better. No team was more open than my Hurricanes. Most coaches closed practices and shielded players from interviews. We opened practices many days, had players talk to media after practice, and opened our locker room after games. Our players were full of riveting stories that could have illustrated that we were more than end-zone celebrations, too.

Take Michael Irvin. He became a centerpiece of our team due to his outsized talent and over-the-top personality. Everyone talked of his arms-in-the-air pose after a big catch. But why wasn't there more talk of how he grew up in a small brick home in Fort Lauderdale with sixteen siblings sleeping four, five, and six to a room? How he painted lines on his street at 40 and 100 yards and came home from high school practice each day to run more sprints? Michael then ran three miles around his neighborhood—literally trying to run to a better life. Michael's father died when Michael was a senior in high school. I talked to him about that, assured him I'd be at Miami for his entire stay. Also, at Miami, if a teammate ran laps as punishment after practice, Michael would sometimes run along with him. Just to be a good teammate. Just because working more than everyone else is what he did all the way to the Dallas Cowboys and to the Pro Football Hall of Fame.

Randy Shannon was another member of that first recruiting class who later joined me in Dallas. He was a quiet, intelligent kid with an unbelievable story in a city full of the unbelievable. Randy was three when his father was murdered. Three older siblings—a sister and twin brothers—became addicted to crack cocaine and contracted AIDS. Randy's mother, a nurse, worked her hospital shifts comforting her children as they died. As a player, Randy was the prototype for the smaller, faster outside linebacker that defined my defense at Miami. In Dallas, I bet on his character more than his talent and drafted him in the eleventh round. He played for two years before starting a career as a college coach. He eventually became Miami's coach for a few years. Talk about a success story.

Jimmie Jones was another name off that team that the Reillys and Parseghians of the college football media world never bothered to meet. As a junior on the Okeechobee High School team, Jimmie started only four games. He was kicked off the team as a senior. Most recruiters passed. Why bother? But Butch Davis got film of those four games and thought we should help him develop at a local community college. I saw his size and speed and said: Why send him to a community college?

We looked into Jimmie's story. He was kicked off the team as a senior because he didn't attend spring practices. Why? He worked to help support his fatherless family of eight siblings. When I heard that, I wanted him on my team more. And he still had to help pay the family bills, by the way. He missed spring practices before his senior year at Miami to valet-park cars and support his family.

He developed into a third-round NFL pick, where we selected him at Dallas.

Here's one more player at Miami: Claude Jones. He was thirteen when his father died of hypertension and diabetes. Claude's boyhood plan was to follow his dad's path into the air force. That changed when he became a Parade All-American offensive tackle at Dillard High in Fort Lauderdale and was offered college scholarships all over the country. Claude, as a freshman, put me on one shoulder to help carry me in celebration after winning our national title in the 1987 season. He won two more national titles at Miami. He played briefly in the NFL, then in Canada, before returning to the path he began at Miami. He went to medical school. A phrase I used when things got tough in practice — "Press on" — became his mantra to becoming a doctor. Today, Dr. Claude Jones works in Cleveland's inner city in internal medicine.

As I said, those teams were full of great stories if you were open to seeing them. I enjoyed coaching inner-city kids and watching them grow as players and men. I was fortunate enough to grow up without racial hang-ups. Later in my career, walking on the Houston field while with the Cowboys, I heard a man calling to me from the front row. Finally, he said something that caught my attention.

"Coach, it's Baby Joe!" he said.

My boyhood friend from Port Arthur and I caught up that day. Years later, when I was inducted into the Pro Football Hall of Fame, there was a congratulatory message from "Baby Joe's son."

I was fortunate to know good people and high achievers from Port Arthur to Islamorada, Baby Joe to World Wide Wes. I built my teams with the same kind of people. They weren't thugs or convicts, as was sometimes depicted by the media.

They were who I am.

They were who I've always been.

4

DEVASTATED TO DOMINANT

I coached the worst game of my career in the 1987 Fiesta Bowl. I suffered the most devastating loss of my life. I cost my most talented Miami team a national title.

Me. Alone.

That loss to Penn State changed me like no other game in my career. I stood before the team in the locker room afterward, telling our players to be proud of their season, to keep their heads up—even as my head couldn't stay up. I could barely talk. My eyes watered. It wasn't sorrow billowing inside me.

It was pain. Pure, gut-wrenching pain.

I collapsed on the floor of the coaches' locker room a few minutes later, crying in agony, all my emotion gushing out in a manner that shook even my crew. I never lived in the middle of the road. It was agony or ecstasy after games. Tony Wise, back in his first year of working with me, was alarmed by my shuddering spasms of bawling after our Pittsburgh team lost to Notre Dame. After years with me, he lost count how many times that happened.

We started losing that Fiesta Bowl long before kickoff. As the top-ranked team, I could have demanded to play closer to our fans in Orlando's Citrus Bowl. Instead, I accepted the school's decision to play in Arizona and watched Fiesta Bowl officials bow down to Penn

State coach Joe Paterno. Penn State, for instance, received first-rate facilities. Ours were so cramped and downtrodden, I demanded an upgrade. The locker room was re-carpeted. When that hit the media, we were labeled as pampered and demanding.

Thus began a national title game with story lines that exaggerated the realities. I sat with comedian Bob Hope at a five-hundred-dollars-a-plate charity function several days before the game when the first theme snapped into sharp focus. Someone said my players had just arrived at the Phoenix airport.

"They're wearing army fatigues," the person said.

That caused a stir. "We're on a mission," my players said, referring to making amends for losing our previous year's bowl game to Tennessee. I wasn't going to criticize them within sight of the game for being arrogant and cocky—just as I coached them. It fit our team's psyche. It also fit like a puzzle piece into the media's pro-wrestling-like buildup of Good Guys versus Bad Guys.

The white hat never did fit me. St. Joe and his Penn State team came out of central casting from college football's nostalgic yesterday, living in Happy Valley, wearing black shoes and uniforms with no names, and coached by *Sports Illustrated*'s "Sportsman of the Year." "Nobody has stayed truer to the game and at the same time truer to himself than Joseph Vincent Paterno, 'Joe Pa' to Penn State worshipers," wrote our old friend at *SI*, Rick Reilly.

Everyone wants to create a hero and an antihero. I demanded our players attend a steak fry sponsored by the Fiesta Bowl organizers. Paterno didn't attend, but I was there. My players wore inexpensive black warm-ups to the function because that's all we could afford with our NCAA allowance. Penn State players showed up in these beautiful blazers. I don't know how they purchased them. St. Joe wouldn't break a rule.

Penn State punter John Bruno then joked in a skit at the steak fry about me keeping the hair spray industry in business. My players thought that joke was out of bounds. They liked his next one far less.

"We even let the Black guys eat with us at the training table once a week," he said.

My players thought about leaving early all night. That joke sealed it. Jerome Brown stood up and said, "Did the Japanese sit down and eat with Pearl Harbor before they bombed them? No. We're out of here." The racial issue didn't draw much attention. We were simply cast as bad guys for leaving the dinner.

But again—I blame myself for what happened next. Not the fatigues. Not the steak fry. Not the media coverage. We dominated Penn State just as I expected. We gained 445 yards to their 162, had 22 first downs to their 8, averaged 4.8 yards per play to their 2.7. But the number that mattered was our five interceptions. The fifth interception came on a pass from the Penn State five-yard line with eighteen seconds left.

Our quarterback, Vinny Testaverde, wasn't ready to play that game. That was my fault. He was involved in a scooter accident toward the end of the season and missed a game and several practices. He then won the Heisman Trophy and other awards, causing him to miss several more practices before the Fiesta Bowl.

Add it up, and I did a poor job of managing a college kid's time and preparation, then a worse one managing our offense in the game. Had we run more, leaned on their defense harder, changed quarterbacks—had I pushed any of a handful of strategic buttons, the more talented team would have won.

I flew directly from the Fiesta Bowl to the Japan Bowl, a college all-star game. I was told there were problems back home from that Penn State game. They greeted me upon returning. Our school president, Tad Foote, reneged on a promise to extend my contract. He also called a news conference and demanded I apologize. For what? Our behavior—or the loss? I'm still not sure. And I didn't apologize.

Decades later, the postscript arrived to that game's nonstop, nonsensical "Good versus Evil" debate. Joe Paterno's career-long defensive coordinator, Jerry Sandusky, was convicted on multiple counts of child sexual abuse. I'm not judging what happened. All I know is Penn State's program wasn't full of saints, as portrayed in that long-ago game, just as we weren't full of sinners.

That loss still haunts me at times. If I had taken more control, demanded to run the ball more, protected the lead; we were national champs.

Was I humbled?

No, I was hardened.

Never again did I take any game, any lead, any advantage in talent for granted. That 1987 Fiesta Bowl loss to Penn State made me a more intense coach, a more detailed-oriented coach—a better coach in many regards. And a more obsessed one.

We opened the following season with the Fiesta Bowl still hanging over us, sophomore quarterback Steve Walsh leading a wave of new players, and a murderer's row of a schedule that began with 20th-ranked Florida, then at No. 10 Arkansas, and then at No. 4 Florida State.

Was it time to be nervous?

Please. That's not my style. As I say at the blackjack table— *you don't play with scared money*. It's how I played in casinos, how I coached in games, and how, after waxing Florida in our opener, 31–4, I sat in our Little Rock hotel bar on the eve of playing Arkansas, having a drink, rather than sweating the next day's game plan. I wanted everyone around my team and in my former college stomping grounds to see that confidence, too. To feel it, even.

I called my brother-in-law Jim Moody to join me for a drink at the hotel bar. I gave him my 1964 Cotton Bowl watch as we talked.

That game made my Arkansas team the co–national champs. Jim knew my full story there. I'd committed to Arkansas out of high school, sight unseen, because Mother and Daddy said I could go to any school I wanted, but they'd watch only if I picked their native Arkansas. "Jimmy Jump Up," my coaches called me there because I never stayed on the ground. Those were good times and formative years for me, right to the spring after my senior season, when I was in the football office as Louisiana Tech coaches visited to learn our defense. Our defensive coordinator, Jim MacKenzie, asked me to diagram our "Monster Slant Defense" on the blackboard for them. The "monster" was the strong safety, who committed to one side. The "slant" was our five-man front that slanted the other way. We shut out five straight opponents my senior season and only one team scored more than thirteen points against us. That's why coaches wanted to learn it.

A few months later, the Louisiana Tech defensive line coach, George Doherty, had a heart attack. They remembered my black-board talk as a student and offered me $1,000 a month, use of a car, and an apartment while MacKenzie recovered that season. I was al-ready married to my first wife, Linda Kay, with a young son, Brent, and planned to get a graduate degree in industrial psychology. But I went to Louisiana Tech to substitute coach and I never went to gradu-ate school.

That watch I handed to my brother-in-law Friday night at the Lit-tle Rock hotel bar symbolized all of that.

"You don't want it?" he asked.

"I'll get another starting tomorrow," I said.

My old college coach, Frank Broyles, now Arkansas's athletic di-rector, made a mistake. He used me to serve as a fake candidate for the Arkansas head coach job while I was at Oklahoma State. It wasn't even a job I wanted. Broyles simply wanted to use me to make his preferred candidate, Ken Hatfield, look better to the public by being chosen over me.

But, that's not the mistake Broyles made I'm referring to here. That mistake was scheduling this particular game against my Miami team. While at the hotel bar, I called up Jerry Jones, my onetime Arkansas teammate. His son Stephen now played for Arkansas. We joked back and forth a bit. I then said, joking-not-joking, "I want to warn you right now, you better have Stephen sit out this game. We're fixing to kick the shit out of them."

We won, 51–7.

Hatfield started his television show the next morning saying, "And Jesus wept." It was such an ass-kicking, President Foote, who married one of Arkansas's famous Fulbrights, grew frustrated with us up forty points and tacking on another touchdown with our second-string players. Foote was always with us as long as we didn't lose. Or win too big.

"Why is he doing this?" Foote asked.

Why? Because I wasn't going to call our reserves off the field. Because they worked hard to taste success and needed the experience, too. Because never letting up was who I am—and whom my teams were trained to be especially after the previous season.

We were cocky, arrogant, and thrived on that mind-set. Down sixteen points the following week in the second half in Tallahassee— "We're comin' back!" Michael Irvin told their Deion Sanders. We indeed came back to beat a talented Florida State team.

We were 8-0 when 10th-ranked Notre Dame came to the Orange Bowl. Lou Holtz had rebuilt their program. In our preparation, we thought a fake punt would work. We put running back Leonard Conley on the punt team the previous game so Notre Dame wouldn't see anything unusual as he lined up against them. We planned to double-check Notre Dame's alignment on their first punt before calling the fake. We had no dedicated special teams coach, so defensive coordinator Dave Wannstedt was up in the press box telling Tommy Tuberville to check the tackles, Dave Campo to watch the ends, Tony Wise to . . .

"What the . . ." Wannstedt said.

I called the fake punt right then. We were at the Notre Dame 41 in the second quarter. Conley took the snap this time, sprinted around the end, got the first down, and we were on our way to a 24–0 win and soon another national championship game.

That fake punt surprise gets back to my blackjack philosophy: *You don't play with scared money*. Ask my good friend Nick Christin how it works. We went to the Bahamas for a getaway weekend with our wives early on in our friendship at Miami.

"If I lose these chips, we'll go to dinner," Nick said to me at the blackjack table.

I erupted. "You might as well hand over the chips to the dealer! You've already lost!"

Winning starts with mind-set, whether playing blackjack or coaching a big game. I gambled a lot through the years, primarily at the high-stakes tables in Las Vegas and the Bahamas. I went to Atlantic City that night after meeting World Wide Wes in the high school gym and won a few dollars. I played blackjack in London the night before a Dallas preseason game in 1993. We were leaving for the airport after the game the next day, so I stuffed a fanny pack full of my winnings and wore it in the game.

"Coach, you look kind of dorky wearing that," said our trainer, Kevin O'Neill. "Why don't you let me hold it for you?"

"Ain't no one holding this except me," I said.

So, sitting at a bar in Little Rock before game day? Coming back against Florida State? Pulling that fake punt against Notre Dame for a first down that surprised even my assistants? These weren't outliers. This is how we coached and played.

I never played with scared money.

I was a "whale," in casino terms, the kind of player who gambled such big money that resorts welcomed them with open doors and complimentary suites. Rhonda and I once walked into the Mansion, an exclusive Las Vegas resort, and there was some issue about bringing our little dog, Buttercup.

"That's a hundred-thousand-dollar rug," the hotel attendant said in showing our suite.

"Buttercup won't pee on your rug," I said.

The hotel manager said it was all good. The next time I came there was a pillow waiting in our suite with the embroidered name "Buttercup."

Shaquille O'Neal once got miffed upon hearing I played at the Mansion. He couldn't get in. He didn't bet big enough. I didn't go for fun or the cackle of adrenaline. I played blackjack for the same reason I coached football—to win. That's where the fun was.

Troy Aikman once sent a message that he was winning at a resort in the Bahamas. Rhonda and I went over from the Keys and surprised him the next morning. Rhonda saw his small bets and joked, "Troy, you just signed a big contract. Bet some *real* money!" By the end of the night, we were having so much fun, we paid the hotel to open its disco.

I would take my coaching crews on all-expense-paid trips each off-season to a casino, too. While I was at Oklahoma State, we took a ski vacation: nine of us in a van, crammed into two hotel rooms, all of us young and having fun. But none of us knew how to ski. That was the end of that. It was casinos and warm spots ever after. We were comped most places because of my whale status. My Dallas assistants and I once even stayed in one of the *Rain Man* suites at Caesars Palace in Vegas, where Dustin Hoffman and Tom Cruise stayed in that movie.

I enjoyed slipping my crew money on our trips as a reward for their good work. For instance, once in the Bahamas, I dropped a $5,000 chip on the table in front of our administrative assistant Bruce Mays. I said if he won that hand he was playing, he'd have to share the money with our strength coach, Mike Woicik. Bruce won. He was so excited he forgot to take the chips off the table as the dealer prepared the next hand.

"Bruce, you better stop him!" I said. "Or do you want to bet ten thousand?"

He snatched the chips off the table. He split it with Woicik. That's the kind of story we laughed about for years. It's also how, in my way, I gave good workers a bonus.

Often while playing blackjack, I took over the entire table, playing four and five hands at a time. The casino sometimes roped off the table to keep back people who recognized me. I didn't always win. I once lost at the MGM in Las Vegas, and the casino manager walked over with a computer printout that extended to the floor. It was a list of my visits and results. He wanted to show on a night I lost that I could afford to give the casino back some money. I've won more than I've lost. But let's be clear: I also never lost more on a trip than I could afford.

The point here isn't to gloat over my blackjack results—well, not too much, anyhow. The point is to show there are two kinds of people who play blackjack: there are those who play with scared money and those who call a fake punt on the way to another national title game while even the assistants didn't see it coming.

5

PYGMALION 'EM

E ach Thursday night, I met with my Miami players without any other coaches or support staff present. It was just the players and me, alone, for an hour.

We didn't discuss the upcoming game on Saturday, or the week's practices. Football wasn't on the agenda at all.

Life was.

"When you graduate," I'd ask a player, "what do you plan to do with your life?"

That's how I phrased it, too. I never said, "If you graduate . . ." I always said, "*When* you graduate . . ." That reinforced a positive seed toward expectation and accomplishment. For the same reason, I never told a player, "Don't fumble." Rather I said, "Hold on to the ball." I never told a kicker before he attempted a field goal, "Don't miss." I said, "Make it!"

Words shape minds, right? And leaders control words. This came from a central pillar of my coaching philosophy: "Treat a person as he is, and he will remain as he is. Treat a person as if he were where he could be and should be, and he will become what he could be and should be."

It's known as the Pygmalion Effect, the self-fulfilling prophecy, the psychology of high expectations. It originally was a Greek myth involving a sculptor named Pygmalion, who fell in love with an ivory statue of his ideal woman and effectively willed her to life. It was the inspiration for a professor transforming a street girl into a duchess in *My Fair Lady*.

We didn't exactly *will* players to life like in the myth. We did, however, inspire them to be all they could be and should be through encouragement and raised expectations. Take those Thursday-night meetings. Some players were the first in their family to attend college. Maybe they never considered a career beyond football until hearing others talk of being a banker, a store owner, or a partner in a lawn service. We discussed each player's answer. I'd always have a story to tell to fit the moment from my career: A player who gave up his college education by getting in some dumb trouble. What did it get him? Or a boss who gave a raise to an employee as motivation, saying, "Now go earn that."

The only rule in those Thursday-night meetings was that players couldn't say football was their postgraduate plan. This meeting, remember, wasn't a football one, even if it served a football purpose for me. Thursday night was also the one night players would go out on the town. And Miami was a tempting town. By meeting late and having McDonald's Quarter Pounders with Cheese on hand, two reasons to ignore that temptation were offered.

Be in bed by midnight was my rule, too.

"I don't care whose bed you're in," I'd say. "Just be in one."

These were college kids. I knew that. But the Pygmalion Effect applied to the full development of the person and the player. When we previously took over the Oklahoma State program with NCAA sanctions and merely forty-odd scholarship players, we sent out word that we wanted walk-on players. That first season, seventy-five walk-ons joined the team. We didn't have enough pads or cleats. We went to Walmart and bought black canvas soccer shoes. Those three-dollar shoes were so bad, several players ended up buying their own cleats. The players tried hard, too. But between the sanctions and a depleted program we had eleven walk-ons and twelve freshmen among the forty-four players in the two-deep lineup our first year. Dave Wannstedt once mentioned in a staff meeting, "We don't even have anybody who can tackle."

"Pygmalion 'em," I told him. "Tell them they can *make* the tackle. If we tell them, we can make them *think* they can. If they think they can, they will do it."

We took a 3-8 team from the previous year and went 7-4 the next.

Years later, Dave spoke at another meeting of the difficulty his Dallas defense would have covering San Francisco star receiver Jerry Rice. He looked at me. We had had this conversation many times by that point.

"I know, Jimmy. Pygmalion 'em," he said.

Establish high expectations. Never forecast failure. Don't permit complaining. Those are some of the fundamental steps of Pygmalioning 'em. *The Wizard of Oz* was a Pygmalion story. The Scarecrow didn't have a brain and the Lion didn't have a heart until they were told they did. That changed how they acted. As coach, I played the role of the Wizard with players.

When Jason Garrett was named the Dallas Cowboys coach, he visited me in the Keys and asked, "What's the best advice you can give me about being a head coach?"

"Jason, before you were the offensive coordinator and your mind was on X's and O's," I said, "you'd walk down the hall, and nobody gave a shit. But now you're the leader, the CEO, the head coach, and you're going to walk down the hall and every head is going to turn. If you're going to get the organization to be as good as it can be, you need interaction with everybody. Every secretary. Every administrative assistant. Every backup guard. Nobody likes to be ignored by the leader."

The key is how you interact with them. I made a point of treating everyone like the best version of themselves—of who I expected them to be. That might mean I'd say, "Nice job," to an office administrator. It might mean noticing someone came in early to work—"I saw you here"—in a way that would encourage them always to come in early. It wouldn't always be praise. Often, in fact, it wasn't. Players often fell short of expectations.

"Hey, you've got to pick it up. I know you've got more than you're showing," I might say in that case.

When Russell Maryland got our final scholarship in 1986, he was raw and overweight. "We're going to take a chance on you. But you better come here to work," I said, setting the expectations.

After he ran an impressive 40-yard dash that first August, I said to him, "That was a helluva run!"

That compliment stayed with Russell decades later. It buoyed his confidence as a young player, he said, allowing him to think he might belong at this level. My give-and-take with another talented freshman, Maurice Crum, who was a linebacker, showed a different way to motivate. He had a root canal one day. He was in pain, could barely talk. He asked to skip the practice.

"Do you want to play for this team?" I said.

"I do," he said.

"See you at practice," I said.

Tough? You bet. It's a tough game. Maurice practiced that day. He reached a higher level of expectation and, like Russell, went on to have a great career. These little conversations nudged them along. Later, in Dallas, I sat by the locker room entrance after a minicamp practice and our third-round pick Clayton Holmes walked by. He was from tiny Carson-Newman College. Now he was practicing with the world champions and had an understandably awed looked to him.

"Hey, Clayton, I saw you doing some really good things out there," I said.

He looked surprised. "Got to learn, coach."

"We think you can play here," I said. "We like you."

He became a Super Bowl starter for us.

Here's the point: How could Maryland know he was noticed, Crum know what he could do with pain, Holmes know we thought highly of him—how can any player know what a coach thinks unless they're told? The words I chose were designed to bring out something from the player. It was the same for the collective team when I spoke in meetings. People often rise to the level of what is expected of them.

Some coaches don't want to set public expectations. I advertised them. It was a good way to Pygmalion the team by announcing where the bar was set. For my Oklahoma State, Dallas, and Miami Dolphins teams it was a measured approach as we ratcheted the bar up each successive season. At the University of Miami, good talent was in place when I arrived. We just needed to develop it. Everyone knew the expectation. I simply reinforced it.

"We're here to win," I'd say. "Winning is what we do."

The Pygmalion Effect didn't work by words alone. There had to be structure, support, and bottom-line integrity. Take those Thursday-night meetings at Miami when I asked players what they'd do *when* they graduated.

Some of that structure was simply laying down ground rules. Players were told to sit in the front row or two in classes. They could not wear team colors like our green T-shirts or orange warm-ups to call attention to being athletes. These weren't stringently enforced for players who kept up their grades, but they underlined the idea of first being students in classrooms. Leaders like Melvin Bratton, Alonzo Highsmith, and Russell Maryland never let the possibility of getting bad grades get in the way of playing football—a discipline that then carried through the rest of the team.

Not everyone kept up, of course. These were kids learning their way. One of the players I released from his scholarship due to poor grades in 1987 was a sophomore tight end named Rodney Hill. He wasn't a major contributor just yet. But his younger brother, Randal Hill, could be. Randal was the top-rated recruit in Florida at defensive back that year. When his plane landed in Tallahassee on a recruiting trip, he was met by Florida State coach Bobby Bowden, actor and FSU alum Burt Reynolds, Florida governor Bob Graham, and rising senior Deion Sanders. But Randal committed to Miami thanks to his grandfather wanting him to play and study nearby.

I called him with the news of his brother Rodney losing his scholarship.

"Is this going to change anything for you?" I said.

"No, I gave my word," he said. "I'm coming to Miami."

The Hills, you see, were raised to understand the demands of academics. Their father was a high school principal and their mother a teacher. School mattered to them. So did accountability. That, again, might surprise some of those who were quick to pigeonhole our players into a convenient stereotype. We switched Randal "Thrill" Hill to receiver, and he became a first-round pick of the Miami Dolphins in the 1991 draft. And what did he do after he graduated and finished football? He became a top U.S. customs agent.

Over my time at Miami, the entire academic support program was reorganized. With the help of athletic director Sam Jankovich, Dr. Anna Price was hired as an assistant athletic director to bring structure and support for our players' schoolwork. Dr. Price, in turn, hired a learning specialist, a tutor coordinator, and an assistant director who oversaw player appearances and summer jobs to ensure that everything worked around the academic schedule.

Dr. Price knew the importance of intelligence in football. She could tell you, for instance, that a quarterback who carried a sub-3.0 grade point average had limited hope of leading a winning offense. Ditto for a middle linebacker on defense. The highest graduation rate, she'd say, involved offensive linemen. But not because they were necessarily the smartest. It was because they did what you told them. *Study this. Learn that.* They followed good coaching. They didn't even move in a game, remember, until they saw the ball snapped.

I had one demand for Dr. Price.

"Get 'em graduated," I said.

And she did, too. In the two years before I arrived, Miami football graduated 9.1 percent and 27.8 percent of its players. By my second and third year, we graduated 72.7 percent and 68.3 percent. When I left, 70 percent was the bar. We ranked in the top tier of NCAA programs. That percentage counted all the players who came in a recruiting class whether they stayed with the program or left school, as the NCAA measures them. If you just counted the players who stayed their full time at Miami, our graduation rate was over 90 percent. That remained the standard after I left, with the help of the developed academic program. That's Miami football as much as winning on the field.

I'm proud players still talk of the impact of those Thursday-night meetings, of how a college education helped them. Dr. Price is still at Miami, still helping players graduate. She doesn't remember my time there with a certain win or our national championship.

She points to the academic support program.

"That's the stamp Jimmy left," she says. "That was his legacy."

6

ONE RING

In the days leading up to our 1988 national championship game against Oklahoma, I chose my words carefully to get players in the desired frame of mind.

"We're going to kick their ass," I said in our first team meeting.

That's how I prepared them.

"Look around the room," I said. "Look at the talent in here. We're gonna practice properly, play smart, and kick the shit out of them!"

Oklahoma's top-ranked defense didn't surrender more than fourteen points in any game that year.

"Look at who they play against!" I said as we showed film of their defensive ends going unblocked against Missouri, their linebackers running free against Kansas State. "That's why they're the number-one-ranked defense. They didn't play the schedule you guys did. Trust me when I tell you this—they haven't seen an offense like ours."

I never followed traditional coach-speak. You know how that goes. The coach worries if his players are ready—and then if they're over-confident. He also doesn't want to motivate an opponent and so calls the other team "great," and "very talented," and tells the media, "We'll have our hands full this week."

I took the opposite approach if we had the better team, as we did in that title game against Oklahoma in the Orange Bowl. The previous year's loss to Penn State was still fresh in people's minds. We had lost three straight bowl games in my three years at Miami. So, our recent bowl game history was a talking point among fans and in the media. It was with us, too.

I just framed history differently.

"We beat Oklahoma in '85 in their place," I said. "We beat them in '86 in this same Orange Bowl stadium. And you know what's going to happen now? It comes down to one-on-one battles. It's beating your man. Danny Stubbs, can I count on you to win your battle?"

"Yes, coach."

"Bennie Blades, will you make something happen?"

Down a line of players I went before saying, "We kicked their ass the past two years and we're gonna kick their ass again!"

It's interesting how my career intersected with Oklahoma coach Barry Switzer's through the years. He was a graduate assistant at Arkansas when I played there, then the offensive coordinator at Oklahoma when Larry Lacewell hired me to be the defensive line coach. I was the best man in Larry's wedding. But that's only because Barry, who was scheduled to be the best man, found someone more interesting to spend the weekend with.

In 1980, Barry's strong Oklahoma team beat my rebuilding Oklahoma State, 63–14. I walked across the field afterward for the ceremonial coaches' handshake and was met by an assistant. He said Barry left the game with five minutes to go.

"He went to his office to call recruits," I was told.

Now I had the better recruits, the better team, and held the hammer, too. I knew it. I made sure my players knew it, too.

"They don't belong on the same field with us," I said.

By the time kickoff came, Steve Walsh remembers, "Our coaches had us convinced Oklahoma was garbage."

The game went as expected. My key decision was to go for it

fourth-and-four on the Oklahoma 29-yard line with the rain falling and us leading 10–7 in the third quarter. Kick the field goal? Play it safe? Walsh threw a first down to Melvin Bratton, we scored a touchdown on that drive to go up 17–7, and that sent us to a not-that-close, 20–14 win.

That ride on my players' shoulders across the Orange Bowl field — arms thrust high, eyes closed in joy, coast-to-coast smile — was defining, exhilarating, career-confirming, and, perhaps most of all, a relief.

We won a title.

Our hard work paid off.

It gave us career credibility.

We. Our. Us. The first-person plural was how I typically talked about our success. The final decisions and buck-stopping accountability fell to me as head coach, but it wasn't just Jimmy Johnson running practice or Jimmy Johnson working late into the night. It was my crew, too. That's why the best memory for me of that 1987 national championship win is spending the night with my staff afterward in Miami's Fontainebleau hotel, laughing, celebrating, replaying the game — replaying our whole journey, really.

I had met Dave Wannstedt while at Pitt. He debated joining the FBI, but I convinced him to move to Oklahoma State. Tony Wise and I met at Pitt, too. Butch Davis was an Oklahoma high school coach, making $18,000 a year, when he initially joined me at Oklahoma State for $300 a month. Bruce Mays became our administrative assistant.

My crew's importance was underlined by their absence my first year at Miami. Since Howard Schnellenberger left in the summer, his staff was told it could stay with me or leave and still be paid. Tom Olivadotti, one of three assistants who wanted the head job, spent our first meeting dropping his keys on the table as I talked. He then said he couldn't work for me. I only wished some others had left with him.

That first year was spent figuring who was with me and who wasn't. Our internal problems surfaced by season's end. We led Maryland at half, 31–0, and lost. We led Boston College when Doug Flutie came to the line for one final prayer in the Orange Bowl. I double-checked our alignment with defensive coordinator Bill Trout up in the press box. He was another one who interviewed for the head job.

"Prevent, prevent," I said into the headset.

No one answered. Trout wasn't there. He had resigned and cleaned out his office before that game. He was already gone. That's how it felt to be on the other side of the "Hail Flutie" touchdown pass.

After we lost to the University of California, Los Angeles, by two points in the Fiesta Bowl, I went into the coaches' locker room and said, "Okay, that's it. I'm bringing in my people now."

I just had to reassemble them now. Dave had moved on to the University of Southern California. Tony and I picked him up at the New Orleans airport before a coaches convention. We went to Pat O'Brien's bar and an hour later he called his wife, Jan, to say they were moving to Miami. The band was back together.

Some of Schnellenberger's coaches stayed and became integral to our success. Joe Brodsky. Hubbard Alexander. Dave Campo joined us later. They went with me later to Dallas. Rich Dalrymple became my trusted media relations director. Leo Armbrust, our team chaplain, became a trusted part of the inner circle.

When I interviewed Kevin O'Neill to be trainer at Miami, I took him to happy hour with my crew to see how he fit. People would ask how a certain candidate sounded in an interview—what X's and O's he knew if he was a coach or what system he ran. I didn't care about any of that. I could teach that. I needed intelligence, chemistry, loyalty—someone who was compatible with my crew.

During my second year at Miami, we took off as a program in good part because my crew joined me. By the time we reached Dallas, Troy

Aikman said ours was the most unified staff of his career. As Troy said, "Position coaches tended to align in some ways with the good players. There was none of that on Jimmy's staff. They'd say, 'This is what Coach wants, this is what we're doing.'"

Our relationship didn't end at the office door. That's not how I worked, how we made the long hours fun. On Thursday nights while coaching college, we'd go out with our wives or girlfriends to the Ancestor restaurant in Stillwater, Oklahoma, or Carlos & Pepe's in Miami. With Dallas it was Friday nights at On the Border in Addison. We'd laugh. We'd joke. We'd enjoy each other's company.

"And the next day Jimmy'd be right back all over our ass," as Rich Dalrymple says.

That was my job.

That's also why the hours after beating Oklahoma meant so much. Sitting there in the Fontainebleau hotel, laughing with my crew, reviewing our journey, celebrating our first championship. Was I ever happier in football?

We didn't blink after that national title. Florida State was somehow ranked No. 1 in our opener against them in 1988. We beat 'em, 31–0. We rallied from down fourteen points with under eight minutes to play and won the next week at No. 15 Michigan.

This was part of a remarkable run even in the living of it. We won 23 of 24 over my final two years at Miami despite a scheduling gauntlet. Half of our opponents in 1987 and 1988 were ranked in the Top 20. Nine were in the Top 10. Twice we played—and beat—the No. 1 team.

We were the show in college football, too. National television most every Saturday, back when that meant something. Magazine covers and sold-out spectacles at any stadium we went. I loved stages like that, loved coaching like that—loved telling my players we were the team people were coming to see. As I've told current Miami players in my talks through the years, "You look down the teams on the schedule and say, 'I can't wait to kick their ass.' That's why you came here."

Even our lone regular-season loss in three years to Notre Dame came with such a swirl of rivalry and controversy it spawned an ESPN *30 for 30* documentary called *Catholics vs. Convicts.*

I got a kick out of that phrase. I also got a kick out of the holier-than-thou school of Touchdown Jesus allowing students to depict us as convicts on T-shirts sold for weeks out of campus dorms. Is hypocrisy worse than dancing in the end zone?

It all added to the fun on some level. It told of the heights we reached that people didn't attack our talent or methods anymore. They attacked *us*. Another Notre Dame T-shirt depicted me as "Pork-Faced Satan," evidently because calling me plain ol' "Satan" wasn't strong enough.

What were we guilty of?

Of winning too much? And gloating all the way?

Notre Dame has an old stadium with one tunnel to the field serving both locker rooms. Its team always warmed up in front of that tunnel. The only way back to the locker room for visiting teams after warm-ups was either walking around the field or going through their players. Other teams walked around. We weren't the walk-around type. We went right through them, and the day began with a back-alley rumble.

And where was I?

Walking right through Notre Dame's team with my players.

Notre Dame coach Lou Holtz told his players after that scrum that if a fight breaks out, "Leave Jimmy Johnson for me." Funny, you never heard his good quips when he lost. Holtz had players wear a

"Rise from the Ashes" T-shirt under their pads the previous year, but that was ignored after we shut them out.

Still, I appreciated Lou's motivational flair. I often joked with my players, too, about wanting to go after someone from Notre Dame. But I wanted someone closer to my size than scrawny Lou Holtz.

"I want that leprechaun," I'd say.

It was a heavyweight fight of a game, one of a dozen classics of my Miami teams. Notre Dame took the lead. We went for it on fourth-and-four in the second quarter and converted a 23-yard touchdown. We got stuffed on a fake punt in the third quarter. Their defensive line had a great game, harassing us into seven turnovers.

We scored a winning touchdown in the final minutes when Cleveland Gary stretched a fourth-down catch over the goal line. The ball popped out of his hand after it hit the end zone ground. Touchdown, right? It was somehow ruled a fumble.

If instant replay had been employed like it is today, that's not a fumble from any angle. It's either a first down if Cleveland's knee hit the ground before the ball crossed the goal line, or it's a touchdown because the ball was in the end zone before he lost it. We then go on to win the game. Holtz never won a national title in his career. I won a second one. No Notre Dame alum produces a *30 for 30* about the game for ESPN. Maybe a Miami alum produces it?

As it was, we lost for the first time in thirty-six regular-season games—on the road, thanks to a controversial call and a failed two-point conversion, 31–30. That's how hard we were to beat.

I made certain we'd have no hangover the next week. Freshman defensive back Charles Pharms said in the aftermath that we needed to get back to our talkative, taunting style that delivered contagious energy inside our team. It made some headlines. I made a point of publicly saying taunting wouldn't be tolerated. I meant that, too.

I also elevated Pharms to a starter, only the second true freshman I'd start at Miami.

I made him captain for the next game, too.

That confirmed who we were, the confident way we were expected to play. We didn't stumble the rest of the year. We went to No. 11 Louisiana State in November and were met by students yelling and shaking our bus to greet us in "Death Valley," as they call it. Our players loved that welcome.

"You don't know who you're playing," quarterback Steve Walsh remembers thinking about those fans.

We won, 44–3.

We then whipped No. 6 Nebraska, 23–3, in the Orange Bowl to finish second in the country. I didn't know that would be my final game at Miami, to end the happiest stretch of my coaching career. The gears were turning toward my next chapter in Dallas in ways I didn't see walking off that field.

It brought me to tears to leave Miami a couple of months later—literally to tears saying good-bye to the players with a final message to "kick Notre Dame's ass." (And they did the next season.) Tommy Tuberville, a graduate assistant, waited with my car for a quick getaway from the media after I spoke to the team. He drove to my home on Miami Beach. You couldn't have picked a more perfect Miami morning. Umbrella-blue sky. Warm and soft weather. The sun sparkled on the water as we drove over MacArthur Causeway. Tommy noticed I was silent in the backseat. He looked at me in the rearview mirror.

I was crying.

"You all right, coach?" he asked.

I wiped my tears.

"I can't believe I'm leaving this place," I said.

7

THE TALENT IN FINDING TALENT

The first time Bill Belichick visited Islamorada to talk football was early in his New England era. He brought a piece of paper listing the names of my draft picks. He wanted to discuss them—all of them.

He'd give a name and I'd say how we scouted the player, why we drafted him, who he became as a pro.

"Leon Lett, seventh round," he'd say, reading from his list.

I told him Leon's backstory: how the coaches at Emporia State said to stay away from him. "He wouldn't go to class," they said, suggesting a missing component of discipline or maturity. I might normally agree. But the more we investigated him, the more we realized Leon didn't go to class simply because he didn't know the material well enough. He was emotional, even high-strung, over how others saw him. He would rather not show up to class than potentially embarrass himself in it. Leon, to that end, skipped his first pregame meal as a rookie in Dallas because he had a nosebleed. He was sensitive to people seeing him with cotton in his nose or, worse, having to answer questions about why his nose was bleeding. So, he skipped the meal before his first pro game just to avoid any uncomfortable interaction with people.

"When he was still there in the seventh round, I went against what Emporia coaches said and my scouts said," I told Belichick. "I saw the upside of his talent. He became an important part of our Super Bowl defenses."

As we continued, what Belichick was really asking as he went down my list of draft picks was more than why a particular player was drafted in a certain round. He wanted some insight into the question every coach and personnel director asks, one that took me years to filter and distill into an answer:

How do you evaluate talent?

My answer was central to our winning. I'd tell my coaches and scouts I wanted the guy who made the four-foot putt with money on the line, sank the eight ball with everyone watching, or made the foul shot with the game riding on it. But what are some traits that define that type of player?

The way we evaluated talent was our road map to success. In an age of sophisticated scouting, where every aspect of an athlete was increasingly scrutinized and measured by numbers, my evaluation began with the player's physical talent. But to build a championship team, you need more than physical talent, of course. That deeper level of analysis involved harder work in solving fragmented and often subjective clues. There is an art to finding the right players. But first you have to know what you are looking for.

I cataloged five characteristics that broadened the chances of draft success and lessened the margins for error. I ordered them by importance, too.

1. INTELLIGENCE

Smart players win games. They listen to good coaching. They can function in complex schemes. They make fewer mistakes. They often self-correct their own errors. They stay out of trouble off the field.

So, how to measure intelligence?

The NFL recently ended its fascination with the Wonderlic Test, consisting of fifty multiple-choice questions on problem solving. I never put much stock in it. It never told me much. I looked deeper than test scores or school grades. I talked with coaches or teachers. Did the player listen? Were outside issues in his life affecting his performance? The main component to measuring intelligence, I felt, was simply talking to the player to gauge if the lights of intellect and ambition were turned on. You coach long enough, deal with enough people, you get a feel for someone just by being around them awhile. At least I could.

Sometimes it wasn't even the answers. It was just a simple observation—one telling moment—that said whether he'd have the behavioral intelligence necessary to fit into my team. The best answers often came without a question. For instance, while at Oklahoma State, I always had barbecue catered in my home for high school recruits. A top running back from Tulsa went through the buffet line one year, dropped a piece of chicken on the carpet, and didn't bother to pick it up. (It was a white carpet, too.) He looked down at it and kept walking. That told me all I needed to know. It didn't matter how talented he was. He couldn't be on my team. I didn't want to coach a player like that.

In our first Dallas draft in 1989, we took Troy Aikman, Daryl Johnston, Mark Stepnoski, and Tony Tolbert in the first four rounds.

Each became a Pro Bowl player.

Each became a foundational piece of our future Super Bowl success.

Each also shared a common denominator coming out of college that buoyed their chance of success in my book. Each player was highly intelligent. Good grades in school. Great grasp of people. Troy was off the charts. Johnston was recruited by Ivy League schools. Stepnoski was the most well-read player on our team, with history and government books his favorites. Tolbert, whom many graded lower than a fourth-round pick, was a two-time captain at Texas–El Paso. Teammates don't vote dummies into that leadership position.

I loved coaching players like that. Troy, for instance, came to my Oklahoma State camp as a teenager. I lost the recruiting battle for him to Oklahoma. Then I couldn't get him to transfer to Miami after Jerome Brown broke his leg in our 1985 game and Barry Switzer opted back to the wishbone offense. Troy went to UCLA. Before the draft, one of our scouts argued to take draft left tackle Tony Mandarich with the No. 1 pick. A left tackle or top quarterback? That wasn't a decision. Troy didn't get away from me this time.

Troy was smart enough to master the mental calculus necessary to play NFL quarterback. But having brains on, say, the offensive line was not just necessary to function in our involved offense in Dallas. It was mandatory, considering how I built offensive lines.

We never drafted an offensive lineman in the first or second rounds. Not with the Cowboys. Not with the Dolphins. That wasn't my philosophy for building a team. The top rounds were dedicated to finding guys who either scored touchdowns or stopped touchdowns. Don't misread that. I valued offensive linemen. I understood the significant role a physical line played in a physical game. But you can find offensive linemen lower in the draft with decent ability and size. And if they're smart, they'll learn to be good.

Take Stepnoski. He was a good, tough guard at the University of Pittsburgh who wore out my good defensive tackle at Miami Dan Sileo, who became a third-round pick by Tampa Bay. Stepnoski, at 245 pounds, was small for an NFL guard. He knew that. He expected to play center in the NFL.

"Can you turn him into a center?" I asked offensive line coach Tony Wise.

This folded into another developed concept of mine: the offensive line coach was more important than any player he coached. No other assistant coach could say that. That is because the offensive line is a world of its own. The linemen block defensive players who are always better athletes. That means if an offensive lineman takes a wrong half-step, the better athlete wins. If he misses an assignment, the play is dead—or the series is dead. Maybe the game is dead.

Tony helped Stepnoski, a third-round pick, develop into a three-time All-Pro center. That's the prototype for how we built the line with smart but undervalued pieces. An undrafted defensive lineman, Mark Tuinei, and another third-round pick, Erik Williams, became our tackles. Nate Newton, a guy considered too fat by many, and Kevin Gogan, a seventh-round pick, became our guards. Each of them didn't just come at a relatively low cost but made at least two Pro Bowls in their careers. Williams, like Stepnoski, became a three-time All-Pro player.

Intelligence multiplies your options, too. One practice in Dallas, offensive coordinator Norv Turner called a play needing a third receiver—the "F" receiver in our playbook. The F receiver typically replaced the fullback on passing downs. No F receiver came on the field in that practice as Norv waited.

"I can run the play," Daryl said.

"You know the F-receiver plays?" Norv asked.

That led to a package where Daryl lined up in the slot or as a second tight end and created match-up problems for the defense. All because he was smart enough to learn that position on his own.

Sometimes I'd fall in love with the physical traits of a player and talk myself into ignoring the mental ones. It never worked out. Dumb players, no matter how talented, find a way to bust a coverage or break a protection. They contribute to losing games and ruining seasons.

Dumb players also get into problems off the field. They're the ones you get calls about in the middle of the night.

"Next time I take a dumb player, hit me over the head with a hammer," I said to my staff so many times it became a mantra on my teams.

2. WORKS HARD

Troy got keys to the gym and weight room at Henrietta High School in Oklahoma to work out on his own. His coach there, Bill Holt, once asked Troy if he intended to stay all night by himself, working out. That work ethic explains how Troy made the Pro Football Hall of Fame.

Cortez Kennedy weighed a flabby 330 pounds at Northwest Mississippi Community College before signing with Miami. I made him run 110-yard sprints, end zone to end zone, often until he threw up. He began to wake early to run a legendary hill at Tropical Park in Miami, did more work at a neighboring track afterward, and was 285 pounds when Seattle selected him as the No. 3 pick in the draft. That explains why Cortez made the Hall of Fame. Cortez had a role model to run with, too. Russell Maryland ran those same sprints to become an All-American defensive tackle at Miami and the No. 1 pick for us in Dallas.

After years inside the game, you learned to recognize how greatness looked, felt, and even smelled. Greatness smelled like sweat. This didn't apply just to individuals, but to full teams. Each Thursday in Dallas, we had a two-minute drill scrimmage of the first-team offense against the first-team defense. They were fierce affairs where it was best on best, from receiver Michael Irvin against cornerback Kevin Smith, to defensive coordinator Dave Wannstedt (or Butch Davis) against offensive coordinator Norv Turner. Everyone wanted to win. The jawing, the competing, the playmaking—it was just like any Sunday afternoon. Norv later heard of an added reason for the fierce play beyond bragging rights: players bet on the outcome.

I was the referee, too, to make sure the work was done well. A long pass on the first play? *Tweet.* I'd call a penalty if we needed to work on a multiple-play drive against the clock. A missed 51-yard field goal? *Tweet.* Someone was offsides. The kicker couldn't end his day with a miss weighing on his mind.

Those scenes were a window into that team's greatness. No one worked harder than our biggest names—Aikman, Emmitt Smith, Charles Haley, Ken Norton Jr. And Michael Irvin? He only knew one gear. At Miami, he demanded to work one summer against Tim Sims, a faster and similarly sized defensive back. Sims could never master our defensive scheme. But as a practice partner, he was a great one-on-one defender. Michael thought that if he beat Sims, he could beat anyone. Once he came to Dallas, Michael would wear a weight jacket running sprints and stay after practice for as long as the quarterback kept throwing.

Steve Walsh was a regular workout partner with Michael and other receivers at Miami and again early in Dallas. When Steve got traded to New Orleans, he couldn't find receivers to work with after practice. They wanted to save their legs for the games.

"Save your legs?" he'd say. "This is how you get better."

That was the first time Steve realized that not everyone worked as hard as my teams did.

3. PLAYMAKER

Nothing about Zach Thomas fit the parameters of an NFL linebacker. He was small at 5'11". He had average speed. Our special teams coach with the Dolphins, Mike Westhoff, worked out Thomas

at Texas Tech and fudged the actual number of repetitions he did
with weights. For example, Thomas did twenty-two bench presses.
Westhoff wrote twenty-four. He feared that Thomas's low-end strength
offered another reason to cross him off our draft list.

Jason Taylor had a similarly misfit story. He was 6'6" but considered too small at 238 pounds to be an NFL defensive end. He also
wasn't fast enough to be an every-down linebacker. The dreaded
tweener—back when people considered it a problem.

All Thomas and Taylor did was make plays. Big plays. Game-
changing plays. Throughout their careers. Thomas set tackling records at Texas Tech, was a two-time All-American player, and the
Southwest Conference Defensive Player of the Year. He also kept
measuring in at 5'11". Did it matter? Sure, it mattered. It meant he
would be available in a lower round because most teams couldn't get
past his height. We took him in the fifth round.

The drafting of Taylor was different. Norv, by then in Washington, had coached the Senior Bowl in 1997. He realized this lanky
kid from small-school Akron was the best player on the field. He
pushed the Washington front office to take him. Too small, he was
told. Washington's personnel department gave him a fifth-round
grade. Turner, knowing he wouldn't last that long, mentioned his
Senior Bowl practices when we talked. I studied Jason's films closer.
The fact he didn't fit the size and shape of a traditional defensive
end again became a bonus. I gave him a second-round grade. When
cornerback Sam Madison was also available in the second round, I
took him. Sam was a playmaker on defense, returned punts, and I
figured wouldn't last until the third round. Jason had a chance to
fall in the draft because of his size. He did, too. We took him in the
third round.

Playmakers come in any shape or position. A guard can be a playmaker if he makes blocks that spring touchdowns. A special teams

player can be a playmaker as a gunner who runs down a punt returner. The important part is opening your mind—not just your eyes—when looking at players.

There's a story Dave Wannstedt tells of our time in Dallas. Wannstedt wasn't alone in liking a certain defensive player. The player's physical metrics were a scout's dream. Big. Fast. Strong. He was a three-year starter at a powerhouse school, too. I took a look at him. One thing stood out to me. He had few sacks. He made minimal big plays. He didn't do much on the videotape.

"I don't see the production," I said.

We took him off our draft board. Another team took him with their first-round pick. He never stood out in the NFL, just as he didn't in college.

So many coaches refused to believe what players told them by their play. Case in point: Tony Wise was a Syracuse assistant recruiting Daryl Johnston. Syracuse head coach Dick McPherson wasn't interested. Why? Because Johnston was only being recruited by Cornell and Colgate. Tony pushed and pushed until McPherson finally agreed to sign Daryl. So, when Tony came to Miami and began recruiting an undersized running back named Leonard Conley, he refused to say only Kansas was also interested. He told me Notre Dame and Penn State were interested in the all-state running back from Medley, Florida.

"Let's watch the film," I said.

Conley's lack of size (5'7") and relative lack of speed (4.6 seconds over 40 yards) didn't turn me off as I viewed him. The other all-state back his senior year was Emmitt Smith from Pensacola. Everyone wanted him. Conley was a comparable afterthought. We signed him at Miami. He averaged 6.4 yards rushing as a freshman in 1987 and became a good part of our success.

Would I prefer to have a big, strong, fast playmaker? Sure. But the most important part of evaluating talent isn't big, strong, or fast. It's making plays.

4. GYM RAT/LOVES TO COMPETE

When I recruited players in college, they often would throw some form of the same line at me, like bait in the water, as if testing my reaction. Sometimes a member of the family asked it, like on my visit to Gainesville, Florida, for a top prospect in receiver Lamar Thomas.

"When do you think he'd start at Miami?" his father said.

I chuckled. "Start? I can't even promise you he'll play. But I'll promise you he'll compete against the best athletes in America at practice. I also promise if he works hard and competes, he'll be further along as a junior or senior than he'll be at most schools if he starts as a freshman."

That was my gauntlet on the table, my countertest to their test. Or like when another player, Claude Jones, was choosing between Miami and Florida State, I said: "You can either come to Miami and win the national titles, or you can go to Florida State, and we'll beat you on the way to winning national titles. It's your choice."

It was a challenge to their ego, their competitiveness—and was pretty much true. We went 4-1 against Florida State.

That pitch didn't work for every player. But maybe those weren't the ones I wanted anyhow. For Thomas, Jones, and dozens of others, my response is what sold them on Miami. They wanted to compete against our top players.

Does a player want to compete against the best? Need to win at everything—at golf, shooting baskets, playing pool? These competitive qualities didn't apply just to players I wanted.

They defined me, too.

I want to be the best at whatever I do—coaching, drafting, fishing, catching lobster in the ocean. Shuffleboard? I had never played the game before I came home, all excited, waking up Linda Kay around midnight to say I had dethroned the defending champion of the Elks Club in Ames, Iowa, when I coached there.

Once, for fun, the Iowa State staff scheduled an ice-skating outing. We were mostly from the South, starting with head coach Johnny Majors, who grew up in Tennessee. Everyone got to the rink, laced up skates, and proceeded to fall in creative manners. Everyone but me, that is. I practiced several times before our outing to make sure I could skate rings around them.

I also played the card game of bridge a lot in college, skipping classes and picking up spending money in the student union. It's an analytical game where you have to read people, meaning that even with the worse cards you can win. That appealed to me. One night in Miami, boxing promoter Bob Arum and I entered a Miami Beach hotel when a limousine pulled up. Arum introduced me to Lucien Chen, a gambler known to drop $1 million on a roll of dice. Chen was a sportsman and fight promoter. He also represented Jamaica in the Bridge Olympics (yes, there is such an event). That got us talking.

A few weeks later, Chen asked me to be his partner in a Miami bridge tournament. I hadn't played bridge in years, but why not? We won the tournament, too. Again: If I get into something, I'm in to win. And if I win, I'll gloat. I mentioned the big bridge title to a *Miami Herald* reporter, who made a little story of it. An FBI agent showed up at my office the next day. He was looking for Chen, who among other things was wanted for allegedly running bolito, a numbers game, in Jamaica. Everything must have worked out because I knew Chen for years. His son, Carey, an artist, even has some of his work in my Big Chill restaurant in Key Largo.

Most days in retirement I wake up and play bridge on the computer. I'm still a gym rat that way. I still love to compete. Just like the players I wanted on my team.

5. CHARACTER

"You don't win championships with bums."

That's the phrase I'd repeat to scouts and coaches to reinforce the kind of player we wanted. *Character* is a catchall word for the attributes that separate the selfish from the selfless. How do you define it? It's sort of like Supreme Court justice Potter Stewart's famous line on pornography: I know it when I see it.

Randy Shannon, for instance, knew that his Miami roommate, Cortez Kennedy, battled weight problems. Randy slept in front of the refrigerator so Cortez couldn't eat at night. That's character.

Aikman could have wanted to throw the ball twice as much as he did to build his stats. He wasn't built that way. After my second year, it looked like we would make the playoffs before Troy hurt his shoulder. That also took him out of the running for the Pro Bowl.

"I tried to get you in the Pro Bowl, but you didn't make it," I said.

"Don't worry about Pro Bowls, coach," he said. "You keep bringing in talented players and I'll go to enough Pro Bowls."

That's character.

Russell Maryland's only scholarship offer after his senior year was from Indiana State. He got letters from schools like Brown and Dartmouth due to his grades. We had shown some interest in him as a junior, and Russell's father sent me a video of his senior year with a note asking to take a look. I saw a fat, 320-pound prospect. A maybe. But we looked into his background. He went to Whitney Young High School, a top academic school, where Michelle Obama graduated five years before Russell. His father was the first Black manager in his Chrysler plant. His mother was an accountant for the Chicago Police Department. Russell became nicknamed "The Conscience" by teammates because he'd have them in his room each night to study video. But first he would oversee a study period.

That, too, is winning character.

8

IT WAS NEVER A DREAM

It all started with a quick phone call and a simple request.

"Could you put in a good word for me with Tex Schramm?" Jerry Jones said.

This was the summer of 1988, and I was friends with the Dallas Cowboys' president, who was charged with selling H. R. "Bum" Bright's iconic franchise. I had sat with Tex, coach Tom Landry, and scout Gil Brandt in the team's luxury suite the previous Super Bowl in Miami. Schramm wanted me to be the team's defensive coordinator. It would be the first step toward my succeeding Landry as coach, he said.

There were other whispers connecting me to NFL jobs at that time. The San Francisco 49ers supposedly considered me before Bill Walsh got his assistant, George Seifert, promoted in 1988. When Buddy Ryan started 1-3 at Philadelphia that same fall, I heard that Eagles owner and Miami businessman Norman Braman was asking around about me.

I wasn't really looking at the NFL, but it evidently was looking at me. Schramm's idea of my succeeding Landry someday didn't work for me. There were too many unknowns, too many ways it could go wrong. I was having too much fun winning at Miami to be anyone's assistant, too.

But I called him for Jerry.

"Hey, Tex," I said, "I want to talk with you about my old college teammate . . ."

It seemed a thread of an idea at the time, Jerry buying "America's Team" and hiring me as its coach. That was his plan. Jerry always thought big like that, from the time I met him three decades earlier. As players, we were hotel roommates on Friday nights before Arkansas away games simply because "Jones" and "Johnson" were alphabetical neighbors. That got overplayed later, the whole idea of "college roommate" fitting a convenient story line of us being best friends. I liked Jerry. But he was a year older than I was in school and played on the offense, meaning he was forever with that side of the team, while I played defense. He also grew up in Arkansas, in a family with some money. I grew up in a Gulf town in Texas, with no money.

How well do you know someone from an occasional night together? Not that much, even if we had some fun. One night in Biloxi, Mississippi, as we practiced for the 1963 Sugar Bowl, Jerry and I broke curfew and found a bar. Some fans bought us drinks. Hey, not bad, we figured.

Suddenly a hand landed on each of our shoulders and a clipped voice said, "You boys gonna pay for these drinks?"

It was our offensive coordinator, Doug Dickey. I was scared to death. I thought we'd be sent home. Dickey took us back to the hotel. Jerry's such a storyteller, he had no problem telling other players about our big adventure even as we walked to our room.

"These guys were buying us drinks and Jimmy and I—"

"I said, get your ass in your rooms!" Dickey said.

We didn't sleep a wink that night. We would laugh about it through the years as our paths occasionally crossed. Arkansas reunions. A random meeting in Hot Springs. Jerry connected me to the right people for the Oklahoma State job in 1979. His son Stephen came to my football camp there while in high school, and Jerry and I had a drink at the Stillwater Country Club, in a small house off the first green. I told him I admired how he'd made money in the oil and gas business.

"Jimmy," he said, "you go to bed every night thinking about football and wake up every morning thinking about football, and that's all you think about all day long. That's how I think about money."

Fast-forward to February 1989: I checked out of my Fort Worth hotel the morning after the Davey O'Brien Award for the top college quarterback (Troy Aikman beat out Steve Walsh) and saw a message from Jerry. I called him from the airport. He wanted me to inspect the Cowboys' practice facility of Valley Ranch, in nearby Irving. There was a $5 million note on it factored into the franchise's sale price. That's when this sale upshifted from a far-fetched fantasy to it-might-happen reality.

"You should have your friend buy the team," Schramm joked at Valley Ranch that day.

I left there and flew with Jerry to Little Rock as negotiations heated up. We got to know each other over the next two weeks more than we had in the previous three decades. We talked plans, structure, people, possibilities. Jerry said he'd run the business side of the Cowboys; I'd run the football side and "We'll make history."

I watched Jerry and Bum negotiate the final steps of the Cowboys' sale on the twelfth floor of the Bright Building in Dallas. All that was left was for the papers to be drawn up and the signing the next morning.

"I know you like Mexican food," Jerry said to me. "I know a good place."

I told Jerry that wasn't a good idea. We should stay out of the public right now, as I'd be recognized. Jerry was new to the public arena and insisted on going to Mia's, a little Mexican restaurant. *Dallas Morning News* reporter Ivan Maisel, whom I knew, happened to be eating dinner there with his wife. That's how a photo of Jerry and me landed on the front page the next morning. I knew we were in public relations trouble as the camera clicked. I just didn't know how much trouble. Unbeknownst to Jerry and me, Mia's was also one of Tom Landry's favorite restaurants. His framed photo was on a wall. So even before we had fired the legendary coach, it appeared like we had brazenly taken over his world.

The next morning, Jerry and Bum finalized the sale. Bum said he would call Landry.

"No, that's my responsibility to tell Tom," Jerry told Bum.

Landry had just teed off on the eighth hole at Hidden Hills Golf Club in Austin when Jerry arrived to tell him the sale was complete, and that I'd be the new coach. It was all over the media by then. Jerry returned to Dallas, I would return to Miami, and he'd do the news conference about the sale.

Dallas was a mix of emotions by then. The same fans and media who wanted change in the Cowboys became upset at the abrupt manner in which it came. Jerry and I were cast as outsiders, Arkansas hicks, tarnishing a Dallas institution. We didn't make it easy on ourselves with some opening missteps, like eating at Landry's restaurant and Jerry's opening news conference, where he told a city that was mourning Landry's exit that it "felt like Christmas" to him.

My plane landed in Miami after midnight. Dave Wannstedt, who happened to be in Dallas for a coaching seminar, flew back with me and we drove down Interstate 95 calling the crew.

"Let's get going," I told Dave Campo.

"Tony, where are you?" I said to the recorder when Tony Wise didn't answer his landline. "We've got work to do."

"Think Gloria would sell the house?" I said to Hubbard Alexander, who had just bought a new home the previous month.

"She doesn't have to sell it," Hubbard said. "I'll sell it."

We were ready to work in Dallas, even if Dallas wasn't quite ready for us. My message was simple when I spoke to the media a few days later: give us a chance to prove ourselves.

"I do believe if commitment, enthusiasm, and hard work are worth anything, we will make progress in Dallas," I said.

That began the most miserable year of my life.

The change began with my marriage.

Linda Kay and I had grown apart through twenty-six years together. Our boys were adults now. At a time when many couples would look to travel, or spend more time together, I took on the challenge of a lifetime. My world rearranged even more around football. I wanted to be alone, to be more selfish with my time and energy, if that was possible, considering our life together had always put my football first.

I came in from a jog early on in Dallas and said, "I want a divorce."

I gave Linda Kay virtually everything: money, possessions, whatever she wanted, because she deserved it and I don't like owing people anything. She was a wonderful wife, a great mother—far better in her family roles than I was while chasing football in a manner that consumed all our lives. That would only hit me like a hammer later.

For this new chapter in Dallas, I selfishly stripped away anything from my life that didn't involve that pursuit of winning. I moved into a place three blocks from the office. I had minimal contact with anyone outside football, except my sons. I began working at 5 a.m. each day, stayed until I was too tired to be productive, and repeated that daily cycle for the next five years.

The job demanded all I had. Everything needed remaking. My first inspection of Valley Ranch for Jerry, for instance, showed something odd. The team's weightlifting area was outside. It got cold in the Dallas winter. How did players lift weights there in the off-season?

They didn't, I was told. They went to individual gyms. Only a couple of teams in the NFL worked together through the off-season at that time.

We built an indoor weight room for mandatory off-season workouts.

The first interviews for my staff included a Minnesota Vikings assistant who said their staff didn't work in the off-season. No draft preparation. Little planning for the season. The Vikings staff reconvened a week or two before the start of training camp, he said. That mind-set wasn't uncommon, I found. The previous Dallas staff often left the office at 5 p.m. They didn't bother attending the second day of the draft, considering they weren't involved.

My crew worked late and year-round, just as in Miami.

Our first practice that spring in Dallas consisted of simple conditioning drills and timing players in the 40-yard run. I knew this was a bad roster from their three straight losing seasons. That first practice revealed the oldest, slowest, least athletic team I could imagine. My 1986 Miami team could beat them. I had no doubt.

My vision to build as quickly as possible can be seen through the prism of the quarterback position. Drafting Troy was just a first step toward our rebuild. We traded the previous year's starting quarterback, Steve Pelluer, for third- and fourth-round draft picks. He could have helped us win a few games that year, like some other veterans we released, including the previous year's receiving leader, Ray Alexander. But the draft picks meant more than a possible win or two.

With Aikman drafted and Pelluer on his way out, I also took my Miami quarterback Steve Walsh with the 1st pick in the supplemental draft. That raised eyebrows. This draft was a relatively new feature for players ineligible for the primary draft. Only three first-round picks were taken over its first eleven years. People wondered what I was doing throwing another first-round pick at quarterback. Does this college rube know that only one quarterback plays? Doesn't he see glaring holes across the larger roster?

Troy and Steve wondered, too.

"Why take me?" Steve remembered thinking.

I picked him up at the Dallas airport and intimated why.

"Hey, Steve, we've got Aikman," I said. "We think he's going to be good. But you never know. And, at the end of the day, I have you in my back pocket. I can trade you."

Steve was smart enough to realize right then that he would probably be traded. That was my vision for how this would play out. It should be every team's plan, considering the value of young quarterbacks. For instance, before the 2020 draft, I said Detroit should draft Justin Herbert with their No. 3 pick. People scoffed at that opinion, considering Detroit had veteran quarterback Matthew Stafford. They instead drafted cornerback Jeff Okudah. Where's the value in that?

I couldn't talk openly about my plans for Walsh that first season and dilute his trade value. Plus, there was a benefit to having a legitimate quarterback competition to ensure Troy was who we thought he was. I purposely called it that, too, stopping reporters who called it a "controversy."

"What controversy?" I asked. "It's a competition—a good, healthy competition. And that's how it's going to remain."

It wasn't easy on Troy or Steve. It wasn't easy for me, either, in a different way. I wasn't able to talk openly with either one. I couldn't build the necessary trust between a coach and quarterback. It took Troy and me awhile to heal those wounds. But everyone understood what was at work after our first season, when Steve was traded to New Orleans for first-, second-, and third-round picks. That's how we built. One good pick became three.

By then, though, that trade was overshadowed by a bigger deal.

The trade of star running back Herschel Walker started out as an ordinary tense day that first season in Dallas. Ordinary noontime jog. Ordinary inner circle of a half dozen assistants or support staff with me. We jogged our ordinary two-and-a-half-mile route to get some exercise and clear our heads. We then always walked back, talking about who should start at guard or how to tweak the game plan. What was a fun excursion amid the winning in Miami was sometimes an edgy one in Dallas.

Tony Wise, with our first season already sinking, remembered on one jog how Philadelphia coach Buddy Ryan predicted doom for me coming out of college because "there's no East Carolina in the NFL."

"There is an East Carolina in the NFL," Tony said. "We're East Carolina."

We were that bad. We were clueless to some NFL ways, too. We went 3-1 in preseason and thought it mattered, especially because our loss came when Denver quarterback John Elway played the entire way in a 24–21 game. Denver coach Dan Reeves played for Tom Landry. That showed how much the old NFL guard disliked Jerry and me: Reeves risked his franchise quarterback in an entire preseason game to eke out an empty win.

We then learned how meaningless preseason was in losing the opener to New Orleans, 28–0. It was painful. We'd lost only two regular-season games in our final four years at Miami. I planned to put an end to it right there, too.

"Let me tell you something—that losing shit, that's over," I told the team before our next game in Atlanta. "We're winning starting now."

Troy still jokes about that talk. That losing shit had a long way to go. We were 0-5 when that ordinary noontime jog became anything but ordinary. I told everyone the roster was so bad we'd be out of a job in two years if we followed the conventional, take-the-best-player process to drafting and rebuilding. I had been on the phone floating trades to help us. It wasn't yet time to trade Walsh. I talked with Al Davis about trading Michael Irvin to Oakland, but my heart wasn't into it.

"We've got to think of something," I said on that jog.

I realized we had one prime asset. Just one.

"We could trade Herschel," I said.

There was a chuckle or two, then silence upon realizing I was serious—that I wasn't playing with scared money. Herschel wasn't just considered a top running back. He was our offense. It would be a public relations nightmare, too—yet another one for Jerry and me. They were stacking up like the losses. But I saw something in Herschel in our opening games that said he was a good back, not a great one. More to the point: He didn't fit our style of offense. Tony Wise would watch Herschel run and say, "Geez, can the guy make a cut? He's running right up the ass of my guy making a block." We wanted a back who would dip and dive and make defenders miss. Herschel would run over people but wouldn't make them miss. Herschel was still our best offensive player, and I wouldn't have traded him unless we got a ransom.

Herschel's name had surfaced earlier in talking with Cleveland's Ernie Accorsi. I called him back. His problem was that Cleveland didn't have a No. 1 pick in the next draft. He said Cleveland owner Art Modell would call that evening.

"We should call some other teams to see what else we could get," I told Jerry Jones.

I suggested Jerry call Atlanta owner Rankin Smith, considering Herschel was from Georgia. Atlanta wasn't interested. We called other teams that night. I told Minnesota general manager Mike Lynn the next morning that we were about to trade Herschel after that day's practice at 6:30 p.m.

"Here's what it'd take if you're interested," I said, listing the parameters.

At 4:30, I came off the practice field and a fax from Lynn was waiting. It was the framework of trading a transcendent talent to Minnesota for the flimsy price of first-, second-, and sixth-round picks in 1990 and five veteran castoffs who had bad knees or bad attitudes. At least that was the trade as Lynn and most of the football world framed it when terms were announced. Minnesota fleeced us, most people thought. Randy Galloway, a popular columnist then with the *Fort Worth Star-Telegram*, wrote the prevailing opinion: "The Cowboys got nothing more than a handful of Minnesota smoke." I can still pull up that column on my cell phone, just for fun.

I saw the trade differently as it was announced. I was in full gloat mode.

"The Great Train Robbery," I called it.

Here's how I saw the deal: we traded a good if overrated running back for three first-round, three second-round, one third-round, and one fifth-round picks and three or four veterans to temporarily fill some holes. Yep, a train robbery.

Most NFL executives, writers, and fans weren't conditioned to view the trade as I did. They saw the five Minnesota players in the trade—not the draft pick attached to each player if we released him at season's end. For instance, we could keep a decent linebacker like Jesse Solomon or have Minnesota's first-round pick in 1991. I only cared about all those rich draft picks.

Thinking I'd keep the players was one mistake Lynn made in that trade. The other one, the one Cleveland was close to making, too: thinking they were one player away from a Super Bowl. You rarely are.

I entered offensive coordinator Dave Shula's office immediately after making the trade and told him there was good and bad news.

"Give me the good news first, since we haven't had much of it this year," he said.

"I set up our team for the next ten years," I said.

"The bad news?" he asked.

"I traded Herschel Walker."

Dave promptly reached across his desk and tore our run-game playbook in half, dropping it in the trash can by his desk. He thought we wouldn't score again that year. He had a short-term point, too. If that represented one immediate problem of trading Herschel, the other involved these incoming Minnesota players. They were better than our players. My assistants wanted to insert them into the lineup. But the plan was the plan. The last thing I wanted was coaches and fans falling in love with average players who would be thrown overboard at season's end for the draft picks. I refused to let any of the Minnesota players start. They couldn't play until the second quarter.

When it came time to complete the trade after the season and get the draft picks, Lynn didn't return my calls. Everyone saw the trade for what it was by then. Herschel had a mediocre season. The draft picks stood out as gold. I sent a letter to the league saying the former Minnesota players were about to be released to allow the accompanying draft picks to be sent to Dallas. Only a word from Minnesota could stop their release, I wrote. I sent a copy to Lynn. He finally called.

There was a point to all this beyond league bookkeeping: I wanted to keep a few of the Minnesota players *and* the valuable draft picks. I had leverage to do it, too. He could get something or take nothing. I proposed keeping three players and sending Minnesota a third- and a seventh-round pick. He grudgingly took it.

Herschel's trade didn't launch us to the Super Bowl by itself. That deal became so famous because we turned Minnesota's draft picks into great players. The Los Angeles Rams traded running back Eric Dickerson in 1987 and received three first-round and three second-round picks. Only one of the six players taken with those picks, running back Gaston Green, had an All-Pro season. And he had just one. Does anyone remember that trade?

We used Minnesota's draft picks over the next couple of years to stock our roster with: Emmitt Smith, a Hall of Fame running back; safety Darren Woodson, a Hall of Fame finalist who should be voted in soon; All-Pro cornerback Kevin Smith; Pro Bowl defensive tackle Russell Maryland; and cornerback Clayton Holmes, a starter on our Super Bowl teams.

In February 2022, I stood at a roofing convention in Dallas and invited the catalyst to so much winning to join me on the stage.

"I just want to thank Herschel for everything he's done for me," I said. "And everything he's done for the Dallas Cowboys."

This was the first time Herschel Walker and I had seen each other since I traded him thirty-three years earlier during my first season in Dallas. He smiled at my line—a little. We hugged. We talked. We were there to discuss, as I said to the roofers, "what people say is the greatest trade in NFL history."

That list is why all those years later, when I stood with Herschel on that convention stage, everyone had come to agree it was indeed the Great Train Robbery.

"You traded me," Herschel said to me before turning to the audience, "but I love that guy."

I love Herschel, too. He helped us build a dynasty.

Still, the losing never stopped our first season. We were closing in on our second win when veteran cornerback Everson Walls was beaten for a 72-yard touchdown against the Arizona Cardinals with a minute to play. That dropped us to 1-9. While trudging off the field, I saw Walls joking with that winning receiver, Ernie Jones.

"Everson, what is going on here?" I yelled. "Get your ass in the locker room."

Walls looked at me. "What's the big deal? We'd already lost eight of 'em. We're not going to the playoffs."

Walls wasn't a bad guy. Nor was he a bad player. He went on to help the New York Giants win a Super Bowl. But he was a bad fit for our rebuilding program in Dallas. That's the first step for any losing organization—recognizing and ridding yourself of the bad people or wrong players. Walls represented the losing culture I had to change. He wasn't around the next season.

"Hey, if we ever get to the point where we can laugh and cut up after a loss, then something's wrong," I told the team after that loss. "You've got to get sick to your stomach every time you come up short."

The losing threatened to eat me and my crew up. Dave Wannstedt wondered as that season trudged on about the effectiveness of our 4-3, hit-the-gaps, read-on-the-attack defense. We had the nation's top college defense at Miami. Now we were one of the NFL's worst defenses. Dave wavered on whether our system worked at this level.

What could he do different?

What, really, *should* he do different?

"Hey, Jimmy," he said at one point, "do you think we should adjust from what we're doing on defense?"

"Dave, listen to me," I said. "Trust me on this. We know this defense better than anybody does. The strengths. The weaknesses. We got the right defense. We know how to make it work. When we get better players, this will excel."

Dave considers that an important moment in his coaching evolution. He would use that story throughout his career whenever a coach's confidence faltered on a proven concept. It was only human nature for us to wonder about what we were doing that first season in Dallas. We used schemes no one else did in the NFL. New York Giants coach Bill Parcells later told me how quarterback Phil Simms said before playing us, "Geez, they're running that college coverage."

"You'd better learn that college coverage," Parcells told him. "These guys know what they're doing."

We played four across in the secondary, for instance, in a design we called the "Switch" or "Double Switch." The switch came in when the two safeties would invert, or move closer to the line, and the cornerbacks would drop back. It involved a man-to-man scheme within a zone at times and required communication and chemistry. Bill Belichick liked the defense and considered that system one of the toughest to play against ("Ask Tom Brady—he'll tell you the same," as Bill said). Belichick also thought the necessary coordination between linebackers and the secondary demanded such attention he wouldn't have time to practice other schemes. A lot of pro players aren't disciplined enough to run it, too. They're wired to run man-to-man coverage or a simple zone. Not one wrapped in the other. You needed the right players. We didn't have them that first year.

"We've seen this work when we have the right players," I told Dave. "We'll get the right players."

Later, when we did have the proper players, Dave directed the No. 2 defense in the league to the Super Bowl. And that college coverage? Well, it was tweaked and renamed the "Cover 2" in Tampa less than a decade later and became the trendy NFL defense for a generation.

We mined every avenue to find the right players that first year, too. Each day, the list of waived players from other teams landed on my desk like a department store catalog. Was there anyone we liked? A nose tackle named Kevin Lilly was signed after a Monday workout, in the team picture Saturday, played Sunday, and was cut the next Monday. The turnover was so constant, a convenient pile of playbooks sat in the corner of our meeting room for players to take upon arriving and return upon leaving.

The process involved losing, too—weekly, painful losing. But you have to understand something: I never dreamed of success at any of my jobs, including Dallas. If you have a dream, a hope, a maybe, a crossing of your fingers . . . Well, crossing your fingers isn't much of a plan, is it?

I'm a believer.

I believed at every stop of my career that we'd be successful. I entered Dallas with the concrete belief we already were champions. If taking that job was like opening a new book, I skipped ahead and read the last page. I wrote that last page, actually. I knew how our story ended. We were champions. This isn't some revised history in reflection. Before my second season, coming off that miserable first season in Dallas, I told Peter King of *Sports Illustrated*, "It's not whether we will succeed. We will. It's just a matter of how long it would take."

That mind-set could be traced to my daily conduct and personal interactions in every job I had. Take Oklahoma State. When we took over that sunken program in 1979, things looked broken at times. We lost five straight games to start our second season before improving the next game. We tied Kansas.

During our usual Thursday happy hour that week at the Ancestor in Stillwater after that tie, I looked at Dave Wannstedt, Tony Wise, Butch Davis, and the crew I'd brought to Oklahoma State.

"Guys, I know it's kind of rough right now," I said. "But you hang with me. We are going to win us a national championship."

I didn't wish-upon-a-star dream that. I believed it was true. I knew it would happen. Those who hung with me won that national championship, too. We didn't win it at Oklahoma State. We took Oklahoma State to its second bowl game in fourteen years. We won a bowl game in our fifth year to get us the Miami job. We won our national championship there in the 1987 season.

The pattern repeated itself in Dallas. I sat with my crew at our regular Friday happy hour at On the Border that first year and reminded them of my talk at the Ancestor.

"Guys, you stuck with me then and we won our national championship, just as I said we would," I said. "I know things are rough. But we're going to win us a Super Bowl here. Just hang with me. Keep working. We're going to win a Super Bowl."

We hung tough. We kept working. We never stopped feeling miserable. It became so bad at games that I pulled my father aside after one Sunday he and Mother had watched. I asked him not to come to any more games. We were losing. I was being booed. I didn't want them to see that, much less have the crowd possibly turn on them.

"Let me go through this alone," I told Mother and Daddy.

There was only one outlet to the misery. While going through my divorce, I began dating Rhonda, a hairdresser I met—imagine this—getting my hair cut. She was positive, upbeat, funny. I needed those attributes that first season in Dallas. Rhonda and I weren't just friends, we were "buddies," as we framed it. She got me to laugh some days in Dallas, a good sign for our years to come. She also wanted to live by herself at that point and became expert at reading my dark moods and giving me space.

There were a lot of dark moods that first season in Dallas, too. By December, my crew and I were empty. We had worked our asses off and had one win to show for it. I saw how beat everyone was at a staff meeting with a couple of games left.

"Well, the only thing we can do now is drink our way through the rest of the season," I said.

Our fifteenth and final loss that year was to Green Bay on a cold, dank day in Dallas. I was in shock from all the losing. I walked down a hallway afterward, emotionally and physically exhausted after talking to the team and the media about our finally finished season. Brenda Bushnell, my television producer, caught up with me.

"Coach, I know you're not feeling good right now, but if we can knock out one more interview for the TV show we'll be done," she said.

I was so drained, I started crying.

"I can't do it," I said. "Get one of the assistants to do the TV show."

I hopped on a plane with Rhonda that night to Miami. The following day we were in the Bahamas. I lay there and bled for a couple of days. The worst year of my life was over. The first step of any rebuild—getting rid of the wrong people—was mostly done.

I was onto Step 2, of adding more of the right people.

9

CHARTING THE FUTURE

Something bothered me in the days after our first draft in Dallas. It wasn't the players we picked. My crew and I felt they laid the foundation to the future.

Jerry Jones, too, offered congratulations for trading down in the second round to expand our chances of success. That move happened when our homework showed the player we wanted, Syracuse fullback Daryl Johnston, would be available later than our 29th pick, the first of the second round. Other teams didn't value him like we did.

Oakland's Al Davis liked talented Penn State guard Steve Wisniewski. So, I took Wisniewski with our pick at No. 29 and sent him and a sixth-round pick to Oakland. We received Oakland's 39th pick to take Johnston plus its third- and fifth-round picks.

"Great trade," Jerry said.

I felt that way, too. We got the player we wanted and added picks. My gut said it was a smart deal. But that was the gnawing issue after that draft. I didn't like building our future on some foggy gut feeling.

"I was just shooting from the hip on that trade," I told Jerry.

There had to be a better manner of weighing the worth of such trades. For all the talk of the problems I'd have coming from the college game, this was another area where my lack of NFL background proved an advantage. I didn't have to force myself to think outside some conventional box. There was no box for me. There was just a bothersome question in this case: How can you calculate the relative value of draft picks to weigh trade options?

I called Mike McCoy, a sharp numbers guy who worked for Jerry in the oil-and-gas business and now was a vice president with the Cowboys. I asked him to call the league and get every trade over the last decade involving draft picks. No players. Just draft picks. The picks involved in those trades were treated as equal value and plotted on a graph. By assigning a random value to the top pick — 3,000 points the No. 1 pick was given — a numerical value was then assigned to descending picks as the arc of the graph demanded.

No. 2 pick: 2,600 points.

No. 3 pick: 2,400 points.

Each pick in that draft era's twelve rounds was given a point value corresponding to the graph. That went all the way down to the 336th and final pick being worth four-tenths of a point.

Just like that, we had a tool to value each pick in the draft's twelve rounds. We also had a distinct advantage over other teams when combined with my desire to wheel and deal. There was no more need to check your gut over a trade proposal. We could calculate its precise value in seconds. I simply added up the points of the involved picks and knew immediately if the trade was favorable for us.

In that deal with Oakland, for instance, we sent out the 29th (worth 720 points) and 140th (40 points) picks. That's a combined 760 points. We received the 39th (560 points), 68th (260), and 119th (60) picks. That totaled 880 points. So we not only got the player we wanted in Johnston at a lower position, but that 120-point difference in the trade meant we effectively received an additional third-round pick, too.

This "Draft Value Chart," as it became known, became a secret weapon during our rebuild in Dallas. We didn't simply use it to view proposed trades in a privileged manner. We used it to study other teams and see who made the best and worst trades. That way we might find a favorable trade partner. San Francisco, which won three Super Bowls in the 1980s, made trades that graded remarkably well against the chart.

"Don't you know what that means?" I asked my lawyer and confidant, Nick Christin.

He didn't.

"They've already got something like this," I said. "They've been using it for a long time and it explains their success."

Years later, I asked San Francisco general manager John McVay about that. He said whenever a trade was proposed involving draft picks, he researched what similar trades received for those picks. That way he had some basis for what was proposed. He hadn't struck on making a chart to measure every pick.

"That would've helped more," McVay said.

Al Davis, meanwhile, made trades that often paid no heed to the assigned value of a draft pick as we charted it. I told him this, too. We had struck up a relationship, being in opposite conferences and similarly questioning convention. I had a policy that no one could call me after 9 p.m. no matter what—even if someone died. What was I going to do, bring them back to life? The only person who broke that rule was Al. He'd call from the West Coast to talk about players or ideas. We had many similar thoughts—just not on draft trades.

"You're a value guy, Jimmy," he said when I told him what my chart said about his trades. "I'm a personnel guy. If I want a player, I don't give a shit what he costs."

Al wanted me to come up with a chart to involve trading players for draft picks. That wasn't possible. There's no set value for players like there is for individual draft picks.

All these discussions came after our success ended the advantage of the Draft Value Chart. Dave Wannstedt took it to Chicago when he

was named the Bears coach in 1993. Norv Turner took it to Washington in 1994. Soon the full league was using the chart. They still do,
too, with some tweaking for the salary cap, as I hear each off-season.
In the winter of 2021, Kansas City general manager Brett Veach told
me they used it in trading their first-round draft pick, and Baltimore
vice president Ozzie Newsome said it was consulted in trading one of
their draft picks. One team, I was told, has constructed another chart
involving the salary cap and consults both when making trades. The
media, too, grades trades by adding points from the chart—just as we
did in the draft room.

My idea wasn't to change the way NFL front offices operated. It
was to make sense of a blurry subject and rebuild the Cowboys with
any edge I could find. If I could expand our number of draft picks
through trades, that expanded our chances to be right. In the twelve-
round draft, we had fifteen picks in 1989, eighteen in 1991, and fifteen in 1992. We also had thirteen first- and second-round picks in
our five drafts—five more than the allotted amount. Jerry once asked
why I was always gathering more draft picks.

"When I was a kid in Port Arthur, the fishermen put three-hundred-
foot seine nets on the water," I said. "They'd pull them in and there
were some bad fish in there. You couldn't help that. But because they
threw that big net there also were a lot of good fish they'd got. The
bigger the net, the bigger the chance to get good fish in with the bad.
That's my idea."

I continually fought the static, stay-in-your-lane theme across
the league. "Owners own, coaches coach, players play" was the idea
when I came to Dallas. Few NFL coaches, for instance, went to college campuses then to look at draft prospects. Why? That was the
scouts' job, the thinking went.

My assistants and I went each March on a two-week tour of about
a half dozen campuses. We didn't just see the players. I had my as-

sistants talk to the schools' assistants, my trainer talk to their trainer, my strength coach talk to their strength coach. The head coach might sell you a bill of goods on a player. But chances are, peer-to-peer, you'll get a straighter answer. Having spent years in college football, my crew and I knew many of these coaches and support staff, too. Sometimes we had worked with them. Why not take advantage of such relationships?

Here's a story: Before the 1991 draft, we went to North Carolina State to look at some prospects. One mystery was defensive lineman Mike Jones. His talent was beyond anyone on their team. But the coaches rotated him in games like any player. Butch Davis's mission on that trip was to find out why he didn't play more. Butch disappeared for a few hours while the rest of us made the rounds. We came back to our plane and he wasn't there. We waited. And waited. He finally came on the plane a half hour or so late, pumping a fist, saying, "I found it." Butch was told Jones didn't play hard and coaches didn't want to reward him until he did.

"Peter, this is why we come here," I said to *Sports Illustrated*'s Peter King, who rode with us that trip. "Now we can scratch off Mike Jones."

Yes, I invited a writer along on a top-secret trip. Big deal. *Dallas Morning News* writer Tim Cowlishaw joined the crew for nachos and beers on Thursday nights after doing a segment on my TV show. Rick Gosselin of the *Morning News* was brought behind the curtain, too. I didn't have a problem in letting people see our thought process. Of course, it came with a caveat.

"Peter," I said the first time I let him inside my world after a game, "if you fuck me with this story, I'll squash you like a squirrel in the road."

He appreciated that. He knew it meant that everything I told him was the truth. That's the thing: I was an open book in showing the NFL what we were doing. Expand the draft? Scout players ourselves? I even doubled down on my speed-over-size belief that was first fought at Oklahoma in 1970. I stepped into an NFC East division that believed the opposite. Bill Parcells's New York Giants, Joe Gibbs's Washington Redskins, and Buddy Ryan's Philadelphia Eagles were big, strong, power teams. Football people chuckled when I took undersized linebackers like Dixon Edwards and Godfrey Myles. They wondered, just like in college, how linemen who were outweighed by thirty pounds could compete against run-happy power teams. They soon realized how when their bigger guys couldn't block our quicker ones.

Not everything I tried worked out. I did contracts at the start until quickly realizing money and financial decisions weren't a strength. I overpaid veteran guard Crawford Ker, who didn't last into our third year in Dallas. I was a couple of drinks in at a bar at the Senior Bowl when I got into a dollar argument with Ralph Cindrich, the agent of center Mark Stepnoski. We actually stepped out into the hall and were going to go at it when, thankfully, another coach stepped between us. Cindrich is a big man. He would've beaten the hell out of me.

I didn't push against NFL convention out of presumption or arrogance that I knew everything. It was to find a better way, one that made sense to me beyond "That's the way it's always been done." Another idea that rubbed me wrong was to "take the best player available" in a draft. What if you don't like the best player available? What if he's not a good fit for your system or isn't a player you want to coach? What if you prefer someone else lower in the draft whom other teams don't value like you—someone like Daryl Johnston, for example?

That again is where an idea like the Draft Value Chart provided a tool to help with trades. In five years in Dallas, I made fifty-one trades. This wasn't the era of fantasy football in front offices like today. The

New York Giants, for instance, made one trade in those five years. It was with us.

In our second draft in 1990, we had the 21st pick and needed defense. We hoped USC linebacker Junior Seau might slip enough for us to trade up for him. He went third to San Diego. Another player we thought had a more realistic chance of falling, Baylor linebacker James Francis, was taken 12th by Cincinnati.

Meanwhile, an unexpected player dropped into view as the draft progressed. Emmitt ranked among my top four players that draft. No one else evidently rated him that high. He was too small and too slow, some said. We didn't know if he could catch the ball, because Florida didn't throw to him. Our running backs coach, Joe Brodsky, preferred Anthony Thompson, a big and strong Indiana back. Thompson broke rushing records that college season and won many big awards—the Maxwell, Walter Camp, Big Ten Player of the Year, and finished second in Heisman Trophy voting.

As Emmitt Smith fell out of the Top 10, a debate we'd had leading up to the draft broke out again in our draft room.

"Smith's too slow," Brodsky said.

"Show me on tape where he's caught from behind," I said.

Thompson played in the weaker Big Ten and didn't have a longer run than 40 yards. Smith played against better competition in the Southeastern Conference and had runs of 96 and 72 yards the previous two seasons.

As teams kept passing on Smith, I got on the phone. There was a run of seven straight defensive players when Pittsburgh agreed to trade its No. 17 pick for our No. 21 and a third-round pick. It was a relatively equal deal by the chart, but a slam dunk for us considering we got our fourth-rated player at a severe discount. We made the move knowing other teams wanted a running back, too. Green Bay took Thompson at No. 19. Atlanta took Washington State running back Steve Broussard at No. 20.

What made the trade memorable is the career Emmitt had. If he was just another running back, if he had the decent careers of Thompson or Broussard, no one would remember it. Emmitt became a centerpiece of our offense right from the start and was named the NFL's Rookie of the Year. By the time he retired, he was the NFL's all-time rushing leader and headed to the Hall of Fame.

And too slow?

His long runs in my four years with him in Dallas were 48, 76, 68, and 62 yards. He still wasn't getting caught from behind. I wasn't surprised. We did our homework and had the answers before draft day. As I told players before games to encourage their practice habits and studying, "You're never nervous taking a test if you know the answers."

I knew the answers as best as possible on draft day. Our process assured that. After all our scouting, each coach then ranked all the players in the draft at his position. Each scout ranked the best players in their region, regardless of position. I had to scout the scouts, too. One might be overly positive. One didn't like anyone. Did they overvalue size? Undervalue intelligence?

I met with each coach and scout individually to go over their rankings. Some scouts gave their report on a player and occasionally added something like "He'll go late in the third round."

"You tell me what you think of the player," I'd say. "I'll decide where he goes."

Our coaches and scouts then met together. We discussed every player. Those were lively meetings that brought different angles of information and ideas. I've had some personnel people visiting me in the Keys saying this was the most valuable piece of information they took back.

The next crucial component of our draft involved scouting other NFL teams. Who did the teams drafting ahead of us like? Where did

others rank a specific player? Our scouts and coaches sought clues everywhere. I'd even talk with the sportswriters covering our team about
what they heard from counterparts around the country. People love to
talk. Information is out there if you keep looking. This was important
to project where in the draft certain players might be taken—and to
align our strategy.

Every team has big draft boards ranking players horizontally by
talent and vertically by position. I had a third draft board. It consisted
of a few names in each round that I kept on an index card in my
pocket. This was the short list of players I wanted to draft, the ones I
specifically wanted to coach. I didn't show it to anyone.

A lot of work went into that index card, and we drafted many of the
players on it. It didn't always work out. Michael Strahan was a player I
wanted in the 1993 draft. His defensive line coach at Texas Southern
was my old friend at Miami Walter Highsmith, Alonzo's father. So I
had an inside report on Michael. I liked him so much, I sent a scout,
Jeff Smith, to Michael's home in Houston on draft day to spy on the
interest around him as the day progressed.

Michael sat there late in the first round, thinking we'd take him as
our No. 29 pick when it scrolled across the screen that we had traded
down for Green Bay's two second-round picks (Nos. 46 and 54), a
fourth-round pick (No. 94), and an eighth-rounder (No. 213). That
was a 220-point win on the draft chart, the equivalent of an extra high-
third-round pick. I projected we'd take Strahan with that 46th pick.
The New York Giants took him 40th. Michael had a Hall of Fame
career. Years later, we're friends and partners on the FOX NFL show
and wonder what could have been.

By our third year in Dallas, all the trading had set us up in position
to control the draft with the 11th, 12th, and 14th picks. We talked to

most of the league about possible trades. We moved up from the 11th pick to take Russell Maryland with the 1st pick, after agreeing he would sign for lesser money than that pick typically earned. We wanted him badly—just at a fair price. We added receiver Alvin Harper with the 12th pick.

Then the value-charting, heart-pounding fun started. I traded the 14th pick down to 17th. Then the 17th down to 20th. That added a fourth- and a fifth-round pick.

Three minutes before the deadline for that 20th pick, the phone started ringing. San Diego was on line one with Bob Ackles and a tepid offer. I was on line two with Atlanta and negotiated second-, fourth-, and seventh-round picks for the trade—a moderate win on the chart. I was about to accept that deal when a third line rang a minute before our pick was due. McCoy picked it up.

"Hold it, Jimmy," he said, listening.

Detroit offered second-, third-, and fourth-round picks for our 20th pick. It represented a 200-point win for us—the equivalent of an extra third-round pick. The deal was done a second before our pick was due. I let out a loud breath. McCoy had to rush out of the room for air.

That was my kind of day. We ended with ten picks in the first four rounds. We turned those ten picks into four prime starters to help us win Super Bowls: Maryland, Harper, linebacker Dixon Edwards, and tackle Erik Williams, who immediately became a point of debate in that first training camp.

That's because it's not just drafting players that matters. It's developing them. Should a rookie start? Should he sit and learn a bit? It's often an art form, deciding when a young player is ready. Maybe the veteran is better now—but the kid will be better in a month if he plays. And who is the kid? You have to keep your eyes and mind open. Leon Lett got a couple of offensive linemen cut his first training camp, because he was a seventh-round nobody from a small college who was beating them badly. It took awhile for us to realize that Leon was somebody special.

I thought Erik Williams needed to play his first summer in 1991. Tony Wise, our line coach, saw a third-round pick beating up on weaker practice competition due to contract holdouts. He wanted to slow-cook Erik's development. We talked back and forth in training camp. I then mobilized one of my leadership ideas:

I wanted assistants to make the decision I want them to make.

That's right. It's their decision. But it's the decision I had them make. Here's an easy example of how that happens: I ask our staff what time we should meet in the morning. I want to meet at 6:30 a.m. But I ask everyone for their input.

"Let's meet at seven o'clock," someone says.

Someone else says 7:30. A couple of people want to get started earlier, at six o'clock.

"Let's compromise and meet at six thirty," I say.

There you have it. They chose the time I wanted to meet.

My discussion with Tony over Williams reached the what-time-to-meet intersection after a scrimmage against Houston.

"He's very talented, but he has to earn the position," Tony said.

"Great," I said. "But how's he going to earn the position if he doesn't get much playing time in the preseason? And once the season starts, he's not going to play at all. How's he going to earn it?"

"Well, I can't bench Kevin Gogan," Tony said of our starting right tackle. "He's a good player."

I asked Tony to name our five most talented linemen.

"Mark Stepnoski. Kevin Gogan. Mark Tuinei. Nate Newton. Erik Williams . . ."

"Oh, you didn't mention the right guard," I said.

"Erik's a better talent than the right guard."

"What about putting Kevin Gogan at right guard?"

"He's six eight, too big," he said.

"Tony, is it inevitable Erik Williams will be the starting right tackle?" I said.

"Yes."

"Then you just made the decision about who to play right now. Let's play Erik now."

Like that 6:30 a.m. meeting time, I allowed Tony to tell himself what to do. If I flat-out ordered him, it might backfire. Tony's a great coach and might subconsciously think Williams shouldn't play. He might tell Gogan or just imply by his thoughts, "Sorry, Coach Johnson is the one who wants you to move to guard."

Since Tony arrived at the decision, he had to work it out with the players, too. He did just fine there. His line became the foundation for our high-powered offense.

The Draft Value Chart, the collecting of draft picks, the scouting of players, the accumulation of talent—none of it would matter if I couldn't straighten out one problem after our second season in Dallas.

We ranked a dead-last 28th in offense our first year and 26th our second year. Our young players weren't developing—Troy, for instance, wasn't even comfortable. I needed a new offensive coordinator and tried to hire the Los Angeles Rams' Ernie Zampese. He instead suggested his receivers coach, Norv Turner. I knew Norv from watching some Rams practices during my University of Miami days. I had Troy talk with him during the interview process, too. That way he would be invested in the decision and help make it work.

"If you come, would you run the Rams offense?" Troy asked.

"One hundred percent," Norv said.

Troy liked that idea, liked Norv's personality. There was some adjustment to the offense. We kept the passing game, though we used verbiage that allowed players to interchange positions more easily. I wanted a power running game to keep it simple for our young guys, too. Wham right. Wham left. Toss right. Toss left.

Hiring Norv meant demoting the previous coordinator, Dave Shula, to receivers coach. I called his father, Don, the legendary coach of the Miami Dolphins, out of courtesy. Don was angry in a way that never left him.

"Why would you do that?" he said. "Dave's a big reason you were named coach of the year last season."

Dave left for Cincinnati, which was better for everyone, and I spent that off-season fast-tracking my relationship with Norv. Other assistants were with me for years. I made it a priority to get to know Norv. On Sunday afternoons, he'd be in his office, grinding away, and I'd look in and say, "Okay, let's go."

Norv would call his wife, Nancy, and I'd get Rhonda. We'd relax over nachos and beers or margaritas for a couple of hours. "Sundays Fundays," we called them. This was during the quiet of the off-season, but it wasn't just coworkers out for a drink. I was out to forge a relationship with Norv. We built a trust to withstand the pressure of the season.

In our third game of the next season, we were mauled by Philadelphia, 24–0. Troy was sacked eleven times. We were 1-2. The outside noise said our third year was going nowhere. Norv had doubts running an offense and calling plays for the first time. I saw it. I had hired him not just to install his offense but also to instill confidence in our young players. For that to work, he needed my full confidence.

"Look, we're doing the right things," I told him. "We didn't play the way we're capable of against Philadelphia. But we will next week. We know what we've got to do. You just stick to what you're doing. We'll get back to playing well and everything will be fine."

Norv says that talk settled him, made some concerns disappear. We won the next four games. We finished seventh in the league in scoring that year. But we still weren't a fully developed team in the middle of our third season in 1991. My challenge was to help us get there. We were 6-5 and playing at 11-0 Washington when I told our players that week to be prepared for any surprise.

"How do you fight an eight-hundred-pound gorilla?" I said. "You don't just go up and tap him lightly. You sneak up and whack him with a big board and then run away as fast as you can."

We went for it three times on fourth downs (converting two). We recovered an onside kick and threw a Hail Mary for a touchdown. We opened up our blitz package on defense. We needed all of it in winning, 24–21.

We met a different challenge at Philadelphia near the season's end. Buddy Ryan won with a great defense—and only a great defense. We had reserve quarterback Steve Beuerlein starting for an injured Troy Aikman, too. That demanded a different way than the gambling tactics at Washington.

"Here's how we're going to win," I said. "Beuerlein, you're not going to take a sack. Get rid of the ball if you see the rush. Just throw it away. No negative plays. Linemen? Tony Wise isn't going to want to hear this, but I don't care if you take twenty holding penalties. I just don't want Beuerlein to get hit."

Beuerlein completed two of seventeen passes the first half. We punted six straight times. We scored eighteen points on special teams. We won, 25–13, and made our first playoffs.

Our young players grew up in the second half of that season. We beat Chicago in the first round of the playoffs for our first appreciable taste of success. We were then run off the field the next week by Detroit, 38–6. Lions quarterback Erik Kramer threw for 341 yards and three touchdowns.

"This moment—remember it," I said in the locker room after that loss. "This is the beginning, not the ending. We've built the foundation of something here. We took a step on the road that'll lead to the Super Bowl."

I then sat in the coaches' room afterward, already moving off-season chess pieces.

"We'll improve the pass defense," I said. "Next year this shit doesn't happen."

10

HOW 'BOUT THEM COWBOYS

We did it! We won it! Standing on the Rose Bowl field at Super Bowl XXVII, I breathed the rarefied air of the mountaintop. What a view this was. What a feeling. This wasn't after we won our first Super Bowl amid cheering and confetti.

It was two hours before kickoff.

I knew then that we had won. Past tense. Mission accomplished. I never felt like that before another big game in my career. I walked over the pregame field as elated as if I held the next morning's headline.

"How many people can say they're the best at something?" I asked the team in my pregame talk. "Can a doctor or lawyer say they're the best? Do they have a competition ranking the number one CEO in corporate America?"

This wasn't just related to professions. Best husband? Best brother?

"We've got that platform to say we're the best," I said. "We've got the team to be the best, too. A lot of people in this room are the best at what they do. Now we're going to show we are the best team. Today we'll go out, kick the shit out of them, and be called exactly that. The best."

None of us starting at the bottom in Dallas four seasons earlier knew the extreme demands and decisions needed to reach that point, both professionally and personally. All of us were different in some form by that day in the Rose Bowl.

No one had changed over the previous four years more than I had. I grew colder. Crueler. Less patient. Less social. More driven. More selfish. Quicker to anger. Tougher on everyone. Petty and unnecessarily sensitive. Unhappier.

And elated.

I raised the bar each year in Dallas in keeping with my Pygmalion belief of a self-fulfilling prophecy. Sometimes we didn't reach that stated goal. But maybe we came close because expectations were set that high.

"I expect to win as many as I lose," I told the media before our season in 1990, raising eyebrows considering we were a 1-15 team the previous year.

We went 7-9 with Troy Aikman suffering a shoulder injury late in the year.

"Not only will we make the playoffs, but I expect to have success in the playoffs," I said before our third season in Dallas.

We went 11-5 and won a playoff game.

"We will exceed what we did a year ago," I said before our fourth year in 1992.

We were ready to sprout wings and fly. The flickering version of the vision I saw, of the one I believed in from the start, came into full view that off-season. We redid our defense as promised, by drafting cornerback Kevin Smith and linebacker Robert Jones in the first round, safety Darren Woodson in the second round, and grabbing safety Thomas Everett from a contractual stalemate in Pittsburgh for a fifth-round pick. They all had impact. Everett and Jones became Pro Bowl players. Smith and Woodson were All-Pros. Woodson is a Hall of Fame finalist after a career that deserves to end in Canton, Ohio.

That made us a contending team.

A phone call just before the season made us a championship one.

"Are you interested in Charles Haley?" asked San Francisco general manager John McVay.

Twenty months earlier, Charles was the NFL Defensive Player of the Year. Now San Francisco had enough of his behavior with teammates and assistants. He even took a swing at coach George Seifert. Our first order of business was deciding if we wanted a player with that kind of baggage.

I had Jerry call San Francisco owner Eddie DeBartolo Jr. Our coaches, our players, our trainer—everyone called their counterpart inside the 49ers with one question I needed answered: *Is he smart?*

That reverts to my first ingredient in evaluating talent. If Charles was intelligent, I could work with him. If he wasn't, there was no hope. All our research discovered three things: Charles was indeed smart. He competed hard. And he was . . .

"Completely bat-shit crazy," as he confessed.

We had our moments. Early on, Charles walked into a defensive line meeting right from the shower, still naked, and lay down on the floor. He once gave everyone—coaches, players, and staff—the silent treatment for two weeks over something. I happened to stand beside him at a urinal during this moment of silence.

"You keep this silent-treatment shit up and your career is going to end like that piss of yours—right down the drain," I said.

Another time, I was upset after a game in Minnesota. The rule was for everyone to be in the locker room when the door closed. Charles wasn't in. He banged on the door to get it opened, then walked to the back of the room.

"Charles, get your fucking ass up here right now!" I shouted. "Get up with the rest of the team!"

He came six inches from my face.

"This close enough for you?" he said.

Uh, yeah.

The next day he came to my office. "I love playing for you," he said. "I'll do anything if you just don't criticize me in front of everyone."

I couldn't promise that. But I listened to him. I also knew players reacted differently to my criticism. If I yelled at Michael Irvin, he would play harder. Emmitt Smith wouldn't play as well if I criticized him. Charles? He'd become aggressive, just as he did in that locker room.

Charles found out after football that he suffered from a bipolar condition that was at the root of his behavior. But let's be clear on something: he worked hard, competed hard, became a great teammate, and desperately wanted to win in the same manner I did. For a second-round pick in 1993 and a third-round pick in 1994, we got the final piece to our championship puzzle: a pass rusher to strike fear in an offense and close out games in the fourth quarter.

Charles immediately noticed the difference in how two contending teams worked. The 49ers didn't wear pads in practice. We wore full pads Wednesday, Thursday, and Friday. We hit hard. Tackles were taken to the ground (except for Emmitt). Linemen battled as if in a game. It was tough. Even our training facility at St. Edward's University in Austin was old, cramped, and minimally adequate, to set a medieval tone. The weather was hot there, too, with the humidity insufferable some days. That's where we bonded, where I constantly tested their character and commitment. One August in our fourth season, when eight players missed practice with various injuries after a grueling run of scrimmages and preseason games, I stood before the best of them, center Mark Stepnoski, with a message for the full team.

"Step, your leg's bruised. It's not broken," I said.

Maybe they hated me at times for pushing, pushing, pushing like that. I would come to hate myself for having to do that, too. But here's the thing: they played for me. I set championship standards from the time we came in the door. I was intense and inflexible. When a free agent kicker quit running sprints at our first training camp, citing asthma, I pointed to the road and shouted, "Asthma, my ass! Get over on that other field and have some asthma!"

When we lost at the New York Giants in sloppy fashion, I threw a garbage can through a blackboard in the coaches' room to underline what I thought of our work that day. I overheard an assistant ask on a flight home from a game who was winning the World Series.

"Oakland's up," someone answered.

"I don't give a shit who's winning the World Series!" I hollered. "I care about our football team!"

Was there room for both? Not in my narrow world. When we started 3-0 that 1992 season, and then let Herschel Walker have a big game in his last stop at Philadelphia, I pushed them, saying: "We'll see who you are now—champions or pretenders." When we won our next five games before losing a hard-fought game to the Los Angeles Rams, I didn't give anyone an out, saying instead, "We play to a standard. We didn't play to it today." When we were 11-2 and lost a December game to Washington that meant nothing in the standings, nothing to the looming playoffs—nothing of consequence, really—I told the flight attendant to stop preparing food service on the ride home.

"No one gets anything to eat!" I shouted. "They don't deserve it!"

After halting food service on that flight, I walked to the back of the plane and yelled at a player to sit down. I told others to quit playing cards. I questioned coaches. I fumed at more players. Was someone across the way smiling?

"No smiling," I said.

Dave Wannstedt, who knew me best, came in my office the next morning and said, "You were kind of tough on everyone. You didn't even allow them to eat."

"I wanted to be tough," I said.

I never had that middle ground of perspective. For me it was win or lose, all or nothing. That's how I wanted it to be for everyone, too. Most coaches talk about "not getting too high or too low" after games. They install the "24-Hour Rule" for players to enjoy a win or suffer a loss. I never talked like that. Every win was an epic triumph to me, like riding the crest of a wave. As Troy said, "There was no better place to be on a Monday after a win than around Jimmy."

Every defeat, by comparison, was a disaster, confining me to a dark place. It was a personal failure as much as a professional one. Butch Davis said some funerals were "happier places than being around Jimmy" after losses. My good friend Nick Christin typically waited to call until Wednesday if we lost, a three-day buffer against my emotions. For big losses, he'd wait until Thursday. There was no sense in reaching me, he figured, when I was mired in an unreachable place.

Here's what most people don't understand about a football team: Not every player is crushed by losing. Some are okay with it. Just look around your company. Some people are intense about succeeding and others don't define themselves by work. It's no different on a pro team. Every player would rather win, of course. Not all of them build their lives around it.

Michael and Emmitt came to me a few years into our Dallas time, as we began to succeed, and said I didn't need to give pre-practice talks anymore. Each day I would speak a few minutes about the day's work, the practice's intent, maybe throw in a motivational story—a few minutes of talk to tell how it all mattered.

"I'm not speaking to you in those talks," I told Emmitt and Michael. "I'm talking to the twelve or fifteen players who need it—who might not think that today's practice means anything or aren't as dedicated to winning as you. We need to get them ready to help us win, too."

For those players who weren't miserable after that loss in Washington, I would make their lives miserable. That, in turn, made them want to win rather than face my tirades. Troy understood my methods as our relationship developed.

"It was kind of like raising a dog," he said. "You reward good behavior to encourage that, and you punish bad behavior to the point the dog doesn't behave that way anymore."

A postscript to that post-Washington flight came from Michael Irvin. He would be in a huddle during a tight game and say, "Guys, if you want to eat, you'd better start fucking playing better."

Michael got it. He understood who I was, what I was about for the most part. But players were still angry with me during Monday meetings after that Washington game. Our company Christmas party was that night. The last thing I wanted to do was stand around and small-talk for a half hour. But I went as coach of the team. Troy went as the quarterback. Few other players showed up.

"How's the team?" I asked Troy.

"They're not good, Jimmy," he said. "That's why they're not here. They're pissed."

My relationship with Troy was strained for much of our first few years, from the drafting of Walsh to starting Beuerlein in our first playoff game when Troy felt he was healthy. He came into my office, fuming over that decision.

So, that night at the Christmas party, Troy and I had a healthy conversation that moved our relationship forward. We didn't talk about the team, the season, or coach-and-quarterback relations.

We discussed fish.

You know how people talk about sports because they're a safe harbor of conversation? Fish became that vehicle for Troy and me. I became interested in big saltwater tanks during my time in Dallas. There was a meditative quality after the workday stress to sitting silently before a sixty-foot tank and observing blue damsels swimming or lionfish eating. That's why I had three large saltwater tanks in my kitchen and four in the living room.

"I've always wanted an aquarium," Troy said at the Christmas party.

After a practice the next week, I told Troy we should get him a tank and some fish. We went shopping together and constructed a tank in his place, setting in rocks and getting the proper fish. Actually, I did that. Troy drank the Heinekens I brought. That started a routine where after Friday practices in the coming seasons I'd say, "Let's go get some fish for the tank."

Fish tanks allowed us to get to know each other and build a measure of trust that carried onto the football field. That was a vital step for us. We developed a partnership, then a genuine friendship. By our fifth year together in 1993, I would call Troy on Tuesday, our day off, and say, "What're you doing?" I'd go over to his place with Rhonda and a six-pack of Heineken, and we'd sit there and talk about anything.

Troy and I reached a fundamental understanding on how the coach-quarterback dynamic worked for us, too. I was the hard-assed coach demanding that players practice hard and play disciplined. Troy was the star quarterback and team leader who encouraged his teammates.

A good-cop, bad-cop routine developed between Troy and me in managing the team this way. I'd stop practice if it was sloppy, curse a player who didn't give full effort, and throw a tantrum to ensure we had good practice habits. That was my bad-cop role. And Troy's role?

"Don't worry about him," he would say in the huddle after one of my outbursts. "Let's just go do our work right this time."

He liked me cracking the whip on teammates if something went wrong so he didn't have to do it. But he demanded my ways be followed. As he says, "I became Jimmy's soldier out there. I'd do what he wanted."

Years later, Troy explained our relationship through the roiling debate over whether Bill Belichick or Tom Brady was more important to the New England Patriots' success. There's no right answer to that. You need both the great quarterback and the great coach in the NFL. But Troy knew the benefit to a quarterback playing for a tough coach like Belichick or me. It allowed the quarterback to come to work each day and just concentrate on being the best player and teammate he could be. And only that. He didn't have to be the bad cop, hammering players into line or worrying about weak practice habits carrying into games. He learned the difference after I left Dallas, when a more relaxed Barry Switzer came in as coach and Troy had to become the team disciplinarian. He didn't like that added burden to his role.

Our fourth season together, we stood on the sideline before a game as Tom Landry and legendary Cowboys quarterback Roger Staubach rode in a convertible around the stadium in a celebration of their careers.

"That could be you and me one day," Troy said.

I didn't tell him then, but that meant something to me.

It was all about building a champion, brick by necessary brick. Every detail counted. Every meaningless game mattered. A few weeks after that Washington flight, we played our 1992 finale in Chicago. Our playoff seeding was set, our bye week assured. That didn't make it meaningless to me. Some starters, like Emmitt, sat out the second half. Our second-year running back, Curvin Richards, was prone to lack of focus and fumbling. Here was a chance to work on that. Emmitt was sure-handed—two fumbles in 432 carries that season. Richards had three fumbles in 49 carries. The final two fumbles came in that Chicago game despite one specific order.

"Just protect the football," I said as he started the second half for Emmitt, making sure not to say, "Don't fumble," and plant that negative seed.

He fumbled.

"Curvin, listen, I told you I don't care how many yards you gain. Just protect the football!" I told him.

He went out and fumbled again. I said nothing to him on the sideline. We won the game, 27–14. We had a 13-3 season. We were the No. 2 seed in the playoffs. We had a bye week coming. All was good.

"See Bruce Mays and get your waiver papers," I told Curvin.

This was a time when I led by fear. That can be risky for a leader. You need respect and credibility to lead a team at all—and I had earned that a while ago from my players. They knew that no one worked harder than I did. They knew my ways were working. The best attribute to combine with respect and credibility for a leader is players liking you. They'll go the extra mile if they like you. Sometimes fear is needed, though, to send a proper message. The thing about fear—if it doesn't work, a team can turn on you.

Cutting Curvin was so unconventional, I got a call from Joel Bussert, the league's director of player personnel, who wasn't sure I understood NFL rules. Curvin couldn't be replaced on the playoff roster, he said, and we still had to pay him a full playoff share.

I didn't care. This was about the fragile nature of a season in the playoffs. One bad play could cost everything. Maybe cutting Richards got everyone's attention and helped us focus even more for the postseason. All I know is our offense didn't have a turnover in three playoff games that year. Our defense caused fifteen. That explains how it all ended.

✻ ✻ ✻

At 4:30 a.m. on the Sunday of the NFC Championship Game, I summoned our staff to an emergency meeting in our San Francisco hotel. The previous afternoon, I had walked Candlestick Park's field with the NFL's groundskeeper, George Toma. It was cool, soggy weather. Some sod had been replaced. There were certain areas of the field so loose they didn't offer secure footing. Toma wanted to ensure that both sides knew the state of the field. It then rained all Saturday night, making a challenging field worse.

I'd been up for a couple of hours when we met. We sat before a whiteboard charted to reflect the field's condition. Wet areas here. Newly sodded areas there. Dry areas were marked, too. I went over our game plan to take this into account, to put players in the best situations. Details, always details.

"If we're returning kickoffs from this end, I don't want a left return," I said to special teams coach Joe Avezzano, showing new sod just out of the end zone there. "You're liable to slip. Give me a right return or up the middle . . ."

I pointed to another patch of newly sodded field.

"Norv, when we're on this side of the field, don't run a pitch-sweep to Emmitt. He's going to have to make a sharp cut and the sod is loose."

And the defense?

"Dave, if we're in this area where they put in new sod, I don't want blitzing," I said. "If we're going to blitz, we'll be in man-to-man coverage and the cornerback might slip. Plus, our linemen can't get a good rush."

San Francisco was 14-2 and the better team that year. We were better that day. We were up 26–14 when I went for it on fourth down at the San Francisco 14-yard line. Emmitt got stuffed. No matter, we weren't playing with scared money, then or ever. We got the ball back, up 24–20, with just over four minutes left. Everyone expected Emmitt to run three times to keep the clock going.

"What's your safest pass?" I said to Norv before first down.

"A slant to Michael," he said.

"Okay, gimme that," I said.

When Michael heard the play in the huddle, he thought the pass was for the curl route on the right side where Alvin Harper typically lined up. He broke the huddle and ran to that side. Alvin went to the left side. We didn't normally throw slants to Alvin because that's not a strength.

There was some soggy, new sod right in the area Alvin ran his slant. The San Francisco defender slipped. Harper was beautifully alone, made a simple catch, and ran 70 yards to punch our Super Bowl ticket.

I've never been part of a more delirious locker room.

"I don't need to put a damper on it—no, no, no—but you do understand we do have one game left to play," I said to the team. "Hey, fantastic, fantastic, fantastic, every single one of you. And I'm not just talking about these last sixty minutes. I'm talking about the quarterback schools, the minicamps, the off-season, the training camp—down in Austin when it was hot and you were tired.

"Everybody, you did one helluva job. And the only thing else I got to say is . . ."

I should have patented this.

". . . HOW 'BOUT THEM COWBOYS!"

As we prepared for the Super Bowl, my challenge was helping our players navigate the big stage. We were the youngest team in football, our players averaging 25.3 years. None of us had played or coached in a Super Bowl. This was such a new experience, a few of our players didn't even grasp we were in the Super Bowl until they were told after beating San Francisco.

Our opponent, Buffalo, had the reverse story. They were experienced at these heights, having lost the two previous Super Bowls. Unlike our rising players, they also had stars at the pinnacle of Hall of Fame careers, like Jim Kelly, Bruce Smith, Thurman Thomas, and Andre Reed.

I needed to address this before perception became reality for our players. I laid a two-by-four piece of lumber on the ground in front of everyone before we left for Los Angeles.

"Buffalo has a good team," I said. "The coming week of media attention will be beyond anything you've seen. We'll play before ninety million people watching around the world."

I called out Emmitt's name.

"Come up here and walk from one end of this two-by-four to the other," I said.

He did with no problem.

"Troy, get up here. You walk it," I said.

He did, too. Then I did. Everyone chuckled.

"Nate," I said to our 330-pound guard, Nate Newton. "Get your fat ass up here and walk from one end to the other."

He did it, no problem, to more laughing—even if no one was sure about the purpose.

"If I'd put this two-by-four just ten feet in the air, what's your thought process then?" I said. "You're suddenly not laughing and thinking, 'It's easy.' You're going to think, 'Don't fall, don't fall.' And you know what's going to happen as you think that? You're going to fall."

I then hammered home the message.

"We know we're the best team," I said. "We know we're going to kick their ass. We know if no one's watching we'll kick the shit out of this bunch. I want you to approach this game like it's being played on the practice field, on ground level, like none of this other attention is even there. Just remember you're the best team."

As usual, I went against the Coach's Traditional Handbook. Telling young players they were the better? Inviting overconfidence on a big stage? But I wasn't sticking my central pillars of optimism and Pygmalion in the closet now. We'd do it our way, the brash way we'd built it, the bold way we'd won all along—and fit our personality.

We practiced those two weeks like we always did. Hard. Physical. Tackling to the ground. Buffalo ran a no-huddle offense when it was novel in the league. To prepare our defense for that upbeat tempo, I had the defense play against two alternating huddles so they could realize the pace of the game and to get them out of breath. As soon as the scout team offense's play was over, the No. 1 offense ran to the line with the next play. Emmitt had to play Thurman Thomas. Troy was Jim Kelly. That was unheard-of in NFL practices. I also explained it was like in college when you play a pro-style offense one week and wishbone the next.

"It might take a few plays to feel comfortable," I said. "But don't panic. We're better than them."

NBC's announcers, Dick Enberg and Bob Trumpy, came to watch us Thursday in Los Angeles and asked Norv afterward, "Are you worried you're going to leave it on the practice field? That practice was like a game."

"If we hadn't done it like this the last eighteen weeks, I'd be worried," Norv said.

Troy considered it my best week of preparing the team. He, in fact, slept so well the night before that Super Bowl, he worried why he wasn't more worried.

In our team meeting that Saturday night, I explained how the game would go. "Buffalo will play hard early, and it'll be a close game," I said. "We'll be conservative early. That's because we have the better team. Don't be alarmed. The longer it goes, the better we'll be."

I pointed to some statistical truths.

"They'll turn the ball over," I added. "That's what they do."

Buffalo had nine turnovers that Super Bowl.

"When they turn the ball over, we'll get aggressive," I said. "They don't have a defense to stop us."

Buffalo went up, 7–0, confirming that idea of their strong start, but our offense found its gear for a 28–10 lead at half.

"We'll beat their ass wherever we play them," I repeated in that Saturday-night meeting.

We won, 52–17, confirming my feeling on the Rose Bowl field two hours before the game. Jerry and I stood there in the winning locker room, holding the trophy high, smiling over our achievement, smelling like champions after a champagne shower. We had played in Japan that preseason and Jerry saw that the winner got a trophy of a samurai. Our starters played one series, we lost the game and Jerry walked by me afterward, silent and somber. I asked his wife, Gene, what was wrong. She said he really wanted that samurai trophy. That became a joke to us later. As we stood holding the Lombardi Trophy, I turned to Jerry, both of us flush with our achievement.

"Better than a samurai trophy?" I said.

No one understood the exhausting journey from rock bottom four years earlier to that night like we did. Everyone celebrated that climb. It was the ultimate win of my career. It confirmed my ways on the biggest stage.

Rhonda and I partied that night before flying to the Bahamas to relax and reflect on our success. I was happy by the water, playing some blackjack, immersed in the golden glow of achievement.

For all of three days.

By the end of that week, I was in Birmingham, Alabama, sitting on a cold bleacher and scouting players to draft at the Senior Bowl.

"What're you doing here?" another NFL official said.

"I'm already behind in preparing for the draft," I said.

That was my life. My whole life. I put football above all my other relationships. I wouldn't measure the stress, the sacrifices, or especially the person I had become until later.

I only chased the next win.

11

SUCCEEDING THROUGH SUCCESS

Just before noon on a soft summer day after the NFL Draft and spring practices—long after I was done celebrating the Super Bowl—I allowed myself one final, intoxicating whiff of that season in southeast Texas. I came off Highway 69 in a black limo, turned on what was Seventy-Fifth Avenue, and was greeted by a stage with red-and-white bunting at the Port Arthur Civic Center.

"Jimmy Johnson Day," the banner said.

Between the hellos and handshakes, between the mayor and the high school quarterbacks, between an *Esquire* magazine writer following me and me craving some local boudin—"Where's some boudin, Mother, tell me how to get to Nick's"—I took in the sights and faces that molded my youth. The past was everywhere in my hometown.

It was here the oil refinery jobs brought Mother and Daddy from Arkansas. Here, on DeQueen Boulevard, I grew up in a duplex beside the local creamery where Daddy then worked, and I did, too, washing out dairy trucks.

It was here on Friday nights that my friend Jimmy Maxfield and I cruised one end of Procter Street in my '53 Dodge with flames on the side, or drank beer at the other, rougher end in the only places that served us at fifteen and sixteen: the bordellos. We soon knew them well enough to give schoolmates tours for a quarter.

It also was here, as an all-state linebacker for Thomas Jefferson High School, Class of 1961, that I lost a tooth one practice, picked it off the ground, and carried it to the sideline.

"Yeah, I see it, Johnson," said our coach, Clarence "Buckshot" Underwood. "Now get your ass back in there. We'll buy you another tooth."

See why I coached tough?

"Buckshot" had played and coached for Bear Bryant at Kentucky. His staff included Fred Akers, who became the coach at Texas and Purdue. So, I was introduced to what good coaching looked like right from the start. We made the state semifinals each of my high school years, and the civic line was that Port Arthur had two priorities: 1) football, and 2) football.

Three decades later, I came back for a day in my honor, back for a charity roast hosted by comedian Don Rickles, back on Seventy-Fifth Avenue after politicians changed a law allowing it to be named for a living person.

"Jimmy Johnson Boulevard," the new sign read.

"This gives little fellows and little ladies hope that they may accomplish much in life as well," said the day's master of ceremonies, the president of a local college and director of the Port Arthur Historical Society.

I didn't prepare a speech. I knew what to say.

"About thirty years ago I was fortunate enough to play a national championship game at Arkansas," I said. "Six years ago, I met President Reagan when I was coach at the University of Miami. He shook my hand and said, 'Congratulations, coach, you have the finest team in college football.' Then, a couple of months ago I shook President Clinton's hand. 'Congratulations, coach,' he says to me, 'you have the finest team in professional football.'

"That was all very special. But what's most special is being back make everyone go back to the practice beginning, all the way back to the stretching, and do it right this time.

"Jump offsides again and I'm going to cut you!" I'd yell at a player. I had a track record of doing that, too.

Charles Haley says I yelled more that season after our Super Bowl victory than all the coaches in all his other seasons combined. That sounds right. I even had another late-season, Washington-style meltdown in Minnesota that represented my season-long concern. We won, 37–20, but two late Minnesota touchdowns put a cloud over the day—over my day, anyhow. I unleashed a barrage of locker room bile in a way some players didn't understand.

I explained why I did the next day.

"Look, I know I was mad about their late touchdowns," I said. "I still am. I'm not going to let us lower our standards. I don't want anybody to look at the film and think they can make these plays against us. Don't show any cracks. That's the standard."

Troy said if being a hard-ass wasn't my real personality, I did a good job faking it. Well, it was a good job. I faked it. I adopted that dictator personality even more that season. I made that dark alter ego my public face. It worked that year for our success. It also wore on me if I looked in the mirror for too long.

What had I turned myself into while chasing success?

A person I increasingly didn't like.

But I didn't examine the pain too much in the moment, because it would have hurt even more if we enjoyed our first Super Bowl so much, we didn't reach a second one.

Bill Belichick visited me in the Keys after his first Super Bowl win and asked the relevant question: "What am I going to deal with? You've been through it. What's coming?"

It cuts to the philosopher's question: What's harder to overcome, failure or success? That's no debate. If you have the right people and

here in Port Arthur, where it all started. Port Arthur, Texas—
and always will be my town."

Mother and Daddy had moved from our duplex to a brick
on the north side. A sign with balloons outside waited there:
come Home, Jimmy—Mom & Dad." I had told them not to co
the Super Bowl. I wouldn't have time for them. That's who I w
reaching the highest level of success and they said they unders
Maybe they did, too, as they watched from Port Arthur. We talke
a while that day. We swapped stories, going back years, Rhonda la
ing with us, until we came back to the present.

I wrapped Mother in a hug.

Then we drove the other way on Jimmy Johnson Boulevard,
past in my rearview mirror, to chase the next Super Bowl.

My assistants thought I drove them mercilessly the season after t
first Super Bowl.

They were right.

My players thought, as Troy Aikman says, "I was a real son
abitch" that 1993 season.

They were right, too.

Coaches, players, media, fans—everyone thought I enjoyed pro
ding players and pushing buttons, because that was my demandin
even demeaning, personality.

That's where everyone was wrong.

It didn't come naturally to act in hard-hearted ways, even as I increased those methods after winning the Super Bowl. I would yell
more often in an uninspired practice, "Start over! Start over!" and

the proper system, failure makes everyone work harder and sacrifice more. Look at the manner in which we progressed from the worst team in football to Super Bowl champs in four seasons. Failure can be your friend in that regard.

Success? It's a tightrope walk for a coach who wants players to gain confidence from success without being spoiled by it. The sports world is littered with one-hit wonders, because winning doesn't increase introspection to make you work harder. It softens you. It means everyone from administrative assistants to team stars wants more the next season—more money, more recognition, more of a role, more pats on the back. More, more, more for me, me, me.

Everyone saw this business side of sports after our Super Bowl when Emmitt Smith announced he would hold out for a new contract. But they didn't see that thinking filter through the whole organization. For example, our talented strength coach, Mike Woicik, thought he deserved a pay raise, too. I told him to take it up with Jerry. He wasn't alone, either.

But Emmitt's holdout affected the whole organization. Let's set aside the dollars, the negotiation, and whether he deserved more money. Let's just talk of how it affected the team—how it affected winning.

It wasn't just the absence of Emmitt's talent that hurt us through training camp practices, preseason games, and into the regular season. It was the effect his absence had on everyone—me included. I didn't do a good job of dealing with it. I didn't prepare everyone properly for playing without him. I kept expecting Emmitt's deal to get done and for him to return to the team, right up to the first game, when he still wasn't there. If that was my mentality, it was everyone's mentality. We lost the opener to Washington, 35–16. So much for a good Super Bowl carryover into the next year.

I again expected Emmitt's contract to get done before the second game. It didn't. We lost a regular-season Super Bowl rematch to Buffalo,

13–10. Charles Haley was so angry after that game, he threw a helmet at Jerry Jones in the locker room, barely missing him, supposedly yelling, "You need to sign that motherfucker now!" Haley was upset. He says he was upset at the offensive line complaining that Emmitt wasn't there. He turned and threw his helmet at the wall and Jerry happened to be in the vicinity. Either way, Emmitt's absence was at the center of it.

There were other reasons we lost those early games the next season, too. We played sloppy up and down the roster. We fumbled four times against Washington. Our kicker, Lin Elliott, a good part of our Super Bowl success the previous season, missed two field goals against Buffalo after missing an extra point against Washington.

"I've lost my confidence," Elliott said to me on the sideline after missing a 30-yard attempt in Buffalo.

He cut himself right there. A kicker with no confidence is like a golfer with the yips on the putting green. That Monday I brought in three kickers to work out. The conditions were tough. There was a gusting, 35 mph wind. They had never worked with the holder. I stood on top of them, applying the pressure of my presence.

Eddie Murray, a veteran kicker, came to me afterward.

"Coach, I don't care about the wind or the holder," he said. "If it's inside the forty, I'll make it."

"Okay, let's get a contract," I said.

That's the kind of confidence I wanted, the kind that fit in the developed psyche of my teams. A kicker with our kind of attitude? Murray tied a franchise record with five field goals against Green Bay that year. His two field goals over 50 yards against Minnesota were a franchise record. He had a career year, making 27 of 32 field goal attempts and all six in the playoffs.

Meanwhile, Emmitt signed his new deal before our third game. He took a handoff the first practice, made a nice move, broke a tackle, and smiles broke out across the practice field.

"We're back," Norv said to me.

Or so everyone assumed.

That became another problem after winning the Super Bowl: everyone figured winning one year meant winning the next year. When Emmitt returned to practice, no one was happier than running backs coach Joe Brodsky, a man as old-school as he was competitively tough. Maybe Joe was too happy with Emmitt's return.

For weeks, Joe had pushed Emmitt's replacement, fourth-round rookie Derrick Lassic, to get him up to speed. He wasn't Emmitt. Who was? But Joe prepared a rookie as best he could. With Emmitt back, Joe still wore out Lassic in those practices. I would look over and see Emmitt resting during drills that first week.

"Joe, I don't mind you riding Lassic and getting him ready," I said. "But get Emmitt's ass in there. He's going to be the one who decides if we win the ball game."

"Ah, coach, Emmitt's a veteran," he said. "He'll be ready."

I blew up. I rode Brodsky from that point in the same manner he rode Lassic. Pushed him. Challenged him. Demanded he stay on top of the situation like his job depended on it. Why? Because it was my responsibility to not let success make us soft with assumptions. That meant exposing any hint of complacency when it leaked into our work habits — even from my coaches. Especially from them. Winning creates a bond between positional coaches and players. That can be a powerful asset toward building trust. It also can enable a coach to let a veteran player get off easy, especially in a violent sport like football. Getting hit isn't fun. Playing hurt isn't smart sometimes. Maybe you could get by with doing a little less in practice? Endure less pain or sacrifice? What's the harm in taking it easy for a few days?

"You have the hammer as the head coach," I told Belichick after his first championship. "It falls on you to use it, too."

All this crap about champions being self-motivated is promoted by people who have never been there. Players are people. A lot of them are lazy, especially with a city like Dallas quick to applaud their previous season. It was my job to make them work. If that made me the team tyrant to players and assistants, so be it.

Oh, my bold and brash personality was still there. It was front and center nationally, too. Just like at Miami, the hate index rose around us when we won. Opponents were readier for us that season. And fans? Before the opener, the *Washington Times* set up a "Cowboys Hate Line," for fans to call in and say why they hated us. There was a common theme in what many of the 277 callers hated:

"Jimmy Johnson's insolent attitude."

"Jimmy Johnson's hair."

"Jimmy Johnson has brought my hatred to new heights I never thought I was capable of."

That was better than being mocked as the East Carolina of the NFL. The way I talked to the team reflected our change in talent and expectations, too. We won two straight games with Emmitt back before playing a bad Indianapolis team. I set the tone for that week in our first team meeting.

"Hey, I get up each day and tell you what we need to compete in the next game," I said. "But, come on, this is the Colts. They have no business being on the same field with us. If we're not playing backups in the second half, I'm going to be pissed."

We won, 27–3.

I wasn't pissed until the following week.

Joe Avezzano was reviewing video with his players when I slipped into the meeting the Friday before our October game with San Francisco. This was no guest appearance by me. I sat in each week on every unit's meeting—offense, defense, and special teams—to oversee preparation and show that every unit mattered.

My working idea was we needed to win two of those units to win any game.

As Avezzano talked, I noticed reserve linebacker John Roper sleeping. He came in through a trade that off-season from Chicago, where Dave Wannstedt was in his first year as head coach. Roper had made a few plays for us in the opening games. He had also been late to a meeting or two.

I thought of cutting Roper some slack and turned back to Avezzano. I looked back a few minutes later. He was still sleeping. This began to bother me. Soon I was boiling. I told Avezzano to turn off the projector.

"Roper!" I said.

He woke up.

"Evidently you're not getting enough sleep," I said. "You can sleep on Sundays. Go see Bruce Mays about your waiver papers."

That was cold, cruel business. No doubt. But what would be the message if I allowed a reserve player to sleep through a meeting before a big game?

People ask what I would have done if it was someone like Troy who fell asleep. That's simple. I'd have nudged him and whispered, "Troy, wake up." Everyone knew the fundamental rule on my teams.

"Listen, guys, I'm going to be very consistent with all of you," I said before each year with every team I coached. "I'm going to treat you all differently. All this fair and equal bullshit, we all know, is just bullshit. The harder you work, the more you meet the guidelines and do the things we ask—and the better player you are—the more I'm going to cut you slack. But understand, if you are a marginal player and are late to meetings or not working hard, your ass is going to be out of here."

Any coach who says they treat players the same is either a liar or not a very good coach. It was a totem pole. Players like Troy, Michael,

Emmitt, and Charles Haley were at the top. Players like Curvin Richards and Roper were at the bottom.

Don't read that wrong. I disciplined stars. Being on time, for instance, wasn't negotiable. Defensive tackle Dexter Manley pulled up
in a car to catch the team bus at Oklahoma State just as we were
leaving for the airport. We left him. In Dallas, we once sat on the
plane five minutes before departure time when Troy said Michael
Irvin wasn't there. Everyone knew to be early.

"Close the doors," I told the pilot.

"There's Michael on the tarmac," Troy said, looking out the plane
window.

"Great, let's go," I told the pilot.

We left him. We checked into our hotel in Detroit and were watching video in a meeting when Michael slinked in and sat next to me.

"Coach, I'm sorry," he said. "I apologize."

"You know you're wrong," I said. "You're not starting."

"Okay, coach."

He didn't start, but after our first possession Norv said over the
headset, "Do you think we've punished him enough?"

"Michael, get in there," I said.

That's how I delivered discipline. Is the salesman who brings in
$1 million in business treated equally with the one who brings in half
that? A star like Irvin was disciplined by missing a series. A reserve like
Roper was released. He didn't play another down in the NFL.

That sliding scale of discipline came into play again during our
Thanksgiving Day loss that season to Miami. It was an odd day, the
coldest Thanksgiving in Dallas history, with a low of 23 degrees during the game. Throw in three inches of snowy, slushy, icy weather and
you had the ingredients for something memorable.

Avezzano thought the bad footing might mean lower field goal
kicks and provide a chance for a block. He suggested putting another

big guy in the middle of the field-goal-block unit. Leon Lett, a reserve defensive tackle, was available.

"Good idea," I said.

We led by a point with fifteen seconds left when the Dolphins tried a 41-yard field goal. Kicker Pete Stoyanovich slipped on approaching the ball. His line-drive kick was blocked by our defensive tackle Jimmie Jones. The football rolled down the field through the snow. It looked like we'd won, and Joe's good idea was confirmed.

The one problem: Leon never had played on that special teams unit. He wasn't versed in the rules. He thought the ball was live as it rolled to a stop in the snow. He slid through a couple of Dolphins surrounding the ball to recover it, sending bodies flying. He touched the ball, making it live, and the Dolphins recovered it. They kicked a 19-yard field goal to win the game. You can't make up stuff like that.

The next morning, Troy was on an airplane for a quick vacation on our extended Thanksgiving break. He was surprised by a *Dallas Morning News* headline: "Johnson, Jones: Lett's job is secure." Troy, like many who lived through my years, thought Leon would be cut. Leon also was involved in an embarrassing fumble return the previous Super Bowl when he raised the football in his hand to celebrate just before crossing the goal line. It was swatted away for a touchback. We led by so much then, it didn't matter.

This one mattered. That's why Troy thought Leon would be cut. But after reading the newspaper story, Troy came to the proper conclusion: I saw something special in this young defensive tackle. That's the kind of person who's higher up on the totem pole, the one who gets more benefit of the doubt on mistakes. I went into the trainer's room immediately after the game and saw Leon, head down, crying. He already asked people if he had a job after that play. I knelt before him.

"You'll be on the football team as long as I'm the head coach," I said. Leon went on to make two Pro Bowls to confirm my belief.

But again: That wasn't his mistake that game. It was our mistake as coaches for putting in a player who hadn't been taught how to handle that situation.

All these years later, I smile whenever that crazy play in the snow comes on TV, because of what came next.

The Dolphins didn't win a game the rest of the year.

We didn't lose one all the way through the Super Bowl.

First of all, I wasn't drinking.

That's always brought up. Troy still insists I was into the Heinekens. It became the second question from the media the next day, right after why I guaranteed a win against San Francisco in the NFC Championship Game at all.

"Were you drinking?" I was asked.

Again: I wasn't drinking. Rhonda and I were driving on Interstate 635 that Thursday night to tape my weekly television show when I made the phone call. Now, if I made the call after that show, they might have been right about being loosened up with a cold one or two.

As we drove, I listened to Randy Galloway's Dallas radio show as New York Giants coach Dan Reeves discussed our big game against San Francisco. Galloway asked Reeves who would win. Reeves hemmed and hawed and . . .

"They want to talk about who's going to win the game, we can solve this right now," I told Rhonda.

I picked up the car phone, one of those early versions about the size and weight of a bowling ball.

"Put me on," I said to the show's producer.

A few seconds later I was on the air. Galloway said later that he thought I was mad about something. I wasn't mad at all. I was confident.

"We will win, and you can put it in three-inch headlines!" I yelled into the phone. "We will win the ball game."

I was having fun, too.

"In my opinion, and I'm a biased person, I think we'll go out Sunday and that crowd is going to be going absolutely wild," I said on the air. "I think we're going to have a very, very tight game for about three quarters. Then, before it's over, I think we're going to wear them out. We're going to beat their rear ends, and then we're going to the Super Bowl. That's my personal opinion."

After I hung up, Rhonda said, "Are you sure about all that?"

"Oh, yeah," I said.

It was so un-coach-like, it started a brush fire. That was fine. It injected a jolt of excitement into a big game, right? It did for me, anyhow.

"Coach, you wrote the check, now we have to cash it," Emmitt Smith said when I walked into the facility the next morning.

Rich Dalrymple, my media relations director at Miami and Dallas, asked why I said that, considering the firestorm it was causing. He wondered how to address it. I wrote the reasons down on a Post-it Note that he kept on his office bulletin board for decades:

1. I believe it.
2. Game is at home.
3. Take pressure off players.
4. Give players bottom-line, no excuses win attitude.
5. Might fertilize seeds of doubt in 49ers.

I signed my name before adding:

p.s.: If we win, maybe it gives us edge. If not, I can't get any lower, so I don't really give a shit what people think!

The only disappointment was that the newspaper headlines were about half of my desired three inches. San Francisco's typically mild-mannered coach George Seifert reacted in good form.

"Well, the man's got balls, I'll tell you that," he said. "I don't know if they're brass or papier-mâché. We'll find out pretty soon."

Back down? Please. I doubled down.

"They are definitely not papier-mâché," I said.

If this was all good fun for me, it underscored my core beliefs from not playing with scared money to having positively Pygmalion expectations. The target audience was my players. It was said on a Thursday night, too, meaning San Francisco couldn't use it for motivational purposes to have better focus in practices that week. Most of their game preparation was done.

"Here we are in the NFC Championship Game, and you think I'm going to tiptoe around like I'm scared to death?" I said to the media the next day. "I mean, I love it. As you can see."

I still love it. This was the big-stakes casino table. I was in my element. A month later, Troy was at the Pro Bowl when San Francisco quarterback Steve Young showed he understood what was at work.

"I know sometimes Jimmy says some things, but he does it in a manner it takes a lot of pressure off your players," Young said to Troy. "He put so much attention on himself, you get to go out and just play."

There also was No. 5 on my list to Rich. A seed was planted in San Francisco's minds. They changed their Friday and Saturday routines to have extra meetings and watch more film, players like Daryl Johnston heard later when talking to their players. And on game day? Jerry Rice, one of the classiest players in NFL history, made an obscene gesture at our bench on the first series and then threw a punch for a 15-yard penalty. That divisive seed was indeed planted in their players' minds.

We led at half, 28–7. We cruised to an easy win where the only negative was Troy suffering a concussion in the second half. He still doesn't remember that game, which is a shame. He was nearly perfect that day.

"I've been doing a lot of talking," I said in the locker room after the game. "If you're gonna talk the talk, you gotta walk the walk! Thanks to you guys! Y'all did the walkin'!"

During the ensuing Super Bowl week in Atlanta, I waited with Buffalo owner Ralph Wilson to go on a television show. Ralph was seventy-three, a gentleman, an original owner in the American Football League. We small-talked as we waited.

"You going to make a guarantee this game?" he said.

I leaned close to him and whispered, "I'm not going to guarantee it to everyone, but we're going to kick your ass."

There was only a week between the conference championship games and the Super Bowl that year. My coaches and I flew into Atlanta on Monday morning to set up. The team followed that afternoon.

By the time they arrived, we had our first crisis: Someone had stolen defensive lineman Chad Hennings's Super Bowl tickets. They had just been passed out before leaving Dallas, so it had to be someone inside the team. Another player, we figured.

I was fuming in my talk to the team.

"I'm going to work with NFL security! I'm going to find out who's holding the tickets! And when I do find out, that player will never play another play in this league! I'll blackball his ass!"

The tickets were slipped under Hennings's hotel room door that night. My favorite movie character is Anthony Hopkins playing Hannibal Lecter in *The Silence of the Lambs*. He talked a fellow prisoner into killing himself. What a study in psychology. Getting a player to return stolen tickets through words was the best I could do.

"How were you going to blackball whoever it was from playing again?" Rich Dalrymple asked me the next morning.

"I couldn't," I said. "But they didn't know I couldn't."

Our second crisis hit as Rich and I sat there talking. Every player except one was on buses to attend the league's mandatory media day. Erik Williams was passed out on his bed. Players didn't have curfew until Thursday of Super Bowl week.

"Listen," I had told the team, "there's no curfew the first few nights, but this is a business trip. We have events we have to go to, and we're going to work our ass off in practice. But you'll have free time to relax."

Now, on our first morning, Williams missed a required event. He got fined $10,000 by the league. I had a different kind of discipline in mind.

"Let's talk about something," I said to the team that afternoon. "Erik, you had a big time around town. You got your Super Bowl ring already. So, you don't give a shit about this team."

I asked everyone who had a Super Bowl ring to raise their hand. Most of the team did. There was no free agency, so most players had been with us the previous year. But some hadn't.

"Eddie Murray, how many years have you been in the league?" I said to our kicker, who had a great season.

"Fourteen, coach," he said.

"Have you won a Super Bowl ring?"

"No, coach, no one in Detroit's got close to winning a ring," he said.

I looked at veteran quarterback Bernie Kosar, whom we'd signed after Cleveland released him that midseason. He helped us when Troy was hurt.

"Bernie, how many AFC Championships did you play in?"

"Three, coach," he said.

"Do you have a Super Bowl ring?"

"No, I don't have one," he said.

I had Bernie talk about the times he came close in Cleveland.

"Hudson Houck, do you have a ring?" I said.

"No, coach, we had great players in Los Angeles like Eric Dickerson and we didn't get there," our veteran offensive line coach said.

I looked at Williams.

"Did you have a fucking good time at the Gold Club?" I asked. "You don't play this game to get another ring for yourself. You play for the team. You do what's asked, you get ready, you remain disciplined in going to events. You do everything you can do to help those other players get the ring that you already have."

We didn't have a problem the rest of that week.

By early Friday evening with our preparation done, I sat in the hotel suite with Nick Christin. ESPN was on in the otherwise silent room. Nick wouldn't talk to me with my mind working overtime before games unless I started the conversation. He tells the story of sitting beside me a few years later on a two-hour Miami Dolphins flight to Atlanta. No word was exchanged the whole way. As he got off the plane, team owner H. Wayne Huizenga said, "Helluva conversation you two had."

"Sometimes we fly to the West Coast, five, six hours, without a word," Nick answered.

So it was silent in that hotel suite except for the television. A report about the Bills came up. One pool reporter and one TV crew are allowed in for the first fifteen minutes of Super Bowl practices. It's a no-frills look to see which players aren't practicing and to collect some harmless video for news shows like the one on our TV. Everyone knows the cameras are rolling these fifteen minutes, so teams do generic stuff like stretching.

As I watched a wide-angle view of their light practice, quarterback Jim Kelly flipped the ball to running back Thurman Thomas in an unusual manner. They were working on something. I immediately paid attention.

"Is that a shuffle pass?" I asked.

They did it again. It was a shuffle pass.

"Hey, where's Butch?"

I got on the phone, tracked down Butch Davis in the hotel lobby, and asked if we had the computer printout of all Buffalo's plays that season. He searched through them and found that Buffalo hadn't run a shuffle pass that year. Then I remembered: Miami had run it against us in preseason. It went for a nice gain, too.

"Let's get ready for it," I said to Butch.

On Saturday, in our final practice, we prepared the defense for the shuffle pass. Sure enough, Buffalo had the ball near midfield in the first quarter and Kelly tossed a shuffle pass in the backfield to Thomas. He got hit immediately, fumbled, and safety James Washington came up with the ball. We converted that turnover into a field goal and 6–3 lead.

Buffalo tried another shuffle pass that game—and, again, it went nowhere. Years later, I talked to Kelly, who couldn't believe we stopped that play. They saw our defensive ends attacking quickly upfield and figured this had big-play potential. (Also, later at the Miami Dolphins I installed guidelines where cameramen couldn't take wide-angle video shots at practices.)

Still, we trailed Buffalo at half, 13–6. We hadn't played our best football. Troy says under the modern concussion rules, he wouldn't have been allowed to play the Super Bowl. He thought he was fine at the time. I did, too. Only later did odd things stick out about his behavior. Mannerisms. Comments. One of his friends, part of our support staff, mentioned a few weeks after the game how Troy stepped off the team bus at our hotel, which was by a mall.

"Hey, I haven't been to a mall in years," he said to the guy. "Why don't we go over to it?" He wouldn't have said that in his right mind, especially during the crazy week of a Super Bowl.

At halftime, I stood at the door to the locker room as our players came off the field.

"We're fine, we'll go out and play our game and win," I said as players went into the locker room.

Normally, I let the coordinators talk to their units during halftime. This time I talked to the offense. I knew exactly what to say. Norv was of the same mind-set. Emmitt, too.

"Listen, you offensive linemen: We've been trying to do a whole lot of stuff so far. But now we're going to go out there, take the ball, and jam it down their fucking throat. We're going to run 'Power Right' until they stop it. Nate, we're going to get you pulling. Emmitt, you're going to carry the load."

Everyone was nodding.

"We're going out in the second half and run it right up their ass," I said.

Daryl Johnston considered that halftime talk my greatest moment. No more finesse. No more pretense. Let's go kick the shit out of them. We were ready to play the best half of our season—a winning statement of our five years together, really.

Buffalo took the kickoff, but on the third play of the second half, Thurman Thomas took a handoff and was hit by a hard-charging Leon Lett and fumbled. That's right, Leon Lett, showing why he wasn't cut on Thanksgiving. James Washington scooped up the fumble and returned it 46 yards for a touchdown. We were tied, 13–13.

We forced a punt, and it was our offense's turn to put my halftime talk into effect. Emmitt began running "Power Right" through the Bills defense. It was a simple play over right tackle Erik Williams— yes, he was ready to play—and right guard Kevin Gogan. Newton pulled from left guard into the hole, Johnston cleaned up any loose bodies, and Emmitt did his thing play after play. Seven times we ran Power Right that drive for 61 yards. The touchdown drive totaled 64 yards.

We punched Buffalo and kept punching until their will was bent, the game ours, and the questions rained like confetti in the aftermath of our 30–13 victory about how many titles we could win. Emmitt was twenty-four. Troy and Michael Irvin were twenty-seven. Our offensive line was mostly young. Charles Haley had just turned thirty. I was fifty-one.

Everyone thought we were closer to the beginning than to the end. I knew otherwise. Winning back-to-back championships was nice. But that's all it felt to me by the end of this evening. Nice.

My sons, Brent and Chad, and Nick Christin waited for me in the parking lot after that game. They noticed that my normal manner of riding the emotional wave after any win—much less this historic win—was missing. In its place was an impatient, even unhappy tone.

"Ready to go?" I said in greeting them.

We had done it—we had won back-to-back Super Bowls. But I was empty of emotion. The next morning, Peter King of *Sports Illustrated* got in the limo with me on the way to a news conference. He picked up on that missing element of elation—of just general happiness, even.

"Are you going to be back with the Cowboys next year?" he asked.

"I can't guarantee that, Peter," I said.

He mentioned that if I stayed another year or two with Dallas, I'd be an automatic selection for the Hall of Fame. That wasn't important to me then. Fabricating some new goal wouldn't solve the essential problem: I didn't like who I'd become. I wasn't happy even on the day I should be the happiest.

Part of it was that playing the role of dictator coach had rubbed me raw. I now knew what winning two Super Bowls required. I would have to wear that dark mask even more the following season.

And the other part?

That had begun to leak out in the Dallas media and elsewhere. NBC's Bob Costas had Jerry and me on together before the Super Bowl and tried to discuss our relationship. We didn't bite. But the clock was ticking on my time in Dallas. And after leaving that Super Bowl, it was ticking faster than ever.

JERRY AND ME

No one understands my relationship with Jerry Jones.

I say that with complete certainty because I don't even understand my relationship with Jerry.

Maybe it's best summed up by a conversation we had in Canton, Ohio, leading up to my Hall of Fame induction in the summer of 2021. This was long after our Dallas success and divorce, long after we had gone our separate ways and lived our distinct lives—long after our story had been told and retold in various, but never complete, ways.

"I know how much you contributed to my success," Jerry told me. "I love you."

"I love you, too," I said. "But at times I hate you."

"At times I hate you, too," he said.

That's our relationship—if you can understand it. Jerry has off-the-charts passion. He has great charisma. No one outworks him. He's the smartest businessman I've ever known. Those attributes helped make the Dallas Cowboys a rare success story and explain why Jerry is in the Pro Football Hall of Fame. They are why I love him to this day.

And why do I hate him at times? Well, that's a longer, more complicated story. Let's start right at the start, when he was signing the papers to buy the Cowboys. He said to everyone in that room, as I sat watching, exactly what we had discussed privately.

"Jimmy, I'll handle all the finances," he said. "You handle all the football."

It was a church-and-state separation that made sense, considering our careers and strengths. It didn't matter if Jerry assumed the "General Manager" title. Jerry and my lawyer, Nick Christin, put my authority over the football side in writing, at least once we got around to writing a contract. People don't believe this, but I took the Dallas job without knowing simple basics like how much money I'd make. Jerry and I were so caught up in the earthshaking idea of buying the Cowboys and all the involved ramifications—replacing legendary coach Tom Landry, handling the public relations fallout, moving to Dallas, and assembling a new organization—that we never got around to talking about my individual deal. I wasn't worried. I just wanted to make as much as I had at the University of Miami. We agreed on $400,000 a year. Jerry said he wanted to make it a ten-year deal. I said he didn't have to do it for that long.

"I want continuity," he said.

Beyond the dollars and years, Jerry and I spelled out that finance-and-football separation just as we had discussed all along. This was important considering the hard work ahead. It became more important as our relationship evolved. The contract read:

> In addition to the duties and responsibilities customarily held by a Head Football Coach in the National Football League, Johnson shall have the following duties and responsibilities.
>
> (1) No assistant football coach, trainer, equipment man or strength coach shall be fired or employed by Employer without the prior approval of Johnson.
>
> (2) Johnson shall have the right of prior approval with re-

spect to the acquisition, releasing and trading of all football players of the Dallas Cowboys.

(3) Johnson shall have complete control of all assistant coaches, players, trainers and equipment men during training, practice, preparation for and the actual playing of games. Notwithstanding the foregoing, neither the assistant coaches, players, trainers or equipment men shall be deemed to be an employee of Johnson, but shall remain an employee of the Employer, nor shall Johnson be responsible for the payment of any salary to any such persons for the performance by such persons of their Contract with Employer.

(4) Johnson shall have the sole and complete control of the Dallas Cowboy players. . . .

For the first few years, that's how we worked, too. Oh, I did some small jobs that crossed that line the first off-season only because Jerry needed some help. He had a $150 million debt from buying the team. The franchise was losing $1 million a month, too. The Cowboys may have been "America's Team," but it was an American nightmare as much from the business side as the football side. That's where Jerry did inspired work. He inherited as much trouble that first year as I did. The first thing he did, just like me, was to get rid of a lot of people. He fired every department head in the transition, except the head of the ticket office, Steve Orsini. Much of the departmental staffs was gutted, too. I got a call from Bob Ackles in the scouting department, saying, "Jimmy, Jerry just fired Chris."

"Chris who?" I asked.

"He answers their phones," Bob said.

I said to find someone else to answer the phones. How hard could that be?

"No, you don't understand," he said. "He's the only one who understands the computer system that powers our computers. We're lost without him."

I called Jerry, asked if he'd fired Chris over in scouting. "Chris who?" he asked.

It turned out, to tighten the budget Jerry fired all the lowest-salary people in every department, figuring they were expendable. I suggested he raise Chris's salary and keep him.

With so many departments suddenly without leaders, everyone jumped in to help. Jerry asked me to sell some stadium suites that first winter. I was on his plane when he sold the first one to Don Tyson, chief executive officer of Tyson Foods. I was told it would take four or five years to sell all the suites they handed me, but the commission could earn me $1 million. I sold them all that first off-season.

I also helped cut the lavish list of complimentary tickets and courtesy cars. The previous Cowboys regime obviously didn't keep close watch on that stuff. I called one woman who hadn't worked for the team for two years, but was a friend of former team president Tex Schramm and still had a company car.

"Well, coach, I knew this call would come someday," she said.

In looking at the company books, I also saw something odd about the team's television shows. I had some experience here. In Miami, Nick and I bought television time, sold advertising, and oversaw production of my television show. I made $300,000 to $400,000 a year. In Dallas, Landry and team president Tex Schramm had television shows and were paid a more moderate amount. The team, too, made a scant profit of $10,000 from the two shows. I called in the officials from the TV station that produced these shows.

"Something's wrong," I said. "I've looked at the books and there's more money to be made than the Cowboys are getting."

Within five minutes I had irked them to the point where one stood up and said, "Evidently you don't want to do a first-class TV show." They all walked out.

Jerry looked at me. "You're so smart, what're we going to do for a TV show?"

I called Brenda Bushnell, who had run my TV program in Miami. She studied the situation and told Jerry there was untapped value for these shows, considering the franchise's name. "Look, American Airlines will sponsor the guy cutting the grass for the Dallas Cowboys," she said.

That first year, the Cowboys organization made more than $700,000 from my television show. That was in addition to the $400,000 to $500,000 I earned. Of course, as soon as Brenda got everything humming along and Jerry understood how to run a television company, he used an owner's prerogative. After she gave her annual talk about the good money made and good plans ahead, he fired her. He didn't need her anymore. He understood how to run a TV company now. He put in one of his people.

From that first off-season, everything we did was to make the Cowboys a success. I worked my ass off on constructing the football side. Jerry worked his ass off paying off that big debt. Everything was reexamined with a bottom-line view. Heading into the second draft, Jerry wondered if he could cut the scouting staff to save some money.

"Jimmy, do we actually need all those scouts?" he asked.

I explained the information they bring.

"You've got your coaches on the road doing the scouting," he said. "I just think that maybe we don't need all those guys. I hear you guys talking about who the top players are. I got *Sports Illustrated* here. It's about the same players."

I mentioned the second, third, fourth, fifth, and sixth through twelfth rounds. Jerry backed off that idea. He was so busy fixing the business side that he rarely made it out to practice those first three or four years. If he did appear, it was for only the last few minutes, standing outside the locker room and watching from afar. He also seldom visited the football offices due to his schedule. Sometimes when he did visit, I was watching game film and he'd be talking about something that felt distracting to my narrow world of X's and O's. I wanted him back on his side of the fence.

Everything hummed along fine at the start of our coexistence, until something reared up that changed our relationship: winning. It wasn't even top-of-the-mountain winning. It was the mere specter of it. We improved from 1-15 our first year to 7-9 the second year. Jerry's business plan was paying good dividends, too. Good? He was raking in money. People started to see the grand blueprint coming into focus and realized these two hicks from Arkansas just might know what they're doing.

Jerry also noticed something disproportionate about how the outside world reacted to us. My football success received far more acclaim than his business success. That didn't sit well with him. He tried to nudge into the football side in ways that added small layers of tension to our relationship. Some ways were obvious: He redid my contract three times to pay me more as we won, but each time, he tried to take out the clauses giving me full control of the football decisions. I refused each time. That wasn't negotiable.

It's not that Jerry wanted to meddle. He wasn't a meddler in the manner owners sometimes are. He never, for example, demanded trading for a player or running a certain play. He just wanted credit for all that. An example came when I traded with Atlanta for veteran defensive tackle Tony Casillas. It was a classic case of buying low. Casillas was unhappy in Atlanta with the gimmicks of coach Jerry Glanville, and they were unhappy with his attitude. Only twenty-seven, he announced he was retiring. I made a few calls and got a valuable player for second- and eighth-round draft picks. I went and told Jerry how we had just added a dynamic piece in Casillas to our defense.

Fifteen minutes later, Jerry was on television telling the world he had traded for Tony Casillas.

"What the hell?" I said to him. "You didn't even know who Tony Casillas was."

This led to the first, scabs-ripped-off conversation about the underlying problem with our growing success as he saw it.

"I can make five million dollars, and no one gives a shit," he said. "You can trade for a backup offensive guard, and everyone goes . . ."

He cupped his hands and made the noise of a crowd cheering. He then uttered the line that became the centerpiece for all the unraveling to come in our relationship:

"I want to have some of that fun."

Even as he said it, I saw it as a wedge in our winning operation. It's an age-old theme of runaway egos damaging winning relationships, from the Beatles to Michael Jordan's Chicago Bulls, to the Los Angeles Lakers of Shaquille O'Neal and Kobe Bryant. Jerry and I hadn't even had a winning season and the temperature was rising inside our relationship.

Months after we traded for Casillas before our third season in 1991, the *Dallas Morning News* decided the theme of their football section was "Power." Absolute power. Their Cowboys beat writer, Rick Gosselin, wanted to talk about my "transforming the Cowboys into contenders by exercising total control over the personnel—drafting, trading, signing and waiver claims," as he later wrote. I had known and respected Rick since he covered me at Oklahoma State for the Associated Press. I heard his pitch for the story and hesitated.

"This is going to be a problem," I told him.

The premise wasn't the problem. Jerry was. He would want to be portrayed as having some of that football power. He did, too, once he found out about the story. It became a constant issue for a few weeks. I finally told Gosselin, "I wish you'd get that story done because I'm tired of spending my evenings with Jerry talking about it."

Jerry worked over Gosselin, too. As Gosselin wrote years later in the *Morning News,* "I spent hours with Jones for a few evenings in camp crafting the few quotes that would appear from the owner in that story to make it appear he was more involved than he was."

This issue with Jerry only increased as we started to win. That 1991 season we beat Washington and had a short week before a Thanksgiving Day game against Pittsburgh. Our team was coming together. Our first playoffs were in sight.

I got a call from the league saying NBC's Bill Walsh and Dick Enberg, who were announcing the game, wanted to watch our practice. This is customary for Sunday games, but the Saturday practice is a simple walk-through with nothing strategic. Due to the shortened week of a Thursday game, our offense ran the same twenty scripted plays in Wednesday's practice that would start the game. I didn't want TV announcers to see those. I was concerned they would watch our scripted plays and might say in the pregame, "I wouldn't be surprised if Dallas ran this swing pass," or "You should look for this early on." It wouldn't be the first time TV gave away something valuable.

I said Walsh and Enberg could watch the final fifteen minutes of practice when it was open to all media. I then got a call from Jerry. He had gotten a call from the league about opening the practice to Walsh and Enberg.

"I don't want to do it," I said flatly.

As we started practice on Wednesday, Jerry walked out with Walsh and Enberg. There's a rubberized track by the locker rooms, then the grass fields. Jerry usually never came on the field. He would stand on the track. This day, he walked to the field with Walsh and Enberg.

I walked over to meet them — to stop them, really. I said hello, but I was angry. I was about to explode.

"You're pissed," Jerry said.

"You're fucking right I'm pissed," I said. "I told you I didn't want them fucking out here."

They retreated but watched from the rubberized track. When practice was over, it was standard for coaches to meet with network announcers. They asked about our offense.

"It's good," I said.

They asked about Aikman. "What you see is what you get," I said.

After a few curt answers, I said, "Guys, let me tell you something. This is not about you. In a different setting, in a different time, I'd be happy to talk with you for as long as you want. I was forced to do something I didn't want to do. Really, I've got no information for you."

Enberg and Walsh, to their credit, didn't mention this in the broadcast. But it was in moments like this where the friction between Jerry and me started to surface. The more we won, the more it was a problem. Before the 1992 draft, I traded second- and fifth-round picks for Cleveland's second-, third-, sixth-, eighth-, and twelfth-round picks. Cleveland's Bill Belichick made the deal to have four of the first seventy-eight picks in the draft. Me? I noted we had a moderate win on the Draft Value Chart.

After making the trade, I found Jerry in the back of the Cowboys' facility with a couple of his friends.

"I just made a helluva trade with Belichick," I said.

Even as I began explaining the trade, I realized my mistake. I shouldn't have said this in front of his friends. It wasn't about actions by this point in our relationship. It also was about appearance. Jerry, I could see, grew more upset that day before his friends with the mention of each draft pick we received.

"I want to have some of that fun."

This was the day before the NFL Draft, and later that afternoon Jerry mentioned that an ESPN camera would be in the draft room. It would have no audio, he said. So, there was no chance anyone could hear private discussions—but America would have every chance of seeing the inner workings, reading our body language, and drawing whatever conclusion we suggested.

"Whenever you make a trade, lean over and talk to me," Jerry said.

It wasn't enough to deal with the stress of managing picks, developing trades, and continuing to build a champion in the pressure cooker of a draft. Now Jerry's ego had to be massaged amid all this, too. I became so upset that draft day, I didn't trust what I would say even to my inner circle. I didn't take my customary jog with my assistants the next day. They noticed, too. They soon discovered the problem. And so sides were taken, walls erected, and emotions rose inside the franchise.

Jerry justified saying he was involved in every deal that was made by noting he wrote the checks. He told me that numerous times. Players couldn't be drafted; coaches couldn't be hired. Herschel Walker couldn't have been traded, he said, unless he wrote a check. Walker threatened to retire after being traded, according to his agent, Peter Johnson. Would he have retired? Doubtful. But Jerry gave him $1 million to report to Minnesota. In Jerry's mind that made the trade possible. Just like he was involved in the trade for defensive end Charles Haley because he picked up Haley at the airport to make him feel wanted in Dallas.

To be fair, I could have handled this better. I could have let Jerry push whatever truth he wanted. He was the owner, after all. He spent the money. But I had trouble twisting truths, playing pretend about his role, appeasing his ego, and having to deal with such nonsense while actually building a championship team. Let's not kid ourselves, too: I had a big ego as well. After all the work in building this team from nothing—all the sweat the coaches, scouts, and myself put in—why shouldn't the story be told as it actually happened?

From there it became a steady drip, drip, drip of issues across the 1993 season that had nothing to do with winning football games, applying layers of lacquered hardness to our relationship. He would claim credit for this player, this trade, this win. He loved to talk to the media. That was noteworthy because of what happened to us in that time: We quit talking. That accelerated our downfall. We talked daily the first three or four years. By the fifth year, my deteriorating relationship with Jerry was compounded by the draining role I played in driving the team to a second Super Bowl title.

I had constructed my persona to be the perfect football coach as I saw it—demanding and demonic, all for the idea of winning. But now I felt trapped by that role I didn't enjoy playing. I felt trapped in a bad relationship with Jerry, too.

Was there only one way out?

I began asking this while preparing for the draft, planning for the summer, and plotting our run at a third Super Bowl.

That's when the worst moment came in March at the NFL owners meetings in Orlando. All the nit-picking between Jerry and me—who gets the credit, who did this, or said that—funneled into an explosive night that started at a hotel bar in Universal Studios. I sat with Rhonda and a group of friends who were all ex-Cowboys: Dave Wannstedt, then the Chicago Bears' coach, and his wife, Jan; Norv Turner, who took the Washington job a couple of months earlier, and his wife, Nancy; Brenda Bushnell, my TV show producer whom Jerry had fired; and Bob Ackles, whom Jerry also had fired.

Jerry had drunk a bit before he arrived at our table.

"Let's toast to the Super Bowl!" he said.

I was in the middle of a conversation. I thought I raised my glass. Some people said I didn't. I'm not sure. But no one else at the table was with the team anymore. No one other than Norv had been part of that second Super Bowl two months earlier. A couple of the individuals had been fired by Jerry. There was an awkward moment of silence as the table didn't join in Jerry's toast.

"Fuck all of you," Jerry said. "I'll toast and celebrate with my friends."

He walked off. No one said anything. There was just a "What just happened?" feel at the table. We then returned to our conversations. I honestly didn't give it a second thought as we sat there. After everyone called it a night, Rhonda and I went to Taco Bell and took tacos back to the room. I don't remember either of us mentioning Jerry's episode.

That changed early the next morning when the phone rang. It was Larry Lacewell. He saw Jerry close another bar with Gosselin and his *Morning News* colleague Ed Werder. Among other things, Jerry said he was going to fire me.

I was angry hearing that. But I wanted to be sure that what was heard late at a bar with the alcohol flowing was what Jerry really said. I met with Gosselin that morning. He said Jerry talked with them at the bar until 5 a.m. They discussed why teams won Super Bowls. Jerry was asked how important it was to have a franchise quarterback like Troy Aikman, a star running back like Emmitt Smith, and a playmaking receiver like Michael Irvin. Jerry was then asked how important the coach was, given that talent, and he dropped the line that was the end of us.

"There are five hundred coaches who could have won the Super Bowl with our team," he said.

I was now furious. There's no other way to say it. After meeting with Gosselin, I fulfilled a previous agreement for a media interview

Arkansas coaches called me "Jimmy Jump-Up" because I never stayed on the ground. As a 195-pound, all-conference nose tackle, I was the prototype of the speed-over-size defensive linemen I later loved to coach.

My hair wasn't always under control just yet, but by the time I coached Arkansas's defense in the mid-1970s I had developed the kind of attacking defense that rattled conventional ideas.

3

I told my assistants to stick together and we'd win a national championship. No one celebrated that first ring as a coach more than I did.

An early misstep by Jerry Jones and me was eating at a little Mexican restaurant called Mia's the night before he bought the Dallas Cowboys. Who knew it was one of Tom Landry's favorite places?

4

5

I didn't intend to change how NFL front offices operate with my love of trading and creation of the Draft Value Chart. That was just a by-product of building a champion.

No one knew the difficult road from a losing franchise to a Super Bowl title quite like Jerry Jones and I did. Winning was the prize for us—and, later, a problem.

6

7

I had one message at halftime of our second Super Bowl against Buffalo: We're giving Emmitt Smith the football. Our smiles tell how it worked out.

Mother, Daddy, and Rhonda gave me love and direction. Mother's death also changed my perspective on my football life.

8

9

Port Arthur left its good mark on me. I left a mark on my hometown, too.

10

I visited President Reagan after winning a title at the University of Miami and President Clinton following Dallas's Super Bowl wins. After his second invitation, I said I couldn't visit because I would be fishing in the Keys that day. But Jerry stepped in to say that we would be there.

11

Miami Dolphins owner Wayne Huizenga was a smart and strong businessman who knew how to close deals. I needed a home in Miami? He wrote a $1 million check.

Dan Marino was a great competitor with a great arm. I only wish I'd coached him in the prime of his career.

12

13

I met a young William Wesley at a high school basketball game and introduced him to the college football world. "World Wide Wes" later introduced me to entertainers like Jay-Z.

14

I never considered the Pro Football Hall of Fame a goal during my career, but being voted in became important to me afterward. Sharing the moment with Troy Aikman made it more special.

15

Bill Belichick has become a good friend in part because we share the same philosophy of coaching. He'll wear one of these Hall of Fame jackets like Bill Cowher and me whenever he wants.

16

My years on *FOX NFL Sunday*, alongside good friends like Michael Strahan, border on a family affair. The program also allows me to still be part of the game I love without being the coach I came to hate.

17

No one is more genuine, funny, or a better friend than Terry Bradshaw. He talks about two-deep zones and barnyard noises in the same sentence.

I'm living the life I want, especially on days my friend Nick Christin, son Chad, and I catch some dolphins (also known as mahi-mahi).

I love my sons, Brent and Chad, but we had some dark times. That's made us appreciate the smiles even more these days.

I didn't enjoy winning enough when it happened, but am doing so these days with people who were big parts of it, like (from left) Rich Dalrymple, Troy Aikman, Dave Wannstedt, Tony Wise, and Norv Turner.

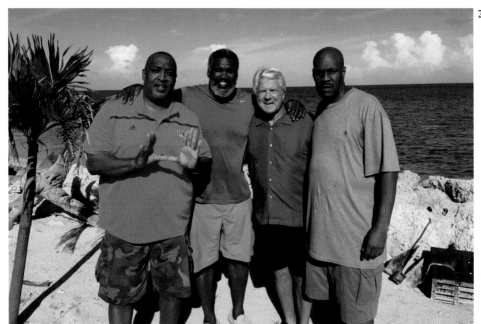

I was never happier coaching than working with the likes of Melvin Bratton, Alonzo Highsmith, and Tolbert Bain at Miami. They remain a part of my life.

Rhonda and I might not be sure what day our anniversary is on, but our marriage is the foundation to my happiness.

but didn't let on about the volcano churning inside me. I then headed straight to the room where the owners were meeting and pulled Jerry out. I didn't even have to say why.

"Jimmy, I apologize," he said. "I had too much to drink."

"Fuck you, Jerry," I said. "I don't care. Too much to drink or not. I'm fucking out of here. I'm gone."

Rhonda and I immediately loaded the car and drove to Miami. I knew Jerry would try to find me and I didn't want to be found. So, we didn't go home. We checked into the Marriott hotel by the Miami airport. Eventually Jerry called me there.

"You quitting?" he said.

"No, I'm not going to quit, but I want you to settle the fucking contract," I said.

"Well, I'm not firing you," he said.

"Well, I'm not quitting," I said. "But settle this contract. Jerry, you don't want me to talk about all the things I know about all the skeletons in the closet. Settle this contract."

Skeletons? There wasn't any lurid bombshell, but as in any business, some dealings and relationships don't want to be held up to a public light. Some are stories I've told here. My contract stipulating he had no football control, for instance.

I soon heard from Jerry's lawyer, Dick Cass, a great guy who recently retired as president of the Baltimore Ravens. He called from his Washington office and said, "Jimmy, you two have to work this out."

"No, Dick, it's not going to work out," I said. "Tell him to settle the contract."

I had promised to make an appearance at Emmitt Smith's youth football clinic in Pensacola. Rhonda and I flew there. I didn't want to do interviews just yet, so I steered clear of the media—sometimes in ways that were humorous as I look back. After the clinic, the car returning us to the airport was followed by Werder of the *Dallas Morning News*. I told the driver to shake him, as if this were some chase scene in a James Bond movie. The driver called security at the airport. Werder's car was stopped, we kept driving to our private plane, and I flew to Dallas to meet with Jerry at Valley Ranch.

We talked for a bit about my leaving. But we stopped short of bringing in the lawyers to work out exit terms.

"Let's sleep on it," Jerry said.

Troy came into my office before I left that afternoon.

"The players want you to stay, Jimmy," he said. "Everyone wants you to return and we'll go win again."

I didn't want to ignore Troy, who was not just a great player but a good friend of mine by this point. I said something about not having made a final decision just yet.

"There's a part of me that would like to come back and win three in a row," I said. "But even if I do come back, it'd only be for one more year."

Troy realized then that it was probably the end, that if I already was saying it was just for another year, everything probably had deteriorated too far for me to return at all. I certainly felt that way. There was a chance, a small one, that Jerry might have charmed me that next morning into staying. Jerry, as I've said, is the greatest salesman. Norv likes to tell how I'd be fuming over something about Jerry during our time and go storming into his office swearing and yelling. "Jerry would say, 'You're the greatest,' and Jimmy would come out feeling better," Norv said.

The next morning, as I went to the office, there was Jerry's quote staring at me from a newspaper headline: "500 Coaches Could've Won the Super Bowl." That slammed the door shut on my decision. I needed out. It wasn't just this quote. It was the exhausting disciplinarian role I would have to play again the next season. That wouldn't get easier. It was all the tiresome antics with Jerry. Our relationship wouldn't improve any.

"Jerry, we can't work this out," I said when we met.

He said, "Jimmy, I want to give you two million dollars."

"Jerry, one million is fine."

Why did I say that? I'm not sure. Maybe to say money wasn't a deciding factor for me.

"No, I want to give you two million," he said.

What I really wanted was to be released from the remaining five years on the contract. I didn't know if I wanted to coach again at some point. I just wanted that option. The expansion Jacksonville franchise had called near the end of the season as word of Jerry's and my deteriorating relationship rumbled through the league. That was fun for my ego, but I was never interested in Jacksonville. My only plan now was returning to the Keys and taking some time off. The papers were drawn up and a news conference called to announce our split. As we walked down the hall to meet the media, Jerry said, "You know they're going to beat me up pretty good in this."

"I'll say the right things," I said.

I did say the right things, too, playing rope-a-dope with some questions and sidestepping others. The newspaper photos that final day at Valley Ranch show us shaking hands, then smiling and hugging in a dog and pony show.

My first thought when I see the pictures from that day is that I was eating pretty good in those days. My face sure looks bloated. My next thought is how emotional it was leaving that team. Daddy drove up from Port Arthur after watching the news conference with Jerry. He and Mother were proud of my accomplishments. He came to my home and wanted to make sure I was doing okay. I began crying in front of him. That reminds me how emotional that decision was for me. We'd won two Super Bowls. We had the kind of players I loved to coach. But I couldn't go on being that drill sergeant. I needed out. I knew it was the right decision. When my tears dried that day, I programmed myself never to look back.

I never did, too.

My departure was best for both Jerry and me. I left a job where success no longer brought happiness, and Jerry assumed the role he wanted in the organization. I'd guess he's more involved in the football side of the Cowboys today, but I really don't know. He did want to be part of the fun as he always defined it: talking to the media, standing in the spotlight, enjoying being portrayed as the epicenter of everything involving the Cowboys. It's his team. He can run it however he wants.

Following my departure, he hired a coach who let him do just that in Barry Switzer, my former colleague and rival. Jerry made his point by hiring Switzer, too: Any five hundred coaches really could win the Super Bowl with that Cowboys team. Barry had never worked in the NFL. He was retired from coaching for five years. He didn't overwork himself those years in Dallas. The Cowboys lost the NFC Conference Championship in 1994 before winning the Super Bowl in 1995.

So that quote about five hundred coaches was right as far as it went. Barry inherited a train running down the tracks and didn't wreck it. The roster was stacked with great players who knew how to work and a coaching staff who knew how to win. He didn't screw up winning in the short term. But to sustain that success over the horizon meant constantly making good personnel moves, managing daily issues, navigating potholes, and playing a disciplined game—all the traits championship organizations must exhibit. As Jerry said, any ol' coach can win with a great and developed team. But how many can turn a 1-15 team into a back-to-back champion? How many can keep that success going into the future?

In 1996, Switzer's third year, the Cowboys went 10-6, won a wild card game, and lost in the divisional round. They wouldn't win another playoff game for twelve years and then it was just one game before being eliminated. They've won two playoff games in the quarter century since that team we built fell apart.

Jerry hired a couple of more coaches who were fine with letting him say whatever he wanted. He then built that great stadium—again, I've never met a better businessman—and hired the sizzle of Bill Parcells to help sell the suites. Parcells took over a troubled roster and improved it. But he didn't win a playoff game in four years. Jerry seized on that point after Parcells left. He noted how everyone wanted him to give up control like he did to Parcells—and the team still didn't win. So he went back to being out front of everything and having all the fun as he saw it.

Here's how I always saw it: The fun is winning. All the other stuff doesn't matter if you're not winning.

Jerry and I have lived our good and separate lives all these years. Sometimes we meet. We always cut up and have a good time. I interviewed him for FOX at midfield in his new stadium in 2009, ending with a hug. I went to a big wedding anniversary party for him and his wife, Gene, in the stadium, too. He and I sat on a FOX set before the 2011 Super Bowl talking with Troy Aikman, Daryl Johnston, and Michael Irvin about our team's success and ending with questions about why I wasn't in the Dallas stadium's "Ring of Honor."

Before my induction to the Pro Football Hall of Fame in 2021, we were interviewed on another FOX panel where we laughed and had a good time. Terry Bradshaw then asked, "All Cowboys friends are asking now, Jerry, when are you going to put Jimmy in the Ring of Honor?"

Jerry, after some discussion, said, "He'll be in the Ring of Honor."

"While I'm alive?" I asked.

That's still up for grabs as I write this. I did stand before the Dallas fans for the first time since I left as coach for a Hall of Fame ring ceremony on a Monday-night game in the 2021 season. I thanked Jerry, thanked my coaches and players, thanked the fans.

"I've just got one more thing to say," I said. "HOW 'BOUT THEM COWBOYS?"

That was a good moment, the cheers washing down as I pumped my arms in the air.

I've never second-guessed my decision to leave Dallas. Others have. Michael Irvin says we would have won five Super Bowls if I had stayed. Troy Aikman has told me we had the chance to be Belichick and Tom Brady years before they kept winning in New England. Maybe he's right. Patriots owner Robert Kraft also has said he uses the schism between Jerry and me as a cautionary tale in his relationship with Belichick.

And Jerry? He's second-guessed himself. "I've never been able to know why I fucked it up," he said with tears in his eyes before the Cowboys started the 2021 training camp.

My guess is he knows why. He didn't respect success. He didn't appreciate how hard it was to build a champion. He didn't understand the job I did. His ego got in the way. Again: I'm not blameless here. But Jerry thought that once the team was formed and we were winning titles it would be blue skies forever, no matter who coached his team. There's a recent book out by former NFL executive Bill Polian about Super Bowl teams in which Jerry says: "Jimmy was an integral part as far as the coaching. Jimmy wanted to be a bigger part as far as a lot of the other stuff. And that was good. I was fine with that. But I got here trading. I got here by making deals every day. Jimmy had never traded for a goldfish when he got here."

All these years later, Jerry is still portraying himself as having a role in football deals he wasn't part of. He still thinks that's important for some reason. And there are fewer people around him these days who know how it really played out.

It's all fine from my view. It really is. I'm happy I left Dallas and have never been happier in my life.

I'm good with Jerry, too.

Looking back at those years, I remember riding in Jerry's car in Little Rock a couple of days before he bought the Cowboys. We were all excited about the possibilities ahead of us. He said he would do the business; I'd do the football.

"Jimmy," he said, "if we pull this off, we'll make sports history."

We did just that. He built a world-class business. I built a championship football team. And I love Jerry. I really do.

I hate him at times, too.

13

A WORLD WITH NO SIDELINE

I didn't just leave a job in Dallas.

I left a world.

Gone were the drama and demands of that oversized Dallas stage. Gone were the stress of running a high-profile organization and my drill sergeant persona. Gone, too, were my name from the daily news cycle and the thought of work when my eyes opened at 4:30 each morning.

For the first time as an adult, I woke up and thought, *What am I doing to do today?* That was a weird sensation at first. Many retired coaches and players talk of voids that can't be filled, that family and free time fail to fill. Their lack of a team becomes a lack of purpose for them.

I felt free.

I *was* free.

After leaving Dallas, my big decision most days in the Keys was whether to take out the boat and go fishing, tinker around the house on some project, or go somewhere with Rhonda like Woody's Saloon and sing karaoke. (Okay, I only sang once. The song? The Beach Boys' "Help Me, Rhonda." Rhonda said I was the one needing help.)

My next connection to football was a chosen one. As I left that farewell news conference with Jerry in Irving, Texas, an old friend literally stepped into my path and surprised me.

"I want to offer you a job," Ed Goren said.

I hadn't seen Ed in several years. He was a CBS Sports producer when I coached at the University of Miami. Back then, I'd fly to New York when my regular season ended and do some college halftime shows on CBS with Jim Nantz and Mike Francesa. It was fun, offered some exposure—and, hey, you never know when you'll want a broadcast job.

"Let's go talk," I said to Ed that day.

We went over to the Hyatt hotel. Ed said he had flown to town to be the first in line for me. He had moved to a new entity called "FOX Sports." The network bought the rights to broadcast NFC games starting the next 1994–95 season in a historic four-year, $1.58 billion deal. It had already invested in big names like John Madden and Pat Summerall to announce the games. Ed wanted to put me on a pregame show with host James Brown and former players Terry Bradshaw and Howie Long.

"Let me think about it," I said.

ESPN and others called soon, too. But because I had worked with Ed and liked him, I chose FOX. It proved to be one of the best decisions of my life. The FOX crew became family to me through the years—good friends and good times. It didn't exactly start that way, though.

That summer, I didn't attend a seminar for our studio show.

"'Where's Jimmy?' became a standard joke with us," Bradshaw told reporters. "I wish he were here. He should be here. We're here. We've been here a whole week. We're not mad at Jimmy. But it just signals that maybe this isn't as important to him."

Terry got a call from Ed about that.

"Terrence," he said, "write this telephone number down: 3-0-5 . . ."

"Okay, whose number is this?" Terry said.

"This is for one Mr. Jimmy Johnson, the newest member of our pregame show. The one that's going to complete it. You might want to apologize."

My contract with FOX stipulated I didn't have to attend the program's weeklong seminar. Just having left coaching, I negotiated to have some free time. Terry called and apologized. It wasn't the best way to kick off a relationship. Now that we're best friends, we laugh about it—well, that and a few other stories from that first season.

I wasn't the easiest to work with at the outset for a few reasons. First, I wasn't sure if my coaching days were finished and so I remained more guarded with my thoughts and personality. I didn't show my full sense of humor and didn't get close with my FOX broadcast teammates. I was also acutely aware there were 30 million viewers of *FOX NFL Sunday* every Sunday and 100 million more for our Super Bowl show and I had never worked in a freewheeling format like our studio show. Terry might talk of a defensive scheme one second, and barn animal noises the next. Everyone ad-libbed. All the ingredients were there for a great show—and for embarrassment. The Super Bowl–winning coach in me didn't want to risk being embarrassed.

I prepared for my role, typically writing a script and memorizing it for any on-air feature. The script would flash up on the teleprompter as insurance. In December that first year, I was reading off the teleprompter, building up to a big finish, when Terry stepped between me and the camera, blocking my view. On live television. Before 30 million people. He simply wanted to stroll over and see the Christmas choir that was on the set. But my big finish had a noticeable wobble. It wasn't perfect! And I was livid. Terry and I had some words later. He said it wasn't intentional. He was just curious about the choir. That's the exact type of thing we would do to each other in my second chapter on *FOX NFL Sunday* in an attempt to screw someone else up. We'd all laugh about it, too.

But I wasn't ready to laugh as a rookie in this live-TV atmosphere.

During another *FOX NFL Sunday* show, I delivered my segment while Howie was seated beside me. Off-camera and out the corner of my eye, he was silently making some chopping motions with his hands to Terry. Like me, Howie was new to television, having just retired from football. I thought he and Terry were making fun of me. When the show ended, I stormed off the set and went to my dressing room.

"He's pissed," Howie said.

"What's he pissed about?" Terry said.

They came and explained that Howie was making hand motions to illustrate how they would segment a piece coming up.

Oh.   ▪

Another time, we were asked to tape greetings to countries—in their own languages—where our FOX show broadcast. Terry and Howie got countries like England, France, and Germany. I got countries like Japan, South Korea, and the Philippines. My tongue had trouble navigating the script in those languages. Terry and Howie were laughing. Again: I wasn't laughing.

The coach in me wanted to be in control of everything.

Still, step-by-step, we made our new team work. I loosened up . . . Well, a little. We developed a relationship . . . Well, sort of. We even worked the ongoing speculation of my returning to coaching after that first season into the show. I was rumored to be considering any open job or potential vacancy for the next NFL season. That wasn't entirely true. I had talked with some teams—namely, Philadelphia and Tampa Bay. On *FOX NFL Sunday*, we had some fun with my decision. In one video, I alternated putting on Philadelphia and Tampa Bay hats in the manner high school kids do before announcing their college decision. After a week of promotion and forty-seven minutes into the hour-long show, I made the big announcement.

I wasn't returning to coaching.

It wasn't a big surprise, considering it didn't come at some team's headquarters. But that show got a 6.4 rating, with millions tuning in—our highest rating of the year. NBC's pregame studio show got a 4.5 rating that day. Yep, the scoreboard still mattered, and I was watching it.

I also signed a three-year deal with a no-escape clause that was announced that day. The conclusion was I was done coaching. Television was my new world.

Even I wasn't sure of that.

14

BACK TO THE GRIND

During my second season out of football, Rhonda and I were talking one day, and she wondered if I wanted to return to coaching. I pointed at the ocean extending into the horizon outside our home.

"Trade that for a film room?" I asked.

Her only question was if I was lying, but not to her. Was I lying to myself? It's true I never looked back after leaving Dallas, never missed that regulated world, never once thought of what was missed by not returning.

I occasionally heard from Dallas. Hudson Houck, for example, called a year into my retirement to ask if he should sign a long-term deal as the Cowboys' offensive line coach. He wanted to rejoin me if I returned to coaching. I told him to sign the deal and guarantee his future, because there were no guarantees I'd coach again.

That's how I felt. I didn't need the money, the fame, or some overriding purpose as others defined it. I wasn't some junkie needing a coaching high. But as I lived my fun life that second season out of football—diving for lobster, hanging with Rhonda, working for FOX—a question crept into my mind.

Would I regret not having tried to win again?

That's what nudged me back to coaching. Not the stage. Not the camaraderie. There wasn't some gnawing biological need to stand on the sideline or in the center of a room again in the manner some coaches miss. It was simply an issue I explained to Rhonda one day: "If I don't give it one more shot, I might think I should've gone back and tried to win another one."

And so, as the 1995 season approached an end, I listened to offers. There always were offers from the time I left Dallas. San Diego owner Dean Spanos and general manager John Butler visited me in the Keys a couple of times to discuss taking over their team. Spanos and I remain friends to this day. But California isn't Florida.

Philadelphia owner Jeffrey Lurie met with me in the Miami home of my attorney, Nick Christin. We talked for three hours. There was a lot to like with Lurie and his franchise. But one element overrode all of that as I envisioned myself in Philadelphia: it was cold there.

Tampa Bay general manager Rich McKay talked with me, too. The Bucs had an interesting roster, draft picks to use, the salary cap in good shape—and they were close to home in Florida. Tampa was tempting. Team owner Malcolm Glazer was scheduled to fly to Miami one weekend in early January to discuss the job with me. A snowstorm hit New York that weekend. Glazer couldn't fly out.

That same weekend Nick got another phone call.

"Is this the Nick Christin who represents Jimmy Johnson?" the man said.

Nick said it was.

"I couldn't get your number, because I was spelling 'Christin' wrong," said Eddie Jones, an old-school southern gentleman and president of the Miami Dolphins.

Don Shula had retired from the Dolphins two days earlier. Eddie called to say team owner H. Wayne Huizenga wanted to talk with me. Some media had already set up outside Nick's office. It was being reported we already were negotiating a deal. The rumor persists all these years later that Wayne and I had some backdoor discussion or wink-wink agreement during Shula's final year. Let's get this straight: there was no previous contact, no wink-wink deal, nothing at all between me and Huizenga or any associates until Eddie's phone call. The first I heard that the Dolphins job might open was that season from Nick Buoniconti, whom I worked with on the Home Box Office show *Inside the NFL*. Buoniconti, a former Dolphins great who played for Shula, said this might be the coach's final season.

"Really?" I asked.

That was news to me. The Tampa job was the one I was considering and might have taken if not for a snowstorm. The day after Eddie called, Nick and I walked through the front door of the Dolphins offices.

Wayne, Eddie, and Miami Dolphins team vice president Brian Wiedmeier sat at one end of a conference table with nothing before them. No papers. No pencils. No apparent questions or agenda. For twenty minutes or so, we talked in generalities before there was a pause, as if they had expended their thoughts.

"I guess you want to know how I'd run a professional organization," I said.

For the next two hours I talked about how I organized the front office, the coaches, the draft and free agency, the support staff—everything down to the daily schedule of running a team's practices. When I stopped talking, there was a pause at the table.

"Well, it's a good time for a restroom break," Huizenga said.

I went to the restroom, too. Huizenga then beckoned me into a side office. There alone, just Wayne and me, he offered the job. I hadn't come to this meeting with the intention of making a final decision on anything. The Dolphins roster was aging, had serious salary cap problems, and they had one draft pick in the top fifty that year. I wanted a day to weigh Wayne's offer and consider taking on that project. Plus . . .

"I need to talk to Rhonda," I said.

"What's there to talk about?" Huizenga said.

A few minutes later, Huizenga's helicopter set down on Islamorada's Founders Park, picked up Rhonda, and brought her to the Dolphins' offices. Wayne didn't build three Fortune 500 companies by accident. He knew how to close deals.

The contract was negotiated quickly that day, but there was one loose end to discuss. I needed someplace to live near the Dolphins' facilities.

And I wasn't going to sell my place in the Keys.

"How much do you think a place will cost?" Wayne said.

"Well, one million dollars," I said.

"Okay, we'll add that to your contract," he said.

One of Wayne's assistants set a check beside the contract when I officially signed. It was for $667,000.

"What's that?" Wayne said. "I said one million."

"We took out the taxes," the assistant said.

"I didn't say shit about taxes," Wayne said. "I said we'd give him a check for one million. Go get him that check."

I got the redone check, bought a place on nearby Williams Island, and had a team owner to appreciate right from that first day. Wayne was smart, strong, supportive. He wanted to be a friend and talk a few times a week about football. But he had no desire to run a team or be on the inside of decisions. It was just the opposite. Wayne prided himself on recognizing and hiring talent. He built Waste Management, Blockbuster Video, and AutoNation into successes by hiring top people. He operated the Dolphins in the same manner.

"All I want to do is win," he said.

We had the same goal from day one.

Overnight, the chase was back in my life, filling me with ambition and adrenaline. I was up at 4:30 a.m. without an alarm again. Before working my final game for FOX, the NFC Championship Game in Dallas, I was so passionate talking about coaching during a dinner that John Madden said it was the first time he wanted to return to coaching himself.

"I hope it's gone in the morning," Madden said.

My first task at Miami was assembling a staff. This wasn't as easy as putting the band back together. Dave Wannstedt and Tony Wise were in Chicago. Norv Turner was in Washington. Butch Davis had taken the University of Miami job. Other members of my old crew were contractually tied to the Cowboys.

I called Bill Belichick about being the defensive coordinator. He had just been fired by Cleveland. We saw football the same way, as we realized from our meeting a few years earlier at the Kentucky Derby, of all places. We were bored during the time in between races, and so we walked around the grounds and talked football. He was interested in working with me. As Bill says, "I came pretty close to taking the job. I was fascinated by Jimmy's defense."

Ultimately, Bill's long relationship with Bill Parcells from their days coaching the Giants swayed the decision. Parcells was now with the New England Patriots. Belichick wouldn't have to learn a new defense to coach, and he would remain in the part of the country where he'd lived his whole life. He had a home on Nantucket. He felt comfortable in New England. Geography was as important to him as it was to me.

I ended up hiring a staff full of new names except for offensive coordinator Gary Stevens, who had been with the Dolphins for seven years and was with me previously at the University of Miami. Not having good friends working beside me represented a significant change. There were no longer Thursday nights out with my crew. I would purposely leave the building around 10 p.m., knowing these new assistants didn't know me and would stay until I left.

That was the start of how different the Dolphins' challenge was from Dallas. There were more visible changes from the outside, too. We tore a bad roster down to nothing in Dallas and rebuilt it through the draft for the long term. In Miami, future Hall of Fame quarterback Dan Marino was a prime reason for my taking the job. He was thirty-five and entering the final stretch of his career. My plan was to rebuild a champion around Marino, before the ticking clock struck midnight on his physical ability.

Some problems that came with coaching the Dolphins couldn't be conveniently swept out the door. For instance, to fix messy salary cap issues, I had to release a handful of good veterans. That added to the burden of a rebuild. The first time I met Shula after replacing him was at a team banquet in his honor. I held out my hand and he shook it while delivering a bare-knuckled message.

"You really fucked up," he said.

"How so?" I asked.

"You let Troy Vincent and Bryan Cox go," he said.

I mentioned that the salary cap dilemma left no choice. (I didn't mention who caused the problem.) He was obviously angry I had replaced him. The NFL's all-time winningest coach had the right to fume if he wanted.

I understood the dynamics of replacing a legendary coach by this point. I followed Howard Schnellenberger at the University of Miami, Tom Landry at Dallas, and now Shula. This became a regular question from visitors to the Keys: *How do you replace an iconic coach?*

The answer? I was never concerned about who came before me. There's a saying: "You don't want to follow the legend; you want to follow the guy that *follows* the legend." None of that mattered to me. I always took a job based on where I would live, the opportunity it offered, and the people I was going to be around—not whom I followed. I took over an Oklahoma State program on probation because

I wanted to be a head coach. I took the University of Miami job, sight unseen, at a coaches convention because of the opportunity and because I wanted to live there. I took the Dallas role because of Jerry's offer and the NFL challenge. I went to the Dolphins because I wanted to coach again and still live in South Florida.

I acted respectful about the preceding era when the subject was raised, but I never looked back, or was hesitant about installing my methods. The past—even my past—didn't mean too much to me while coaching in a particular season. I was always about the present and the future.

Media, fans, and many people inside the organization made comparisons to the previous coach because of the good memories and point of reference. I was usually good about sidestepping those issues, but I made a mistake a few months after replacing Shula in talking at a Dolphins awards banquet for their previous season. Many of the team's greats were there and references were understandably made to the franchise's history. The previous season was reviewed. Don Shula was lauded. Awards were given to players like Cox and Vincent, whom I had released to get the salary cap under control. The entire night was about yesterday.

"I know I'm supposed to say congratulations to all the people in the past," I said when it came time for me to talk. "I'm supposed to talk about the great tradition, to pay tribute to all the great people who laid the groundwork . . ."

I gave a dismissive wave of my hand.

"Well, forget that," I said. "I only care about one thing: the present. The people who are here to win *now*."

That caused a stir. It's how I felt. It's how I always felt in any job. That night's message was directed at my current staff and players, that what happened before doesn't matter to us. But some things need a gentler touch or are just better left unsaid in a public forum.

Still, if others were upset at how I came in the door, I was more concerned with the minefield of inherited issues: An aging roster. Dan Marino's physical health. A mediocre team. A limited array of draft picks. Salary cap problems. And maybe worst of all: a general, comfortable feeling from the players they had a good team since they made the playoffs the previous year before being blown out by Buffalo in the first round. As Peter King wrote in *Sports Illustrated*, "It may be stretching things to say the Dolphins of 1996 have as many problems as the Dallas Cowboys of 1989, the year Johnson began his pro career. But not by much."

My grand plan was to clean up those problems the first year, draft like I did in Dallas, and use Scotch tape and baling wire to hold Dan Marino together, if necessary, to make a quick run at the Super Bowl. There was a small margin for error. Dan was on board with everything right from my first day. I made sure to talk to him privately after my first team meeting to underline his importance in my plans.

"Coach, I've set enough records," he said. "If I throw ten passes and we win, I'll be happy."

Dan still could throw the ball as well as anyone when healthy and proved to be a true pro, a great competitor, and, despite some media reports, a good partner with whom I had a solid relationship in our years together. I would have loved to have coached him in the prime of his career.

But if I foresaw the potholes involving the Dolphins' roster, salary cap, and draft options when taking the job, I was surprised by the state of Dan's legs. This was the era before quarterbacks were bubble-wrapped under protective rules. Dan's gait remained affected by the aftermath of a torn Achilles tendon. He had minor knee surgery, as usual, after the previous season—"a tune-up," he often called them. There were other effects from thirteen years of playing NFL quarterback.

It took one practice to reveal what it all meant. I had the team run a couple of laps around the field to loosen up. Dan came to me and said he could run a couple laps with everyone, no problem.

"But then my knees won't let me practice," he said.

Welcome to Miami.

The morning after our first preseason game against Tampa Bay, I called veteran Dolphins linebacker Jack Del Rio at his home. I needed to see him. He was a strong, smart player who had played for me in Dallas. His veteran presence might be needed on our young team, I thought when I signed him.

"I wonder what he wants," Jack said to his wife, Linda.

"Maybe he wants to make you captain," she said.

Jacks knew that wasn't the case, as I selected captains before each game.

"I'm going to have to release you," I told Jack that morning. "I didn't bring you in here to be a second-teamer."

I found Zach Thomas before the meeting that day. "You're the starter," I said.

Zach was too small and slow by NFL standards. That's why we got him for a fifth-round pick. He was so good from his first practice, veteran teammates asked him to take it easy. That's the kind of player I needed to build this team. I watched him closely, too, to be sure he was that player, day after day, in the physical practices that told these veterans how my way was a different world.

After stretching and some special teams work, we jumped right into the "Middle Drill," where five offensive linemen, a quarterback, and a running back went against a defensive line and linebackers. Every play was a run inside. You want to see who will play physical? Who will be tough in a tough game? That drill also told everyone the kind of team I'd be building.

That first summer was about finding the right players. In a team meeting in mid-August, I ran a video of Marino placing a touchdown pass between two defenders in our second preseason game against Chicago. I turned off the video.

"That's the kind of plays we need. So, Dan Marino, you have a job on this football team," I said. "You're number one."

I turned the video back on to show Larry Izzo making a special teams tackle. Izzo was the opposite of Marino on the food chain — an undrafted rookie linebacker who excelled on special teams. He also started a fight against Washington's offensive line in a scrimmage. The next day, as the whistle blew to end a play, there was Izzo flattening another Washington player in a borderline hit that started another fight. Some coaches hated fighting. I loved it in the context of building a new team.

I asked Izzo where he was from in that team meeting.

"I'm from Houston, sir," he said.

"You have family there?" I said.

"Yes, sir," he said.

"Well, call your family and tell them you have a job on this football team," I said. "You're number two."

The underdog stories of Zach Thomas and Larry Izzo were put in perspective for the players by a couple of other surprises in that training camp. Third-round cornerback Dorian Brew, my second draft pick with the Dolphins considering we didn't have a second-rounder, was cut before the season. So was fourth-round linebacker Kirk Pointer. Many coaches and general managers hang on to a player they invested in rather than admit a mistake. I was never afraid of admitting mistakes, of taking some accompanying criticism. The important part was not to compound the mistake by doubling down on it. You're going to swing and miss in the draft. That's the nature of it.

Hopefully, you're going to hit on some Zach Thomases and find some Larry Izzos, too.

We worked hard. We improved. In our first season in 1996, we won our first three games. We were 4-3 when Dallas came to Miami for a game I wasn't looking forward to playing. The issue wasn't so much my Dallas background, having coached most of those players, or the media's obvious focus on the Jimmy-versus-Dallas story line.

I knew the game would be a struggle. That was the problem. I almost wanted to get it over with more than I was looking forward to it. The game played out as I expected: we couldn't get anything going, Troy threw for three touchdowns, Michael Irvin had 186 yards receiving, and Dallas whipped us, 29–10.

"They don't have a player who could start for us," Barry Switzer said.

That sounded about right. Our youth, inexperience, and shallow roster showed as that first year played out. We weren't ready to challenge for anything. We ended up that season 8-8.

That wasn't my prime problem as the season developed, as I gauged our developing talent, as I looked three years down the line, when I knew we *had* to win.

You know how I mentioned I never *dreamed* of success—how I firmly believed our plan would bear champions at Oklahoma State, the University of Miami, and at Dallas?

I couldn't find that tingle of belief with the Dolphins by the end of that first season. I didn't see how the dots could be connected quickly enough, given the depleted roster and our short timeline. Approaching the final game, I was downcast as Rhonda, Nick, and I got together for some nachos and drinks after taping my Dolphins television show. I put a question to these people I trusted most.

"How would it be if I left after one year?" I asked.

"You can't do that," Nick said.

He was right. I couldn't. I knew that. But I also knew I'd have to alter my central philosophy from believing my plan would lead to winning it all to . . .

We would win as many as we could.

That became my realistic goal moving forward into the second season. It meant a shift for me, subconscious or not, from the bold and brash coach who demanded his teams play that way. Oh, we still had attitude—and I still worked hard, still worked long hours, still worked to the detriment of family and friends and any outside life in ways that became my life's regret.

But all the previous stops of my career were fun to me.

The Dolphins became my first job.

Our first three draft picks in 1997 were receiver Yatil Green, cornerback Sam Madison, and defensive end Jason Taylor.

Green blew out his knee on the first day of camp, did it again his second training camp, and never had the career we hoped. Madison became an All-Pro cornerback. Taylor is in the Hall of Fame. That summed up my Dolphins personnel moves. We couldn't get a break on offense. We built the league's best defense by our third year—a physical, attacking defense built around young players.

On offense, I took low-cost, short-term gambles like troubled running back Lawrence Phillips from the Rams and my former college player Lamar Thomas, who was released by Tampa Bay. That was in the hopes of getting Dan immediate help. I didn't care if it was a short-term Band-Aid. Those two moves reflected the stark difference from our long-term building plan in Dallas. Phillips didn't work out. Thomas became a good contributor for us.

We took a progressive step that second season. We made the play-offs with a developing roster around Dan. We then lost our first-round game in New England in a manner that didn't just make me angry—it made me angrier than I've ever been in my life.

I had a routine of watching the DVD of the game's television broadcast on my laptop in my front left seat on the plane ride home. We hadn't even left the ground when I'd seen enough.

I slammed the computer down in the aisle.

That game had a backstory—several backstories, in fact—that all spiked my anger. In my first summer in Miami, veteran Keith Byars took a pay cut to help get our salary cap situation under control. He wasn't happy. Then, as we rose to 3-0 in beating the New York Jets, 36–27, he was the starting tight end and threw a tantrum because his streak of catching a pass in 130 consecutive games ended. I never knew such a streak existed. I was just thinking of winning. Byars was so unhappy, I cut him a couple of weeks later. Then he signed with New England.

Now here we were going to New England for a playoff game. We had just played them the week before, too, and something was obvious.

"They have our audibles," I told Gary Stevens. "We've got to do something about it."

The idea when I came to the Dolphins was to keep everything constant for Dan. The system stayed the same. Gary remained the offensive coordinator. We also kept the same checkoffs and audibles. This consistency caused some problems. One issue was that we had five new starters on offense that first year. Our entire backfield—starters and reserves—were rookies. They weren't comfortable with the full playbook, much less the audibles and necessary protections. The second year we added more newcomers. That added to the audible concerns, considering that no one was as comfortable as Dan was in using them.

The other problem was that NFL defenses had changed over the previous seasons. Dan, with his great arm, had tremendous success against man-to-man coverage throughout his career. He would come to the line, see one of his receivers like Mark Clayton or Mark Duper in single coverage, and audible a pass to exploit the backfield's weakness. He tore up those defenses.

Now the zone blitz had entered the game. It presented a different problem. A quarterback read man-to-man before the snap, but then a defensive end or linebacker dropped off the line into the area where you expected to throw. For that reason, many teams changed to audibles that didn't involve the larger playbook. The idea of an audible was limited to getting out of a bad play.

I went to Gary a second time the week before the playoff game to say we had to change our language against New England.

"They've got our audibles," I said to him. "We've got to be careful."

We trailed 7–0 at the end of the third quarter when Dan studied the defense at our 38-yard line. It was third-and-two. He read man-to-man.

"Forty-six!" he called out.

That was an audible to pass, as numbers in the forties always were. New England knew that thanks to Byars, as we suspected, and they admitted it after the game. Linebacker Todd Collins had studied Marino to know he liked the slant pattern on these short-yardage downs against man-to-man coverage, too. On the plane, I watched the video as Collins turned to his teammates and made a slashing motion with his right arm, signaling a slant. He then moved right into Marino's passing lane at the snap, took the easy interception, and ran it back for a touchdown.

That's how our second season ended. It's why the computer was in pieces on the plane. It's also why I fired Gary Stevens that week and why I decided during the off-season to bring our audible system more in line with the times. People made an issue later that Dan didn't have an offense tailored for him. That wasn't true. The entire offense was built around Dan. As for audibles, we kept "check-with-me's" and dual calls, meaning we called two plays in the huddle and Dan chose the better one in seeing the defense.

He could still audible, too. But the idea became to audible only out of the wrong play. For instance, he would audible if we had a run called and the defense showed an eight-man front. That's what the league began to do in the face of the zone blitz and what most teams have done for years since then.

That broken computer said we had to change some things after the 1997 season.

Before the 1998 draft, I got a surprise call from Archie Manning. He asked if I could work the draft so his talented son Peyton would land in Miami. I was intrigued. My hope was to find a franchise quarterback to set up the Dolphins for the next ten or fifteen years. That's always a prime responsibility of any general manager. And as coach? I hadn't watched much tape of Peyton playing at Tennessee because he was expected to be the No. 1 pick in the draft, and we had the 19th pick.

But what if the Mannings helped me to draft him?

What Archie wanted to know was whether I could pull off a trade to get Peyton. Archie didn't want his son's career being dictated by the whim of the draft order. Archie, of all people, knew the problems of a young quarterback going to the wrong franchise. He spent a decade getting beat up on losing New Orleans Saints teams. Neither he nor Peyton was afraid of challenging the NFL's draft system or risking some public opinion polls by doing what was in their best long-term interests. That was shown a few years later when Eli Manning forced a draft-day trade from San Diego to the New York Giants.

Archie's idea could solve both of our concerns. I planned to let Peyton sit behind Marino and get a graduate school education in NFL quarterbacking. It was win-win as I saw it.

I went to work on that. Our 19th pick was the problem.

No matter what I offered—and I offered my entire draft—there was no feasible way to jump from No. 19 to 1st or 2nd in the draft to get Peyton. Trust me. I tried.

Indianapolis had the top pick. It wasn't passing on a generational quarterback like Peyton. That was that.

I ended up trading back from the 19th pick in the 1998 draft, in keeping with my strategy of adding value and expanding draft picks. We took a pass-catching running back, John Avery. Avery didn't work like I hoped, but I also traded a future pick to take cornerback Patrick Surtain in the second round and defensive end Kenny Mixon in the third round. Surtain became a star. Paired with Sam Madison, he soon gave that defense bookend All-Pro cornerbacks. Combined with Jason Taylor and Zach Thomas, the Dolphins had the foundation of a great defense for the next decade. But drafts are also filled with missed opportunities. I missed receiver Randy Moss, who was drafted 21st by Minnesota. Lots of other teams passed on him, too.

But what could have been? Our first game that 1998 season was Peyton's debut in Indianapolis. We won, 24–15, as Peyton had a rookie's day of throwing for 302 yards but also having three interceptions. Afterward, I found Archie standing by the team bus.

We mentioned our previous draft talks. But one thing was certain.

"Peyton's going to be great," I told his father.

15

MY CHANGING LIFE

Did your perspective ever change in life?

What happened?

Mine changed standing before my mother's coffin.

My knees buckled, my breath stopped, and my controlled world crumbled right there. I took a few stumbling steps toward my sons, Brent and Chad, sitting in the first church pew with Rhonda and my father, and through a veil of tears did something I never had in all our lives together.

I kissed them.

"I love you," I said.

There was a sudden clarity to my life in that moment of who I needed—of who I needed to be, too. It was time to start loving the people who loved me back, to live in a manner that football didn't allow.

Even the mourning of Mother was folded into the suffocating idea of football over family, of football over life, and now death, too. I couldn't attend Mother's viewing. I couldn't put football aside. This was late December of 1998, when I arrived home that Sunday night after team meetings for our Monday-night game against Denver. Rhonda was waiting. My sister Lynda had called. Rhonda didn't want to tell me the news over the phone when I was with players and coaches.

"I've got something to tell you," she said softly. "Your mother died."

I stood there shocked, silent. Three weeks earlier, I had had a private plane fly them from Port Arthur to Miami to watch a Dolphins game for the first time. Their health had been a problem for a few years by then. Mother was so weak from dialysis and Daddy from colon cancer, they weren't sure they could make the trip. But I took them on my boat. Mother actually hummed with excitement on the water. They attended our game. I wheeled Mother through the stadium in her wheelchair. They always enjoyed watching my teams play. Daddy said the only time Mother got animated anymore was seeing my teams play on TV.

The son who once had his parents watch the Super Bowl from home because he had no time for them? I tried to be better. I invited them to come live near me in Miami, but they refused. I got them a cook, a housekeeper, and a yardman. I regularly called them on the drive home from work. I called them on Sunday nights after wins, but it would take me until Wednesday to be in a better mood to call after losses. I ended those conversations with a difficult phrase for me: "I love you."

Now I stood at home before Rhonda, hearing the news, all the breath gone out of me.

"Really?" I finally said.

Rhonda hugged me. "I'm so sorry," she said.

Even in that moment, I saw through the pain, through my tears, to the looming decision about the Monday-night game. I felt the two men inside me—the obsessed coach and the guilty family man—struggling against each other. The coach demanded being on the Dolphins sideline the next night. *Aren't you the leader? Don't you demand players play hurt?* Our tight ends coach, Pat Jones, lost his mother that season and didn't miss a game. Our defensive backs coach, Bill Lewis, lost his twenty-eight-year-old son in a military helicopter accident and didn't miss a game. This is the world we lived. The good son, the guilty father, the happy partner of Rhonda who wanted to be happier—this side of me already regretted the decision I knew I'd make, the one I always made, the one everyone around me never doubted.

I coached that Monday-night game. We beat Denver, 31–21.

We moved to 10-5 on the season.

All that shrank from view as I flew to Port Arthur for the first funeral of my life. I know that sounds odd. I've always struggled with death. I'm not sure why. Is it the finality of it all? On the FOX show, everyone knew not to bring me into the conversation if death was involved. I broke the news to Bill Lewis about his son, Gregg, and had to be consoled by people almost as much as him. Was it the tragedy? The pain? The opening of an emotional valve kept closed to be the hard-hearted dictator? I had never attended a funeral because I don't want my memory of someone to be of that person in a casket. Jerome Brown, for instance, was one of my favorite players, and I didn't attend his funeral after a car accident. My University of Miami players asked about me. Others have through the years at funerals for friends or players, too. I would rather take the criticism for not attending a funeral than remember them that way.

I hurt at Mother's funeral, the great coach and not-so-great family man struggling with her loss and confronting who I was.

Seeing Mother in the coffin made me look at life differently.

I decided to bury that part of me I didn't like, the obsessed coach, that day, too.

I told Dolphins owner H. Wayne Huizenga about my decision to retire after that season, after we beat Buffalo in the playoffs, after I celebrated in that postgame locker room by stomping on a box of "Flutie Flakes" cereal, named after Buffalo quarterback Doug Flutie. I was still that coach in the winning-locker-room moment. I still had that emotion. But we didn't compete the following week against the same Denver team we'd just beaten in that Monday night game.

That was that, I felt. The great personal toll of coaching no longer seemed worth the chase of winning. I was honest with myself after that last game—and with the Dolphins organization.

"I'm going to retire," I told Eddie Jones.

"Let's talk about it," he said.

I emptied my office. I made plans to meet with Wayne the next morning. Dave Wannstedt, who was just fired in Chicago, happened to call from Tampa, because he'd run into mutual friends.

"Hey, listen, I've had enough of this," I told Dave. "I'm calling a press conference tomorrow and stepping aside."

Dave was stunned. "What? Really?"

We made plans to meet the next day at my home in the Keys on my first day of retirement.

I drove to the Dolphins facility the next morning as promised, to meet Wayne at 8 a.m. This would be a tough good-bye. Wayne wasn't just a great team owner; he had also become a good friend over the previous few years. He had tremendous success in the business world and, like me, had fun along the way. We had fun together, too. Rhonda and I once had him down to Islamorada and went out on my fifty-three-foot Ocean Sport Fisherman with his wife, Marti, and another couple. This boat needed a high tide to navigate into my docks. It was low tide when we returned. So my captain, Terry Moore, swam the hundred yards to shore, retrieved my thirty-one-foot Contender boat, and drove out to get us.

"You make him swim to shore?" Wayne asked while Terry was in the water.

The next day a crate arrived from Wayne—an underwater scooter with a note saying, "Don't make your captain swim anymore."

That was Wayne. He invited my staff for a golf outing each year to the Floridian, a private course he owned. I didn't golf anymore except on this day. I pulled up in my Corvette. He noted it was dirty and said he'd have it cleaned while we played. He had gifts on the course, like hundred-dollar bills tucked in each hole so whoever made the first putt on a green got a cash prize. When we came to a par three, up a hill, he said a hole-in-one won the car up there beside the green.

"It's a Corvette," Wayne announced at the tee.

When we reached the top of the hill, it was *my* Corvette. Thankfully, no one got a hole-in-one that day.

Wayne understood my struggles, as he had his own with "QTL," as he called it. "Quality Time Left." How much did he have? How much do any of us have?

As we sat in a meeting room, he suggested we try a new way, a different way, to have me coach the team.

"Go home to the Keys, now that the season's done, and don't come back until the draft," he said.

That wouldn't work. "If my name's on it, the only way I know how to do it is every day," I said.

We talked a little more. He suggested I delegate the duties to others, to put less on my plate.

"Hire this guy Wannstedt," he said. "Let him coach the away games."

That was creative, if unrealistic.

"No, I can't do that," I said.

"Then just bring Wannstedt in, and you can spend more time with Rhonda and your family," he said. "You'd have someone you respect here to fill your shoes if you're not here."

I felt myself softening. That made some sense to me. The more Wayne talked, too, the more I realized how difficult it would be for me to leave him in this manner. It took him all of thirty minutes to end my retirement. Dan Marino waited outside the room. When I finished talking with Wayne, Dan said he wanted me to stay, that our team was on the verge of winning big.

"We're close," he said.

Well, yeah, we were in a sense. The defense, full of young stars, ranked No. 1 in the league that year. We had made the playoffs the last two years with a rebuilt roster, the salary cap was cleaned up, and we'd taken the progressive step of the playoff win that 1998 season.

With a few moves on offense . . .

With that young defense . . .

If Dan stayed healthy . . .

With a little time for me to recharge that off-season . . .

My phone rang. It was Dave, driving down from Tampa to meet me in the Keys.

"How's retirement going?" he said.

"Not so fast," I said. "How'd you like to come to the Dolphins with me?"

"What?" he said.

"What city are you near?" I asked.

Wayne's helicopter picked up Dave and his wife, Jan, from the Fort Myers airport. We had to find him a dress shirt to wear at the news conference announcing my staying and his hiring as assistant head coach. It was a hectic day for our good media relations director, Harvey Greene.

"I might stay one year," I told Dave. "I might stay five years. There are no strings attached. Let's just see how it plays out."

That night, Dave and Jan slept on my boat amid the boxes I had packed from my office. They joked that they might wake up to find I retired again. I knocked on the boat's window at 6:30 a.m., to talk with Dave about the work ahead.

And so, as if by some gravitational force, I was pulled back into football. I was done with coaching while standing over my mother's body only three weeks ago. I was done immediately after the season with the consuming sacrifice and myopic life that came with it.

Coaching, though, wasn't done with me.

That off-season, former Miami police chief Bill O'Brien asked me to give a motivational speech to the top FBI agents in the Southeast region. This was in Fort Lauderdale and, driving there with Bill and Nick Christin, I mulled what to say. My motivational speeches are usually geared toward teamwork or getting individuals to improve. I tell some football stories, some jokes, and might tell car salespeople about the guy who everyone said was lucky to be the top seller each month—the same guy who also got to work early and stayed late.

"These agents are already successful, so my typical talk won't work," I said.

I struck on a relevant subject that was on my mind: the difference between trying to improve the Cowboys and the Dolphins. Nick said it was the best speech I gave.

"When I arrived at the Cowboys, everyone was scared for their job," I said. "Few of the players were secure. I had tryouts every Monday to see if I could find someone better than I had. Everyone on the roster knew they had to work. Plus, we were losing. So, everyone was already uncomfortable and motivated. The great players wanted to get better and sacrificed to do that. They demanded to have a winning team. That's how we zoomed from one-and-fifteen our first year to Super Bowl titles by our fourth and fifth years."

I looked over the room.

"When I came to the Dolphins, it was a completely different situation," I said. "Everyone was in their comfort zone. They'd made the playoffs the previous year. Even if they weren't close to a championship, they thought they were successful. Many of the veterans knew they weren't going to be fired. They worked. But did they work hard enough? They sacrificed. But how much? They weren't a great team, but they were a mediocre-to-good one. There was a comfort level there. That's the problem in trying to build a championship team."

I related this to these successful agents not being comfortable with their good careers.

"The enemy of great is good," I said.

In keeping with our short-term model, I once again took low-cost chances chasing immediate help: running back Cecil Collins, arrested for breaking in and making sexual advances, was a fifth-round pick; Tony Martin, a veteran receiver, faced federal money-laundering charges; another receiver, Robert Baker, was out of prison on drug charges and needing a second chance; and defensive tackle Dimitrius Underwood, a first-round pick in Minnesota who walked away after one practice, was signed a couple of weeks later.

People wonder how teams decide to take chances on players. Look at the talent, the cost, and the situation. In Dallas, Charles Haley had proven talent and was the missing piece to a championship roster. In Miami, we needed any help to win that season. Each player we signed came at minimal cost. I crossed my fingers that they would stay out of trouble long enough to provide some immediate help we needed.

Only Martin helped, scoring five touchdowns that year.

We started strong, though, playing like the team we could be if our pieces aligned. Dan was named AFC Offensive Player of the Week twice in the opening four weeks. We were 3-1 entering a game against New England, where, after two series, he came out of the game with a pinched nerve in his neck. Damon Huard stepped in at QB, moved the offense, and threw a winning five-yard pass with twenty-three seconds left to beat New England, 31–30. Huard won the next four games, too, as a controlled offense coupled with a strong defense and special teams vaulted us to 7-1.

I kept pushing, pushing, pushing, too. Jason Taylor, for instance, started slow. He'll tell you he discovered South Beach that third season. And his production suffered from it. He had no sacks the first five games of the year. He didn't want to be confronted, even purposely hiding from coaches, ducking into some side room.

"Where's Jason Taylor?" I said to start one team meeting.

He sat where he always did, a row from the back on the right side of our meeting room. He raised his hand a few inches.

"Anyone seen Jason Taylor?" I said, not looking at him.

He raised his arm.

"Where the hell is JT?" I yelled.

"Coach, I'm right here," he said, standing up.

I looked to the other side of the room.

"If anyone sees JT, let him know the season started five weeks ago," I said.

There are all sorts of ways to motivate people. Jason was full of healthy pride. There was no need to yell at him—at least too much. His rookie training camp in 1997 was so tough for him, my demands so high, he called his mom ready to quit after five days. She set him straight. That was good because veteran Dan Stubbs got hurt that training camp and Jason had to start. He didn't know the system, much less the league. Now it was my turn to help him.

"Don't worry about all this shit that's going on, the schemes and checks," I told him. "Go out and do what you know how to do. Go tackle the football. You're ready to do that in this league."

He had five sacks and two forced fumbles as a rookie and nine sacks his second year. That's why I called him out in the meeting room the third year. He went out and got a sack that sixth game against Philadelphia. He came right to me on the sideline and stuck out his hand to shake.

"*Jason Taylor*, nice to meet you," he said to me.

I found him a few minutes later on the bench with his hands on his knees. I bent down before him with big smiles on both our faces as I congratulated his play. Jason has a framed photo of that scene in our 16–13 win against Philadelphia. He was a dominant player, a dominant personality—just the kind of player I loved coaching.

We were 8-2 going into a Thanksgiving game at Dallas. After missing five games, Dan split practices with Damon that week. I suggested Damon start, but that Dan dress for the game, and then we'd see where the day went.

"If I'm dressing, I'm starting," Dan said.

Nothing went as hoped against Dallas. Dan threw five interceptions, including a pick-six that broke a scoreless game in the third quarter. We lost, 20–0. He never did fully regain his way and we had a late-season slide, losing five of our final six games and having to open the playoffs across the country in Seattle.

By then, I had told Wayne and Eddie Jones what people were starting to conclude: This would be it for me. All the issues that made me contemplate retiring the previous season returned that year. I wasn't having fun. I didn't want to make the great personal sacrifice needed to coach. I didn't believe we could win it all—or even dream it at that point. Having Dave helped, but it wasn't like having my full crew in college or at Dallas, who jogged together each noon and met for a happy hour each week. That relaxed me at necessary times, took my mind off football.

My only break from football in a workday came by day-trading on the stock market. I bought my first stock, Mattel, in 1966 and remained active in the market. I would sit in my office for a few minutes, trade some stocks, take my mind off football, and make some money. Some people thought I was less invested in coaching because I'd take a break with stocks. It was no different than jogging or happy hour, as I saw it. I was just as committed to winning.

The only difference in my work habits that final year came near the end of the season when I spent a little more time with Rhonda. That helped me emotionally. By then I knew that whenever that season ended, my coaching career would, too.

"You'd better think what you want to do," I told Wayne and Eddie.

We followed a conservative plan in that playoff game in Seattle. We kept the score close, didn't turn the ball over, got 87 efficient rushing yards from J. J. Johnson, punted eight times, and played great defense. Dan then came alive that final drive. He completed a third-and-seventeen pass and took us down the field for a touchdown and 20–17 win. That was a moment. We were one of only three teams to make the playoffs all three of those years and now had two wins in them. As I said: *We weren't going to win it all, but we'd win as many as we could.*

You don't get to write your ending, though. We couldn't even schedule our ending properly. We landed in Miami after a nearly six-thousand-mile round trip just before sunrise Monday morning and kicked off early the following Saturday afternoon at 14-2 Jacksonville, which was coming off a bye. Some sports journalists like Peter King called it the worst playoff schedule the league ever made.

That doesn't explain our meltdown. Our first play, a pass by Dan, was intercepted. Our third series ended with him fumbling and was returned for a Jacksonville touchdown. Our defense gave up a 90-yard run for the longest touchdown in playoff history. Our initial first down came with us trailing, 38–0.

It was still the second quarter.

"Man, I don't think I've ever been through one like this," I said to my longtime trainer Kevin O'Neill.

"Yes you have," he said.

I looked at him, silent.

"You were on the other sideline," he said, referring to that first Super Bowl win against Buffalo.

It all comes full circle, I suppose. I felt useless, standing amid the rubble in Jacksonville that afternoon. I had been called and felt many things during my career, good and bad, before retiring and after, but useless wasn't one of them. By halftime, I could see players like Jason and Zach looking at me for some purposeful words to help them. I had one word left in coaching.

"Pride," I said. "At this point, you've got to play for pride. You've got to have some pride, not in the name on the front of your jersey, but in the one on the back, or they're going to run you right out of the building."

It ended 62–7, and I walked down the aisle on the plane home, trying to apply some balm to the players' hurt. I don't remember what I said. It didn't help much anyway. At our team meeting the next morning, I told our players what many suspected: I was retiring.

"I have no more to give," I said.

The news conference that morning was delayed an hour when Wayne had a contract drawn up to promote Dave Wannstedt to head coach. It became a joint talk to the media—me going, Dave staying.

"This time, it's final and forever," I said. "I'm retiring from coaching. As much as I'd have loved to have brought a championship to Wayne Huizenga, who—and I've said it as many times as I've been asked—is the best owner in professional sports."

I turned to him, tears in my eyes.

"We gave it our best shot and it didn't work out," I said.

I went out the door to my Corvette, where Rhonda, our little Yorkie, Buttercup, and a small cooler of Heinekens waited. I sucked one down.

Islamorada was less than two hours away.

"Be careful of those I-95 roadblocks," Dave said to me.

"High tide is two o'clock," I said. "We've got to get out of here."

16

A LIFE OF RETIREMENT

I returned to my world of boating, fishing, and hanging out with Rhonda, while informing a disbelieving football world I was done with coaching.

"But it's in your blood," San Diego general manager John Butler said in Islamorada in offering me their coaching job. "The NFL needs you. You've got to be in coaching."

I had him look out my floor-to-ceiling window to the ocean. It wasn't in my blood anymore. I was cured.

John Shaw, the St. Louis Rams president, came and asked me to run their draft. Nothing else. Just the draft. That was impractical from a football side. It didn't matter, though.

"Look around you," I said to him, too. "This is the life I want."

There was only one football question left for me: FOX, ESPN, CBS, or ABC's *Monday Night Football*?

A broadcast job allowed me to be near the game I loved without being the person I hated. I could enjoy football without being consumed by it. I met with ABC's executives in a Miami airport about the *Monday Night Football* job. Bill Parcells gave me some good advice about that one.

"If you do *Monday Night Football*, everybody's going to have an opinion on Tuesday morning about what kind of job you did," he said.

"If you work in a studio, you can say whatever you want; people will laugh about it, and you go on about your business."

Parcells also had an idea. "Why don't you and I go to CBS together in their studio?"

Bill wanted a job in New York, close to where he lived. But since I had to travel regardless, I wanted to return to the good people at FOX in Los Angeles. I was ready to enjoy television this time, too. With no chance of a return to coaching, I let my guard down, showed my sense of humor, laughed with everyone—especially at myself—and became friends with everyone on the show.

The FOX crew became more than friends over the years, too. They became family. There's a simple reason our pregame show has won the ratings battle every year: We like each other. We really do. Our show is like sitting at a bar listening to good friends talking and laughing about football. The most fun time of my career—fun, mind you—has been my years with FOX.

On Saturdays, I watch college football with Terry Bradshaw, Curt Menefee, NFL insider John Czarnecki, and sometimes Howie Long at our hotel. We set up three TVs in one suite. We have beers, and I'll have my nachos, too. We might trot out an occasional thought for the show the next day, but much of what we say won't be repeated—just laughed over in that hotel room as we sit before the games.

All those times I grew upset on the air during my first stint with FOX are the same kind of moments we have the most fun with on the show now, too. Any mistake or hiccup in delivery becomes a target for the rest of the program. Terry once called an ambidextrous player "amphibious." We had fun with that. He once talked about quarterback Russell Wilson's injured finger, explaining, "Without this finger you can't grip the ball."

"Terry, it's not that finger," we told him, showing another finger. "It's this finger."

"Okay, forget it," Terry said.

One show, I noticed James Brown, the host at that time, make a surprised, high-pitched sound while reading off the teleprompter. Terry had reached under the table and grabbed James by his private parts to liven up the show.

"Ah, Terry's at it again," James said.

It's rare for men in their fifties, sixties, and seventies to work together and enjoy each other's company in the manner we do. We've all succeeded in our world. The temptation could be to one-up everyone on these shows. We're too good of friends for that and besides, we'd rather laugh at ourselves. Michael Strahan is as nice a person and as good a television personality as you'll meet. But once in a while, he'll rattle on about a subject until we go to a commercial. "What did I just say?" he'll ask us.

Howie, a guy Terry calls "a boring individual," is another all-around good person. He'll also be "Mr. Long-Winded," using up everyone's time with a thought until someone jokes, "Howie, take a breath, please!"

I'm the most, uh, experienced one. Hey, I scouted Terry at Woodlawn High School in my first job at Louisiana Tech, and coached Howie in the Blue-Gray All-Star Game before he joined the Oakland Raiders.

The running joke is they can't believe I'm a guy who used to be feared as a coach. Troy Aikman will come on, see me laughing, and explain to the others how I'm totally different today than those Dallas years.

"I don't even know you anymore," he'll say.

Having fun, enjoying friendships, being relaxed while watching games—this is the person coaching didn't allow me to be. The entire FOX team has visited me in the Keys for a couple of days and stayed at my restaurant. Howie has come for my fishing tournament. Terry has visited several times, always following my one-night rule. Yes, it is a rule. I still have limits on tolerating people—even good people like Terry.

I also have the rule about not calling after 9 p.m. When the host's job opened up on our show, Curt was leaving on an overseas trip and so called me late one night. Curt had worked at a local Dallas station when I coached the Cowboys and asked if I would put in a good word for him. I wasn't happy it was late. I joke with him now that I hung up the phone after we talked and thought: *Who the hell is Curt Menefee?* We got lucky when he joined our team.

Our behind-the-camera friendship has produced an on-show chemistry that was the exact vision of those creating it. David Hill, the executive producer of FOX Sports when I started, is a funny Australian and one of the smartest guys I've known, a member of Mensa. Ed Goren, like a good coach, assembled the right team. Bill Richards, our producer now, is the most talented person I've met in television.

Then there's Terry.

Where to start? Terry and my lawyer, Nick Christin, are my best friends. No one is more genuine and generous than Terry. And entertaining? I bought a private plane to ease the traveling to the show and would touch down near Terry's Oklahoma ranch to pick him up. The first time we landed, he wasn't there. I was mad. I'm still particular about time. We were refueling when he arrived.

"What's the matter?" he said.

"I didn't buy this fucking plane to wait on people," I said. "It's on my time, not your time."

"Jimmy, they're still refueling the plane," he said.

The next time I picked up Terry, he was lying on the runway, head propped up on his luggage like he'd slept there. He can make you laugh anywhere—for any reason. We were in Seattle for a playoff game when a movie that Terry was in, *Failure to Launch*, debuted.

Everyone from our show went to a private screening. Terry sat by me. When his nude backside scene came on the screen, he turned to me and said, "Geez, I wish I'd lost a little weight before this thing."

The scene called for Terry's nudity to surprise Matthew McConaughey. Terry was offered a big, medium, or small prosthetic to wear over his private parts. He said he couldn't take the large, was too embarrassed about the small, and so, just like Goldilocks, took the medium. After a couple of takes, the director encouraged McConaughey to act more surprised. Terry decided to help. Seeing how there were just the three of them and a cameraman in the room, he took off the prosthetic for the next take.

That got the right reaction from McConaughey. Oh, and Terry forgot that a few dozen other people were watching on the monitor next door, too.

Our friendship has taken us down other paths. We did a Geico commercial together—I was the bald one, he had hair. I had a cameo in the television series *The Shield*, where I played a bearded prisoner in lockup who shouts, "Terry is the guy you are looking for!" Yep, that Terry.

Terry once mentioned being offered a nice sum of money for a series of TV commercials for a male-enhancement pill. He couldn't bring himself to do it. I did it instead.

Add it all up and do you see why I enjoy my time at FOX? All of us mature men laughing and playing boyhood pranks on each other? We're serious about putting on a good show, of course. I've given mock pregame speeches as a coach, run (okay, walked) pass routes on our fake TV field, and addressed the big issues of the day concerning the game's best quarterbacks, like Patrick Mahomes:

If I was drafting a number one player to start a team, I'd take Justin Herbert over Patrick Mahomes.

Or Aaron Rodgers's deceptive words about a COVID-19 test:

I love watching Aaron Rodgers play. I think he's the best quarterback in the entire league, first-ballot Hall of Famer. And I respect his attitude toward being an individual. But this is a team game. In all honesty I'm disappointed in his play on words and his explanation. I'm disappointed in some of his selfish actions.

Why Jacksonville coach Urban Meyer failed:

Going to Jacksonville, just like when I went to Dallas, you knew you're going to lose, you're going to have adversity. The difference is, in Dallas, I had my entire coaching staff from college. I had my administrative assistant. I had my PR director. I had my trainer. We were all on the same page when we had adversity. He didn't have that in Jacksonville. There was a lot of backstabbing, one thing or the other, because he didn't have his people.

I've interviewed Jerry Jones on the show a few times. Bill Belichick will talk only with me, so I go to Foxborough at times during the season to interview him. Through the years, we've had good conversations about his team or the state of the NFL.

Once we talked about Bill's youth in Annapolis, Maryland. His father, Steve, was a renowned Navy assistant coach and Bill knows all about the school's history, which is wrapped in the larger military history.

That fit in with our FOX show's trip to the U.S. Naval Academy. We do a Veterans Day salute every other year in a military setting. Pearl Harbor. West Point. Fort Benning. These are my favorite shows. Dealing with the young military personnel, seeing their hard work, discipline, and everyday politeness gives me renewed faith compared to some of the stuff you see on television.

We even took our show to Bagram Airfield in Afghanistan for five days in 2009 during the war there. That was a rewarding trip. We flew on a cargo plane to Kabul. Michael Strahan and I slept in the barracks with a little TV in our room. Or at least he slept. I couldn't. I watched ESPN's *SportsCenter* over and over.

We ate with the servicemen and servicewomen. We toured the facility. It was a great experience—right until it was time to leave the country.

I couldn't leave.

David Hill and I had our visas denied. A woman who handled the visas for FOX had accidentally entered our names twice in the paperwork. We were red-flagged. The Afghanistan officials refused to listen to the woman's explanation, maybe because their culture refuses to listen to women.

All the other FOX crew members flew home. David and I were stuck. FOX had built a bar during our stay, in which everyone was rationed two beers a day. Well, I went back and got Terry's two beers, Michael's two beers, Curt's two beers, and Howie's two beers and tried to enjoy myself.

We spent the night, got our visas straightened out, and an air force general lent us his plane to fly to Bahrain. We caught a commercial flight from there to London and spent another night. I was exhausted, still not sleeping, moving through time zones. I broke down while phoning Rhonda.

"I'm so tired," I said.

I've been threatening to retire for the last decade because of the dreaded cross-country travel from the Keys to Los Angeles. FOX allowed me to do shows from home during the pandemic. That helped.

And now when I walk to the studio at 4:30 a.m. on Sundays, it's to have coffee with Dave Wannstedt, who works with FOX, too.

All those years ago at Pitt, Dave talked to me about staying in coaching, or joining the FBI.

"You can go as far as you want in coaching," I told him.

Who knew we'd end up together on a TV set?

CHAD AND THE ULTIMATE VICTORY

To understand what I lost while winning, what I sacrificed for success, what I fear my addiction to football cost in human terms, sit with me for a tortured night in a rental car outside a suburban home in Dallas. It is cool outside. Dark. Quiet, too, except for my occasional bouts of crying.

This is in 2009, nearly a decade after I've retired from football, and the car is parked outside the unlit house where I'm told my son Chad is staying. Chad is approaching forty now. He said we would meet at my hotel when I stopped in Dallas. He didn't show. He then didn't answer my phone calls. I'm guessing by now, deep into the night, with no movement in the home, that it isn't about him refusing to take my calls anymore.

He's not capable of taking them, I'm sure.

He's lost for another night.

This isn't his actual home. He lost that 4,500-square-foot home in upscale Highland Park, near where Jerry Jones lived, a few years earlier. He's staying with a friend now, probably just passing through, like he has various places for a while. I had to make some calls to find where he lived now. Some places he's lived in recent years aren't even homes. Some I only find out about later. He's slept on a lawn chair by a hotel pool, for example, entering the lobby the next morning like a guest for the complimentary breakfast. That's how he gets through some days.

Everything Chad had to define his successful life disappeared in a two-year spiral in the early 2000s. He lost a job with a Wall Street firm that once paid him a $1 million bonus. He then lost his home, his expensive artwork, his Mercedes, and two Porsches—all his possessions, all gone, piece by forfeited piece. He rides a bicycle now for transportation. He didn't have a wife or children to lose, but his money is all gone, like most of his friends and certainly his health. Doctors found his immune system in such bad shape their initial diagnosis was leukemia.

The actual disease was what it's been for years, what I neglected to see—what I wasn't around enough to detect.

Chad was an alcoholic.

And the cause? Well, that's my additional fear. I don't know that my life of prioritizing football over family led him down this dark road. I just know it didn't help that I wasn't around much.

Once, after his freshman year in college, my older son, Brent, stayed out most of the night. I came into his room the next morning and said something about following some rules if he was to live at home.

"Dad, why should you question what hour I come in, when all those hours I wanted to talk to you while I was growing up you weren't there?" he said.

Only too late did that resonate with me and make me face up to some facts about the absentee father I'd been to my sons—my two different sons.

I never worried about Brent. I've spent nights crying in bed over Chad, inconsolable to Rhonda. I've helped him into treatment centers from Florida to Texas. They didn't solve his problem. I've called bars he frequents, asking them to stop serving him. One bartender once answered that Chad was sitting right across from him drinking, as we talked.

I'd give $1 million to anyone who could help him through his troubles. But only one person can get him through this wilderness. And he can't answer the phone right now.

And so, I sit in the car, this grand football coach who is just a common man. This common man who has become a desperate father. This desperate father who fears the son he wasn't around to help then, can't be helped now.

I think. I wait. I am looking at the house for a sign of life—a light, an opening door, something that would allow me to see that my son is okay. I fall asleep for a few minutes. I cry for a few more. I mostly stare into the darkness for answers that aren't there. Even as the night lifts for the coming day, nothing lifts around me.

Do you see what I sacrificed for winning?

Can you sense the regret I'm carrying?

If you can, if you feel my burden, if you can get out of the car with me and watch me knock on the door with a demand that might turn my son away forever—only now are you ready to understand why Chad's turnaround is greater than any football win I ever had.

We never had a sit-down family dinner in all the years my two sons, Brent and Chad, grew up.

That's the example Chad uses to explain to people how different his family was from other families. People think he's joking. Or has some odd definition of a "family dinner." But it's true. I was never home for such a dinner. I was always chasing the next win, the next recruit, the next job—there always was a "next" something, keeping me from sitting at the head of a table as everyone talked about their day. We came close to having a traditional sit-down family dinner once, as Chad remembers it. I was actually home one Thanksgiving while coaching in Pittsburgh, not having a game or preparing for one. Linda Kay spread some food out for us to eat, buffet-style, to pick and choose for the day. That was as close as we came to a family dinner.

You hear football coaches list their priorities as faith, family, and football. They then might spend an hour in church each week, a few hours with their families, and eighteen hours a day with football.

I never pretended what was important. Football was my faith. Football, in many ways, was often my family, too. That's not to say I didn't live with my family. But besides Son No. 1 and Son No. 2, I had Sons 3–88, or whatever the roster size was in a particular season. I spent most of my time with those sons, too.

Neither Brent nor Chad questioned things like not eating dinner together. Why would they? That's the only life they knew. When they grew old enough to have dinner at a friend's home and saw everyone in their customary chairs and the dad asking about school or going over his day, that felt strange to my sons initially. Uncomfortable, even. They wondered why this family ate together like that, until realizing at some point that we were the unusual family.

The Johnsons weren't the Cleavers, the Bradys, the Huxtables, or whatever your perfect sitcom family was in your childhood years. I was too busy with All-American players to be the All-American father. My sons were living their lives, too. If you want to put a positive spin on it, you'd say my boys *were raised to think independently.* That translated into our day-to-day relationship in a manner people also can't fully understand.

Asking how their day went?

I went weeks, literally weeks, without seeing my sons, between getting up early for football and working late into the night.

Helping them with homework ever?

Chad just laughs at that idea now.

Birthday parties? Christmas gift exchanges?

The Johnsons stopped traditional celebrations when my sons were in third or fourth grade. They were given a JCPenney catalog for Christmas to choose their gifts. Chad picked a Nerf football one year and took the rest in cash. That's how it was for anyone in my larger family, too. My mother once found a wrapped gift on her porch in Port Arthur on her birthday. She felt touched I'd remembered. She then opened the gift. It was a box of power tools from the sponsor of my Dallas television show that coincidentally showed up on her birthday. I had thought maybe they could use some tools. I did, however, later send her a diamond ring. I wasn't exactly cold. I just wasn't tied to a calendar.

Brent and Chad have talked about all of this with me as adults. They wouldn't change anything of their youth, they say. They understand what it takes to succeed at the highest level. They have no regrets—though I do. My boys don't even remember having a conversation with me—a real conversation, something beyond an exchange of "Hey," or "How you doing?"—until they were deep into adulthood.

All the normal activities of normal families weren't part of our routine—of my routine, really. Many coaches could ration their time. They could delegate responsibilities. They made free time for their families. That's not the way I was made up. I either had to go 100 percent in something or not at all. I knew the kind of commitment I needed to win. Those coaches who took weeks off in the summer and spent family time during football season—those were the coaches I'd laugh at. I knew we were working extra hours, sweating for that extra yard, searching for any edge.

I spent decades compressing the vast game of football into something so small and simple it fit in the palm of Vinny Testaverde's hand. Or Steve Walsh's hand. Or Troy Aikman's or Dan Marino's, or whichever quarterback's hand held the football and our fortunes for that season. I was obsessed with controlling that world. The greatest ones are in any profession.

But was it a healthy obsession?

That's what I wrestle with some days. I can sidestep the question by saying there are unhealthier obsessions. I can answer that question, too, by saying that by locking on football each day, by filling my mind with competitive thoughts, by coming home at night when everyone was asleep and leaving the next morning when they were still asleep, I achieved everything a football coach can. I couldn't have succeeded to that level without that locked-in mind-set. My family understands that to be true, too.

The full truth is, I also pushed everything else aside to succeed to those heights. *Everything*. Family? No one bothered me with trifling issues or small talk of their day. Friendships? I had little time for those outside my football world. No one bothered telling me to see a particular movie or eat at some new restaurant. If I ate out, it was typically nachos and beer at an open table with my crew, to allow for a quick exit when desired. If I was somehow stuck at a restaurant where the waiter went around to each person at the table, I would typically call out orders for everyone to get things moving pronto.

Time, you see, was always the enemy as much as the next opponent. How much could you stuff into a day? Where did you schedule yourself to be and for how long? Why waste eight hours of sleeping when four would do? My football schedule didn't revolve around Saturday and Sunday games in the fall. There was never a day I didn't think of football, never a meal where third-and-four didn't enter my mind.

Linda Kay ran the home and raised the boys. She was great at it, too, especially with all the yo-yoing around the country we did for my football. Brent was born in Arkansas, learned to walk in Louisiana, and attended kindergarten in Iowa. Chad lived in seven states by the time he was eighteen. Neither lived in a childhood home for more than two and a half years. One of their childhood memories is watching television at our new home in South Carolina six weeks after I took a job at Clemson University with the legendary coach-turned-athletic-director Frank Howard. I walked in the room.

"You guys want to move?" I said.

"What?" they said.

It wasn't anything against Clemson. I was offered the defensive line coach's job and a $2,000 raise at Oklahoma. So, six weeks into a new home, we moved again.

It was only later, years later, that I realized what I put my family through. And what I missed. I never really saw my sons play football. Think of that. I've coached hundreds of games across five decades on football's biggest stages. I've watched tens of thousands of players and thousands of games.

But making a priority of watching my sons play? I didn't do that. I even enjoyed hearing of opposing coaches taking vacations or attending family functions. *It gives us an advantage*, I thought. We were winning. After I left Dallas, I chuckled when Barry Switzer missed a Friday meeting with his Dallas Cowboys to watch his son play high school football in Oklahoma.

I was too busy preparing the team for our Saturday games at Oklahoma State to drive across town to Stillwater High School to watch Brent play. He was a star linebacker. I did see him play once (Oklahoma State must have had an off-week) and suggested afterward he try a slightly different technique in a certain alignment. He said that's not what his coaches wanted.

"I'm going to do what the coaches who see me every day tell me to do," he said.

Brent received twenty-six scholarship offers for football. He was that good. He received thirty-eight academic scholarship offers. He was that smart. Stanford. Harvard. Rice. He could have gone any-where he wanted. It broke his mother's heart when he chose the University of Texas for football.

My fatherly input? Well, he had to read in the local newspaper that I didn't want him to go to a Big Eight Conference school and have to face me. That was about it as far as my advice went on what school he should attend. When he signed with Texas, a Stillwater reporter asked Brent what my involvement was in his recruiting process.

"He wanted tips," Brent said.

That's right. I picked his brain about recruiting—the coach in me curious about what worked and what didn't on a high school senior. Mail-outs and unsigned letters weren't read, he said. Handwritten letters or ones written by alumni were interesting.

Even my son's recruitment process was filtered through one idea: *Can it give me an edge?*

Chad attended Christopher Columbus High School in Miami. I saw him play part of one game there in 1984 on a Saturday night. A quarter. Maybe a half. Even that came with a story. Columbus was playing national powerhouse Cincinnati Moeller. My University of Miami team played Michigan earlier that afternoon in Ann Arbor. I jetted down after what was our first loss at Miami to watch the Moeller game. That's right—the Moeller game. Even Chad knew I wasn't there to watch him, but to recruit some players on the other side of the field.

I did offer Chad a nugget of fatherly advice that his brother didn't need. Chad says it's the only significant advice I gave him growing up. He was considering playing college football and asked what I thought. Hey, I wasn't good at birthdays or homework, but evaluating talent was right up my alley.

"Look, here's your choices," I said. "You could go to an I-AA school, sit on the bench the first couple of years, and possibly start as a junior or senior with a lot of hard work. Or you could go to an I-A school like Miami and the most you'll ever be is a special teams player."

There it was for him on the table. Honest. Direct. And a bit harsh for a hopeful son? Well, that was the only unflinching way I knew to discuss football, whether with my players or my sons.

Brent and Chad were best friends throughout their youth. They bonded like, well, brothers due to being yanked continually into some new town where they knew only each other. They were opposite personalities from the start, too. Chad explains their differences by pointing to the movie *Twins*, with Danny DeVito and Arnold Schwarzenegger. There's an exaggerated element of truth there. Brent was quiet and straitlaced. Chad had a big personality and hung with a louder crowd. Brent was a star athlete and scholar, as the college scholarship offers showed. Chad was a decent athlete who didn't study too hard. Brent's good looks allowed him to be a model later in life. Chad looked like, well, me at every age.

Brent went to the University of Texas law school after college, where he met his wife, Belinda. He became a lawyer. She rose to be chief operating officer of Airbnb. They raised two children: Lola and Ro. They became a happy and successful family.

Chad, with my football evaluation, went to Florida State as a regular student. Actually, that's not true. There was never anything regular about him. He used his good personality and leadership abilities to become president of both the Alumni Association and the Intra-fraternity Council. He joined Merrill Lynch after college and won awards as their top rookie salesman. He stayed single, enjoying that lifestyle.

They were adults when I became the Cowboys coach and divorced Linda Kay. That wasn't easy on them. They started down their successful careers, and we had a better relationship now that they were adults. We talked regularly, if briefly. I would stay in touch with quick calls or small thoughts. I once, for instance, sent Chad a book,

The Ten Commandments of Success. This was from the motivational author Og Mandino. Commandment No. 5 was "Thou Must Smile in the Face of Adversity Until It Surrenders." I wrote in the margin: "It surrendered on Nov. 5, 1989." My first win in Dallas.

By my time with the Dolphins, I told a reporter that my sons and I had talked more in the past year than we had all the years of their childhood. And when I walked over to kiss them at my mother's funeral, with tears in my eyes, I needed them for support in a way I hadn't needed anyone before.

I changed after football, too. When Lola, my first grandchild, was born in 2002, it showed me a new side of life. Brent and Belinda came to Los Angeles to spend a weekend and watch the FOX show. They left Lola with Rhonda and me. It was a new world, watching my granddaughter and realizing the universal truths of love and family. Later, as Lola and Ro grew up, Rhonda and I met them at Disney World, or we'd go fishing in the Keys—just another grandfather and his grandchildren enjoying time together. (I left Disney at three o'clock, though. It's tiring playing Grandpa.)

I enjoyed this next chapter in life after football. I thought all was good with Brent and Chad.

"I saw a glimpse of who he could've been," Brent said of such moments.

I knew nothing, as it turned out. I was blind to a problem that consumed Chad for years.

It began in high school in a commonplace manner with friends at parties, in homes, sometimes simply with beer taken from our house. That's where Chad first felt alcohol's dark pull on him. He seemed like any other kid having a few beers, like I'd done growing up in Port Arthur. I remember Mother crying one night when she realized I was drunk, her golden child tarnished.

Brent, as usual, was altogether different from his brother. He didn't drink. He didn't even toast champagne at his wedding. His aversion to alcohol dated to a high school ski trip when he was offered a shot of whiskey. He hated it, called it the dumbest thing he ever did. He then saw how crazy people got drinking in high school and college and went the other way. He never had another drop of alcohol after that high school incident until his mid-thirties.

Chad was one of those crazy people his brother saw drinking. His problems with drinking weren't recognizable in high school or college as he partied the same as many students.

He began working as a Dallas stockbroker in 1989, the same year I started with the Cowboys. During Chad's first several years as a success in the financial world, he never thought alcohol was leading him down a dark path. He drank hard on weekends at first. Then he began drinking after work. Chad had a big house and expensive cars, so no one questioned his work-hard, play-hard lifestyle. About a decade into his career, though, the boundaries quickly loosened in ways Chad never expected as the stress of work increased. He would have an afternoon drink during work. Then one in the morning to get him going. Drink by drink, day by day, his life quickly unraveled to where alcohol was his last thought at night and first thought in the morning.

Chad's manager at work was the first to recognize something was wrong. His manager had a brother with alcohol issues and saw some familiar warning signs. He confronted Chad, telling him to get help or get a new job. Chad opted to get help. Sort of. He went in for counseling—in a manner of speaking. He later learned the therapeutic word for this: *appeasement*. He didn't go to therapy for help. He went through the motions simply to appease his boss, to say he *got help*. He tried to paint himself as a picture of success, even as he sat in therapy discussing his issues.

An alcoholic?

Chad?

He left there and didn't change anything. He made the turn from a functional alcoholic to a dysfunctional one in his early thirties. He drank to be drunk. He kept drinking to stay drunk. Did you see Denzel Washington in the movie *Flight*? That's a good portrayal of the everyday alcoholic Chad became.

The descent came quickly when, true to his word, the manager fired Chad. He didn't have a steady job again for seven years. Part of the reason was that he didn't want to take a lesser job than his high-paying one. He also was incapable of following a disciplined workday. He wasn't tethered to anything by this point except the glass before him.

Back when his career was rising, he and a friend had looked for an open bar one Christmas Day. They found one in a downtrodden part of Dallas, took one step in, and immediately turned around; it was so bad. "If you ever hear of me going in here, put a bullet in me," Chad joked with his friend.

Two years later, he was opening that same bar at 7 a.m. His daily routine: wake up, get sick, drink, get sick, and continue drinking. His full personality never waned, though. He never looked a mess. That contributed to making everything worse. He could be an inch off rock bottom and talk a drink out of a bartender.

He soon lost everything material that defined his life. He was at a point where he scratched each day for money. He hit up friends. He called family. He just needed some support through a tough time, right?

I gave Chad money.

He asked for more.

It's hard to stand by and watch your son become a wreck. In football, I was used to controlling and improving people and situations. I had to accept that the only way to help Chad was by not helping him, by letting him fail to the point he felt the need to change. I told him money would only be there for him to get help. He found odd jobs to cover some costs. One was as a bartender in a hole-in-the-wall bar. One day he was serving the people who used to be his Highland Park neighbors. He saw the shocked look on their faces, heard them say as he walked away, "Wow, this is how far it's gone for him."

That hurt. He tried a treatment center. He drank upon leaving it. He tried another. Same result. We didn't know it at that time, but these were all painful steps toward something better. All I knew is that it hurt like hell to watch him go through this. There were nights when he'd call and beg for money. He would make promises through slurred speech of how he'd do better.

"You've been drinking," I once said.

Chad heard that and thought, *Of course I am drinking*. It's all he did. He had no illusions of who he was after a few years of this life-style. Everyone in the family knew his condition to the point where he later condensed our descriptions of him into one-liners.

Brent: "Life is good, you should join it."

Linda Kay: "You're going to die before forty."

Me: "What a waste of a life."

Physically, he was a mess even if he didn't look like it. He had no health insurance. A doctor friend offered help and performed oc-casional tests. Chad was told he had the immune system of someone with AIDS. I went with him once to the doctor when he got results about the condition of his liver.

"I don't give him more than two years to live if he doesn't quit drinking," the doctor told me.

He kept drinking. He might have hit physical and emotional bot-tom, but he still hadn't fully hit rock bottom. I had, though. I still of-fered to get him treatment, but I took a necessary step, given the way everything looked. I took him out of my will.

"I'm not going to sit around and watch this," I told him. "When

I die, you get zero. I don't want to pass away and leave you with this sum of money and you just kill yourself with it."

I wasn't alone. Chad called his brother for money, too. And called. After ten or fifteen times hearing the same spiel over several years, Brent was numb to the pain, too.

"I need some money or I'm going to die," Chad told him.

"Okay, that's one way to fix it," Brent said.

Several years passed like this. Nothing changed. Nothing helped. This was the one problem I couldn't solve by watching more film or making a big trade. I blamed myself for not being aware of Chad's problem until it was too late. Maybe I could have helped him if I'd known earlier—if I'd had a better relationship throughout his life.

I felt defeated.

And so I sat in that rental car all that night in 2009 with a plan. I didn't know if it would work. I didn't know if Chad even would listen. But when there was some movement in the home that morning, I knocked on the door and waited.

"It's your dad," Chad's friend told him inside the home.

Chad came to the door.

"Look, I'm going to take you to get help," I said.

He didn't commit right away. This was all about him committing, too.

"You've got to make a decision," I said.

A few hours later, we were off to the Father Joseph C. Martin–Ashley Treatment Center in Maryland, as suggested by my old team chaplain, Leo Armbrust. It was the fifth one Chad tried. Rehab, as he said, wasn't failing him. He was failing rehab.

After ninety days in the center, he looked ready to start his life again. We had a plan, too. He would fly back to Dallas, gather his belongings, and move to Tampa. He needed to get away from his old world. We had found a sober house there for him, a place where a normal life could be led while surrounded by a support group.

Chad was driven from the treatment center to the airport. He had a two-hour wait.

"You going to be okay?" the driver asked.

"No problem," he said. He went to his gate and saw ESPN on a television. He hadn't seen sports in three months. The television was in a bar, and he walked in and sat down at the only available chair. It was at the bar. The bartender asked him if he wanted a drink. Chad ordered a Coke at first, then a beer. *Just one*, he told himself while watching the TV and waiting for his plane. That led to a second. And a shot of tequila. Next thing he knew, he was two hours out of treatment and right back to where he was upon entering it.

He flew drunk to Dallas and took up his old ways again. He revisited the same places, saw the same wrong friends. For several days, he was pulled back into that addicted life, drink by drink. I was broken.

"Look," I said, "if you're not out of Dallas by the end of the week, lose my number. Not only are you out of the family, but there's also going to be no communication. I'm not going to stand by and watch you destroy yourself."

Finally, Chad came to some personal resolution. He packed up his stuff and drove to Tampa. He still didn't immediately move into the halfway house. He had a little money left on him and used that for alcohol. He lived out of his car. When he ran out of money, he woke up one morning and drove to the halfway house. One more humbling experience awaited him there. They realized he'd been drinking.

"There's one requirement to live here and you don't meet it," they said.

He slept one more night in his car, returned the next day, and only then was allowed into the home.

That was his first sober night.

He lived in the house with twenty-four other guys. Everyone shared a refrigerator and living space. There was counseling there that had Chad follow short-term goals at the start. Not just one day of sobriety at a time. Ten minutes of sobriety. Thirty minutes. A morning. The idea wasn't just to stay sober. It was to have a healthier and happier life.

There was valuable structure to living there, too. A curfew was in place. Everyone had to attend recovery meetings and attempt to find a job. Chad's first job in that new life was washing dishes and making subs in a deli. You know how we talk in sports about getting better every day? That was Chad's path. One day became two days. One week became two weeks. He surrounded himself with sober friends, made better decisions, constructed an improved life for himself. Two weeks became a month.

It wasn't about people convincing Chad to stay sober anymore.

It was about Chad deciding to live that way.

He stayed in that halfway home for nine months. As he says, "That's where it started. I remember accepting that, whatever my life is, it's my life to lead."

We had an important conversation nearly a year into his sobriety. He grew up thinking that since I succeeded to a high level, I expected similar success from my sons. All he saw was my hard work growing up and the sacrifice to win the next game. He willed himself to be that kind of hard-charging person, too. The president of Florida State clubs. The No. 1 stockbroker in his firm. If he wasn't succeeding at that level, he felt he was letting me down—letting himself down, really.

I never felt that way. I certainly didn't feel it after his emotional journey to sobriety.

"I don't care what your job is," I told him. "I don't care if you flip burgers at McDonald's. As long as you're sober, we can get through anything together. I don't care about anything else."

I meant that, too. I still do.

At about this time, Chad was still living at the halfway house, but he was wondering what to do with his new life. He only knew two worlds well, he figured. He knew the financial world as a high-level stockbroker. He also knew the recovery world of alcoholics and treatment centers. He realized which one had more meaning to him. That led to his decision to open a treatment and rehab center himself. People were surprised, even unsure, about him making such a quick turnaround from being an alcoholic to leading people's recoveries. One governing idea to sobriety is not taking on big projects at the start. Chad knew how to answer that: the Johnsons are always capable of quick rebuild jobs.

One of the few remaining friends from his previous life, Scott Roix, lent him some property on Madeira Beach, near St. Petersburg. It was in a beautiful spot overlooking the Gulf of Mexico. It took six months to get the proper licensing and set up the place. He opened Tranquil Shores in 2010 with three employees. It grew to thirty-three employees within a couple of years. It counsels between twenty and thirty people at a time. Students. Housewives. Business executives. Younger. Older. Everyone is linked by the same problem.

All those down years of bouncing between treatment centers and struggling with demons can be viewed now as a business education for Chad. They helped him create the best place for people in his previous condition. He understood what worked and what didn't, where to focus attention and where to ignore.

For instance, he learned that the thirty-day stay he had at some centers wasn't long enough. His clients stay ninety days. He also saw previous treatment staffs stretched too thin. Tranquil Shores has a ratio of one counselor for every three clients. And while group therapy mattered, he saw one-on-one sessions as vital. They became a priority for clients in his center.

I finally gave him some good coaching advice, too. We would talk about constructing his business and I stressed the importance of creating an atmosphere where people are confident and feel fulfilled — where you make them confident and fulfilled. If he could achieve that, everyone working there would become everything they could and should be in the team.

Yep, the ol' Pygmalion Theory.

In retirement from coaching, I've tried to become a better father. Chad and I have a scheduled call at 6 a.m. each Wednesday. It began as mechanical conversations of what we were doing or planned to do. With time it developed into sharing our thoughts and hopes.

The boys noticed my small gestures of change. For instance, I once called Chad when the Cowboys played in Tampa and asked if he wanted tickets.

"You've never done that before," he said.

Another time, Rhonda and I got ambitious and rented an RV to drive and see my sons. This idea floored my Brent and Chad. Me driving across the country? In an RV? Who was this guy?

The RV broke down.

We ended up flying to see them.

The point is, I don't take family for granted anymore. I'm not trying to make up for lost time. Yesterday is yesterday. And today? Well, Brent's family is doing great. Chad met a beautiful woman, Mary, in his new chapter. They had a son, Cooper, near the end of 2021. That tells you how well he's doing. Tranquil Shores was such a success, he recently opened a second treatment center, Cedo Ranch, in Austin, Texas. It was previously an actual working ranch. Long-horned cattle are in the fields. Of course, my first thought when he told me of adding another center was one of a concerned father.

"You sure about this?" I said. "You haven't bitten off more than you can chew?"

Chad said he's got it under control.

He does, too.

There's a client reunion each year at Tranquil Shores. Every person who has gone through the program and stayed sober is invited with their families. I've been to a few of them. I've sat by Chad as the mothers and fathers of sober children went to the podium and talked of their journey. They were emotional talks, full of pain, in a manner I could relate to and appreciate. Somewhere in each talk came a common line of gratitude.

"Chad, thanks for saving my son's life . . ."

"Chad, you picked my daughter up at two a.m. and drove her around for four hours before you took her to detox . . ."

"Chad, we wouldn't be here without you . . ."

I sat there, listening, crying once again over Chad. These weren't tears of pain and frustration, as they were for so many years. They were tears of joy, of thanks—of a father's unmatched pride, most of all.

I spoke at one of these reunions.

"I've won national championships," I said. "I've won Super Bowls. I've had a lot of success in the football world. But nothing I've accomplished in my career can come close to anything you're doing at Tranquil Shores."

I looked at Chad, talking through tears.

"You're saving lives."

18

SURVIVING *SURVIVOR*

When I arrived at the harsh beauty and searing reality of Nicaragua, a journey that spanned ten impatient years, I was greeted about as I expected.

"You look like Jimmy Johnson," someone said.

"No, he'd never do this," someone else said.

"You're, like, a look-alike of him."

"An exact look-alike."

"Wait, you really are Jimmy Johnson."

This was in the coastal town of San Juan del Sur in 2010, at the start of my adventure on the television show *Survivor*. The question from the nineteen other contestants was the one I've been asked ever since:

Why would someone like me do something like this?

I understood the surprise. People identified me with football, only football. The hard-driving coach. The Super Bowl–winning celebrity. The studio expert on *FOX NFL Sunday*. And now I was standing in the middle of a wilderness? About to suffer hard days and sleepless nights? Volunteering to live off the land, interact with strangers, and exchange a posh life for such a primitive one that palm fronds were used to clean your teeth (they didn't do such a great job, either)?

What everyone didn't realize is that this was exactly what I wanted to do since my youth. I dreamed then of living in the wild. I tried to talk Mother and Daddy into letting me get a marmoset, a little mon-key. I imagined an untamed life living off the land on the Amazon River. No cars. No electricity. No civilization at all. That sounded like a grand adventure to me. But then my coaching career started, and I went off the grid in an entirely different way.

My family and friends questioned my going on *Survivor* for a dif-ferent reason. Rhonda and Terry Bradshaw, for instance, worried about my health. Imagine that. Imagine being worried about the old-est contestant ever on the show with a stent in his heart disappearing into a remote part of the world and subsisting off the land for weeks. What could go wrong?

So, again, I understood the questions. But this wasn't just a child-hood fantasy by this point in my life. I loved the television show, too. I watched it every week—live, not recorded, making football and *Sur-vivor* the only events I watched at the times they aired. I wanted to go behind the curtain and see how the show was made. You know how football fans wonder what it's like in the locker room or in the huddle during a game? That's how I looked at *Survivor*.

There was also a philosophical component to my decision. I once read a quote that resonated with me, especially in my chapter after football: "Live your life from the start to the finish, but don't just live the length of it. Live the width of your life, too."

This trip was living the width for me. It was the w-i-d-t-h, actually, considering it became a wider and wilder adventure than I expected. It didn't just take me out of my comfort zone, but into a place I never knew existed. I can talk about it all now, too—now that I didn't die. That's not entirely a joke, either. My experience had an important bonus, one that was entirely separate from what happened in Nicara-gua, one I'm grateful for to this day.

Being on *Survivor* might have saved my life.

It started a few weeks after I retired from the Dolphins. Rhonda pointed a video camera at me standing in a floral shirt on the beach behind our home in Islamorada. I had already filled out a stack of papers applying to be on the show. Now came the application video.

"My name is Jimmy Johnson," I said. *"I can be your ultimate survivor. I've watched every minute of every episode of* Survivor. *You've had some good people on there. But I believe I can beat all comers."*

No playing with scared money, right?

"I'm in good physical health—although my wife, Rhonda, says I'm crazy," I continued.

Rhonda, in fact, suggested dropping me off on one of the uninhabited little islands off the Keys for a weekend to cure me of this *Survivor* itch.

"I've won two Super Bowls," I said in closing on the video. *"I've won two college national championships. What better way to end my career than win* Survivor?"

I sent off the application. I was all excited.

And I was rejected by the show.

No reason was given. None was necessary. They receive thousands of applications, and maybe they thought mine was a celebrity stunt. Maybe they thought a FOX broadcaster on a CBS show wasn't good for business. Maybe I was too old. I was still disappointed. This was to be my first venture in a life after football. And I didn't make the team.

I filed that away as a missed opportunity. I had forgotten all about it several years later when I was in New York and bumped into Les Moonves, who was the chairman and CEO of CBS at the time.

"Coach, I hear *Survivor* turned you down," he said.

"It's true," I said.

"Are they nuts?" he said. "That'd be great for ratings. You still want to be on?"

I nodded. "Yes, I do."

"We'll get you on next year," he said.

That was for the 2007 season in Estuaire, Gabon. I had never been to Africa. I was pumped at the renewed possibility of being on the show. Again I went through the application process. This time I was approved, no doubt with a call from on high. To finalize everything, I flew to Los Angeles and went through the requisite psychological and medical tests every contestant must, probed and prodded like a prospect at the NFL Combine.

Driving back to the airport for the flight home, I called Rhonda. "I'll be going to Africa," I said.

A minute later, the phone rang. It was Dr. Richard Horowitz, the show's medical chief.

"Coach, we'd love to have you on the show," he said. "But you need to see your cardiologist. You've got one artery one hundred percent blocked and one artery seventy percent blocked."

I saw my doctor the next day. I had surgery a week later. A stent was put in one artery. The other couldn't be unblocked, but the cardiologist said not to worry, my body had adapted to it properly. That began a disciplined regimen to improve my body and get me back to health. Rhonda put me on a strict diet. I exercised more, running and lifting light weights. I lost twenty pounds. I went on a medicine to drop my cholesterol from 220 to just over 100.

Instead of suddenly dropping dead one day from my heart problems, I felt better than I had in years thanks to the doctors and nurses who helped.

I also didn't give up my *Survivor* hopes. I applied again. A decade after my first attempt to get on the show, I made the team. I was excited, the little boy in me ready to live in the wilderness, even if the grown man wondered where it would all go. Some things didn't change from my coaching days, even as the game did. Organized? Prepared? My son Chad called one day and asked what I was doing.

"I'm packing for *Survivor*," I said.

"When do you leave?" he said.

"Next month."

I couldn't wait for my last big game.

At the start of each episode of *Survivor: Nicaragua*, a sequence of stunning scenes of nature unfolded to the viewer as a voice-over said, *"Into the wilds of Nicaragua, an untamed land of active volcanos, rain forests, and fierce wildlife . . ."*

It looked wonderful on a big-screen, high-definition television. Inspired. Picturesque. That was the perfectly edited and dramatically presented show I watched from my sofa all those years with a cold drink.

It was another experience altogether living inside that show. All day was spent foraging for firewood, scavenging for food, boiling water, repairing a leaky hut, and attempting to sleep for a few hours at night. Where were those relaxing hours on the exotic beach, watching sunsets and contemplating your adventurous nature, that I expected to have?

There was none of that because the fire was low, the water needed boiling, and the cycle of fundamental needs started over as soon as you completed them. No wonder why primitive man had such a short life span.

There was an added issue for me. My celebrity status changed everything. It started when I was kept out of the orientation meetings in Los Angeles before leaving, to maintain my presence as a surprise. I understood why. It was just an opportunity lost. It wasn't just that contestants met and, in some cases, made tacit alliances that later came into play. They also were afforded a practical outline of how everything operated. Here's an example: food was plentiful the first week we were on the grounds before filming started, but it was cut to a severe daily ration thereafter. The other contestants knew to bulk up that first week to help get through the second week. I didn't know that. And why didn't anyone tell me?

Well, that gets to a part of the experience that was uncomfortable for me. It was called "Lockdown." Anytime cameras weren't around, there was no communicating with anyone. No words. No nods. No hand gestures. There could be no exchanges in any way unless a camera was there to capture it. This was a television show, after all, and the producers didn't want anything done that viewers would miss.

Lockdown was enforced stringently, too. I once stepped aside simply to let another contestant go first in the food line.

"You go ahead," I said.

"No talking," a show official said.

And people thought I was tough on players?

We lived the primitive life for a week in Nicaragua before the show started filming. So just getting to the starting line felt like a long, uncomfortable journey. Seven rough days. Seven sleep-deprived nights. It was a nonstop week of rummaging for firewood, being hot during the days and cold and wet at nights, with no change of clothes while barely talking to anyone. Fun, right?

Out in the wild, you discover what separates civilized man from our primitive forebears, too.

Toilet paper, for one.

Showers, too.

We had nothing for simple daily hygienics. Razors? Nope. Deodorant? Forget it. We didn't even have combs, with which everyone had fun, considering my existence with perfectly coiffed hair. But I came prepared for that. My hair was cut like a zealot monk's—ragged and just over the ears, the shortest it had been since high school.

A week in, the cameras started rolling, and our diet was essentially reduced to a small cup of rice. I never went a couple of hours at home without finding a snack here or there. Now I ate so little in Nicaragua I didn't go to the bathroom for eight straight days. *Eight!*

The worst part was, I couldn't sleep. No one could. The rain dripped down on you through the bamboo. The cold settled into you. We were middle-aged people—and, ahem, older—spooning with each other at night for some measure of warmth. By the time we made it to the starting line of filming, I felt like a zombie. We all did to some degree. It was so difficult, two women quit near the start. That wasn't good for the show, the producers agreed, and some of the more taxing demands were loosened starting the following year. Food, for instance, became a more available prize of the competitions. Bamboo and tools were provided upon arrival. I watch the shows now and realize how football players from earlier generations consider the current game so mushy-soft.

So much of my energy was expended simply staying intact and upright, the art of playing the survival game became almost secondary. That was the purpose, of course. You had to survive just to play *Survivor.*

The dilemma of my strategy in the game reverted to my celebrity status. Nineteen of the show's contestants were strangers in name and reputation, blank slates to be introduced and invented however they chose. I was different. Everyone presumed who I was and projected what they saw or heard from my coaching days. That was understood. It also meant I needed a plan that took that preconception into account. The show, after all, was built on strategic relationships or Machiavellian manipulation to become the last person standing and win $1 million.

I decided to play the game by not playing it. No lies. No manipulation. I wouldn't pretend to be someone I wasn't. That wasn't just because my inner compass struggled with not being truthful or outright deceiving people. Being open and honest was my best chance to win as well.

Let's be honest here: I wanted to win going into this experience, too. Are you kidding? Throughout my life, I've wanted to win at shuffleboard, ice skating, bridge games—anything I encountered, big and small. I wasn't heading into the wilderness for a month just to lose on a show I loved. But this game was different for me because I was different from the other contestants.

"All the adventures I've had in the past, I was in charge," I said in an aside on the show. "I could fire players. I could recruit players. I could sign them. Out here I don't have control. Maybe somebody's going to be infatuated with me being Coach Jimmy Johnson, Super Bowl winner. Well, I'll play on that superstar status. Some of these other players may resent that. Maybe they're Philadelphia Eagles fans or Washington Redskins fans. So, I have got to work on each particular contestant and try to win them over."

In the opening minutes of the first episode, the show laid out the prime plotlines. There were the primitive challenges of our Nicaraguan setting. There was Kelly, a contestant with a prosthetic leg. Then, four minutes into that first show, another contestant, Marty, spoke privately in a way that explained my central problem.

"As I'm looking around at the group right now, I see Jimmy Johnson, an NFL coach," he said. "Okay, I want nothing to do with Jimmy Johnson in this game. Frankly, I have no idea why the hell he's even here. And I'd rather him on the other tribe, frankly."

Marty considered my celebrity status a threat. The other side was shown when contestants were divided into the under-thirty team (La Flora) and over-forty team (Espada). The younger team liked me.

"Damn, I wanted the old football coach, man!" a La Flora member shouted.

"I'm young at heart!" I shouted back, giving the title to the first episode.

And so it began. My personality and my tribe's expectations

nudged me into a leadership role. It was simple things at first. Were those knots on the hut right? Who's fishing or collecting firewood today? I kept true to my open-book strategy right through the oddest pregame speech I've ever given.

"Okay, folks, team huddle," I said, sitting on a log by the beach, addressing my tribe of older contestants. "First of all, the reason I'm here is I'm here for the adventure. There's no way in the world a jury is going to give me one million dollars. I know that. But the thing that I can do, I can help somebody win a million dollars. And the winner can come from one of you guys. Nothing would make me happier than to see one of you win a million bucks. And I'll help you all the way. I promise. Just as long as we're psyched up for it and we know what we've got to do, we'll kick their ass."

Cheers. High fives. It was all true, too. I was there for the adventure. I didn't need another million dollars. I'd be happy if one of them got the money—I really would. I had already told the producers that if I ever made it to the final three contestants, I was giving the money to charity anyway.

With each passing day, my struggle to survive became more evident. It wasn't just the bull's-eye on me as a celebrity, as Marty described. At sixty-six, as the oldest contestant, the primitive living took a physical and mental toll on me. I was wet, hungry, dog tired—and worse. That first night of filming—our eighth day of rough living—I began retching, hands on knees, as the cameras rolled. I was dry-heaving, really, considering there was nothing to bring up from my hundred-calories-a-day stomach. Coach Johnson might have pointed Contestant Johnson to the "asthma field" right then.

"Zero sleep, sick, throwing up, ants and mosquitos biting me everywhere, and cold and shivering until the sun came up," I told the team. "I don't think I've had a twenty-four-hour period where I was in that much discomfort and that miserable. I watched every second of *Survivor*. I never imagined it was this difficult."

"Coach needs to be careful," said another contestant, Jimmy T. "He's getting his ass kicked out there."

I rallied and tried to help people. Holly, a middle-aged woman from South Dakota, was struggling worse than I was. She admitted to problems. She lost her bearings. She grew upset with another Espada teammate, Dan, a sixty-three-year-old from Brooklyn. She took Dan's $1,600 alligator shoes, filled them with sand, and dropped them in the ocean. That was her state of mind. By the fifth day of filming— nearly two weeks since our arrival—she looked broken sitting with me on driftwood on the beach. She said she couldn't go on. This brought out the coach in me.

"You can do it for one day, can't you?" I asked her.

She broke down. "I can't do it," she said, crying. "I've never failed anything in my life, but I have to be honest."

As I said on the show, Holly's situation was "no different than a football player wanting to quit the team. We all go through some adverse times. And our minds get weak."

I talked to Holly like one of my players. Well, sort of. My voice was softer, my words more encouraging.

"The only thing I ask you to do is give it your best," I said. "But we need you. We really do need you."

Holly collected herself. She later defined this talk as a turning point. She became the last remaining member of our Espada tribe and the final woman on the show. She wrote a motivational book of her experiences called *Your Winner Within*. Who did she ask to write the book's foreword? The coach pushing her to make one more day.

Day by day, crisis by crisis, we moved forward. Food was a forever issue. We saw some howler monkeys and wanted to share their food. I imitated their call. Someone said they were looking at me. What did they say?

"They said, 'Get your ass out of here,'" I said.

Hey, it was all in good fun. But it wasn't all fun and games by that point. The subtext of *Survivor* is deceit and trickery. I put myself out there, trying to play my open-book game, the ol' coach with his new team. There remained the two views of me.

"His soul is inspiring," said one teammate, Yve.

Or . . .

"Why do we get stuck with a celebrity on our team?" Marty said. "Everybody's got glitter in their eyes. If Jimmy Johnson walked across the lagoon, everybody'd believe it."

The third competition came on the eighth day. I had already held a bamboo pipe as part of a waterway in one competition and crawled through mud in another. Now we had to run for ten wooden barrels, roll them to a common ground, place them individually on platforms, and throw small bags to land on each barrel.

Tyrone was our bag tosser. He took a good lead—*Ride the wave*, right? But then Tyrone began missing the barrels, fell behind, and Jimmy T. wanted to get in there.

"You're wasting me," Jimmy T. told me.

I soon subbed in Jimmy T., but he didn't let it go when we lost. No one did. The bag-tossing controversy was worth an ESPN 30 *for* 30. Tyrone was upset he was pulled. Jimmy T. was upset he wasn't in earlier—like he was the Troy Aikman of bag tossing.

"Coach, I want you to evaluate me," he said. "Maybe you could look at me a little better. I've got some skills. And if you leave me on the bench, it's going to cost us."

Only Marty was happy. He thought the tension all worked against me.

"I need to remove him so that people will lose their daddy," Marty said.

That is sort of what happened, too. But I have a confession: I was looking for a way out. You know that Vince Lombardi line "Fatigue makes cowards of us all"? He was right. I was physically exhausted and mentally spent after this run of wilderness living. I wanted the white courtesy phone to hail a limo and take me back to civilization. It was provided after a two-hour ride over dirt roads to our second tribal council meeting. Jeff Probst, in his role as moderator, asked each of us if we were one of the weaker players. No one admitted they were.

Until it was my turn.

"I'm the oldest player and one of the weakest, too," I said.

In my coaching days, I used words and ideas so people arrived at the answer I wanted. This was no different. I was voted out. After my torch was snuffed out, I turned and offered a final word of encouragement to the others.

"One of you, win your million bucks, okay?" I said.

I meant that. I was also delighted to be driven soon to a plush resort.

"What's the first thing you ate?" people always ask.

Ate? I sucked down three Kalik beers in rapid succession. Civilization never tasted so good.

When I arrived home and rushed back to the Keys, ready for my good life . . .

. . . *Survivor: Islamorada* was waiting for me.

Rhonda wasn't home, as she was finishing a trip across the country with friends. So, as I pulled in to my home, people whom I didn't know began scattering like cockroaches as the lights went on. Some jumped out of the pool. Others hurried off the dock.

"What's going on here?" I asked my caretaker, a fifty-eight-year-old man who lived in a separate cottage on my property for several years. "Are all these people living here?"

That led to a confrontation, which led to an argument in his family. As all this escalated, he barricaded himself in his shack. He threatened to commit suicide.

Police were called. That led to the next odd scene, which was straight out of Barney Fife and *Mayberry R.F.D.* The policeman and I knocked on the caretaker's door. And knocked. Finally, when he didn't answer, we opened the door and walked in. There he was, holding a gun.

"Gun! Gun!" Barney Fife yelled, running away.

In the process of retreating, the policeman drew his gun and fired over his shoulder. The bullet could have hit me. It hit the hot-water heater instead. Like I said, Barney Fife all the way.

That led to a real lockdown at my place. A SWAT team arrived. A Marine patrol team took control of the docks. A helicopter circled overhead. A perimeter was set up on my property. I stood there watching it all, concerned for everyone's safety.

The SWAT team's negotiator talked with my caretaker, who could be seen on occasion walking by the window. He was heard on occasion, too.

"Shoot me!" he shouted.

And: "Kill me!"

I sat back and drank a few beers and considered my welcome back to civilization. I ended up in the police truck watching a bomb-squad robot enter the cottage. I listened to the negotiations. And I waited.

The standoff lasted five and a half hours. It ended with police coaxing my caretaker out of the cottage and taking him away.

I still watch *Survivor.* I'm also a fan of *Naked and Afraid*, a Discovery Channel show where two survivalists meet naked in the wilderness, each carrying one item, like a machete or fire starter. They have to survive for twenty-one days. Sometimes I think there's one more chapter waiting, think what tool I'd choose, think of the ways to navigate those twenty-one days.

Rhonda will give me a look.

"I'm only thinking about it," I tell her.

19

ENTERING THE HALL

Twenty-two years after I left the NFL sideline, I arrived at the FOX television studio in Los Angeles at 4 a.m. on a playoff Sunday feeling back on the sideline.

Except I was more anxious.

"Hear anything?" Troy Aikman texted from Green Bay, where he was the analyst for a FOX broadcast—my former Dallas quarterback's good mind and spirit still serving him well.

"Nothing," I answered.

None of my fellow FOX broadcasters arriving that morning even mentioned my Pro Football Hall of Fame candidacy. I couldn't blame them. There was nothing to say. I hadn't slept more than two or three hours since the voting that Wednesday.

Bill Cowher got surprised with news of his election Saturday on the CBS pregame show by the Hall of Fame's president David Baker. I was happy for Cowher. I also figured they wouldn't pull that TV surprise on back-to-back days. Beyond that, was Baker going to fly from CBS in New York to the FOX studio in Los Angeles?

All those years in coaching, the idea of making the Hall of Fame didn't occupy a moment's thought for me. I had always lived in the moment—the game, the draft, the season. I was so obsessed with succeeding, I never cared about what my legacy would be decades later.

I cared now.

I wanted confirmation that the journey was worth it—and not just the public work and sweat and Super Bowls and inexplicable relationship with Jerry Jones.

The private sacrifice. The guilt I carried in some form. My career consumed me. Maybe it cost my marriage, maybe my son's health. Getting in the Hall wouldn't change any of that. It would confirm my career, though.

So, yes, this Hall of Fame vote meant something more to me than I once could have imagined. As we prepared for that day's show, I mentioned to Terry Bradshaw that they might bypass me.

"Forget about it," he said. "Put it in the back of your mind and get ready for the show."

I did just that. I went out and did the pregame show, hoping in the back of my mind that Baker would surprise me like he had Cowher. He never did. Our pregame show ended. I didn't say anything, but felt like that was it, my good chance gone. No one said a word.

Two hours later, I stood on our mock football field set at halftime of the playoff game, ready to talk about Seattle's defense, when host Curt Menefee said, "There's always room for one surprise guest, especially when it's this man coming in right now, from the Pro Football Hall of Fame, David Baker."

I went numb.

"Hall of Famer," Baker said, walking out and shaking Terry Bradshaw's hand.

"Hall of Famer," he said down the line to Michael Strahan, Howie Long, and Tony Gonzalez.

He then stood before me.

"It's my great honor to tell you that you're going to be the three hundred and twenty-eighth Hall of Famer, and your legacy is going to be in Canton, Ohio, forever," Baker said.

I teared up. I couldn't breathe.

"The only thing I can think of is all the assistant coaches that worked for me, all the great players that played for me," I said. "They're the reason I'm here and . . ."

I gasped for air.

"I can't talk," I said.

Finally, I got a breath. "This is so special, because when you put the work we put in, it's nice to know people appreciate it."

It came out later that only a few people at FOX knew of the surprise. Bill Richards, our producer, knew days ahead of time to prepare the show. Curt knew to be ready for when Baker came on our set, too. Eric Shanks, the CEO of FOX Sports, wanted the presentation at halftime rather than the pregame show because the audience would be larger.

More than 33 million people watched. Troy watched, wiping away tears, from the broadcast booth in Green Bay. Bill was bawling as he produced the show. Our wardrobe director, Victoria Trilling, called it the greatest moment in her twenty-three years with FOX. It certainly was my favorite moment.

That night after our show, I took the FOX crew to the Dan Tana's restaurant in West Hollywood. Dinner turned into a party with the other people in the restaurant. "Congratulations, Jimmy Johnson" was sung to the tune of "Happy Birthday." Drinks were sent over. ZZ Top guitarist Billy Gibbons came over, then played the guitar, as my day of days became a night to remember, too.

The Hall of Fame weekend in Canton that summer was like a class reunion of my career. I bumped into Dan Marino, who said he'd just had both knees replaced.

"I wish you'd done it while playing for me," I joked.

I saw Archie Manning.

"Remember that phone call . . . ?" I asked.

I was talking with Bill Belichick and Bill Cowher when Bernie Kosar saw us.

"Here's three guys I was a pain in the ass to," he said. "But it's all good now."

We laughed. All the old battles didn't matter anymore—everything was tucked into yesterday.

I had been to Canton only once before my induction. That was my choice. A lot of University of Miami and Dallas players invited me. The reason I went in 2017 was that Jason Taylor asked me to introduce him. Jason was so nervous about asking, he kept putting it off, passing the Hall deadline, telling the officials he would do it the next day. Then the next.

"Of course I'll do it," I said when he asked.

That night Jason turned to me in his speech and said, "When you drafted me in 1997, guys built like me did not play defensive end in the NFL. But you didn't care. You took a chance. Back then they were called *tweeners*, a derogatory term. Now they're *hybrids* and everyone wants one."

Four years later, it was my turn. I had one goal for my speech: make it short and sweet. The Hall asked who I was going to thank so they could run the names at the bottom of the Jumbotron, but I couldn't come up with a list. There were too many people. How could I thank them all?

But then as I sat there, listening to other speeches, I began to think I'd better thank some people.

Troy introduced me.

"First of all, about Troy," I said to open my speech. "I had a lot of great players, but more than a great player, he's become a great friend. And I think that's one of the great things about our game—the relationships that we make with one another, players, coaches, each other. It's a special, special game."

I paused and looked over the crowd.

"I guess you're wanting to know what I'm going to say about Jerry Jones!"

People laughed and applauded as I looked at Jerry.

"Well, Jerry, you told me . . . He said, 'We're going to make sports history,' before we ever bought the Cowboys—before *you* bought the Cowboys because I didn't pay a damn cent."

"And you know what? We—WE!—did make sports history. Not only for the Dallas Cowboys but for the NFL. We go from the worst team in the league two years in a row to winning back-to-back Super Bowls and building a heck of a football team.

"We did it and let me tell you, from the bottom of my heart, thank you. Thank you for giving me that opportunity.

"You know, I look back, and so many things have happened to me in my career and it's because of others. You know, I didn't do it, they did it. But before I give you the thank-yous, I want to say something about the people who really sacrificed.

"My sons, Brent and Chad, and their mother, Linda Kay. She was a great, great woman. Bill Cowher knows, as a coach, he has to struggle with the family life and wives put up with a lot of crap. Fortunately, Rhonda doesn't have to put up with much crap because I'm pretty good."

I smiled at her.

"Well, getting ready for this thing I'm saying, 'Okay, who am I going to thank?' Started a list and said, 'No, no, I can't do that.' You know, I went back to Brent and Chad. I said, 'You know, I wasn't here for you.' I felt like I had to outwork my opponent and that's why it's hard on coaches' families.

"My two sons played football. I never saw them play a down. That's a shame. Fortunately, I corrected that, and we have a relationship now that I wouldn't trade for any. It is the best. I've got the greatest two sons in the world, and I love them with all my heart.

"I love my wife, Rhonda, with all my heart, and I appreciate she puts up with me. I started putting together a list and I said, 'Okay, Troy, Emmitt, Michael, Charles, Nate, Dan, Jason, Zach, Russell, Daryl, Step. My coaches Dave, Tony, Norv, Butch, Camps, Bruce . . . I said, 'The hell with it, I can't make a list.'

"There is too many to say thank you, so I'm not going to say a whole lot of thank-yous. I went into the College Football Hall of Fame a long time ago because I had great assistant coaches and great players. Maybe I had something to do with bringing them together, but they won the games. Those players won the games. I didn't win the games.

"I went in the Broadcasting Hall of Fame and, hey, listen to this, when you're sitting there with Terry, Howie, Michael, Jay Glazer, Curt, and you've got the best producer in all of television with Bill Richards, you're going in the Broadcasting Hall of Fame. It's because of those folks.

"And now I'm in the Pro Football Hall of Fame. Again, great assistant coaches, great players, and a great organization. Looking back—I went and counted—I coached, recruited, or drafted thirteen players in the Pro Football Hall of Fame. Let me tell you what: Zach Thomas belongs up here. Darren Woodson belongs up here. Those two players, they were key factors. . . ."

It was fun looking out and seeing the people who helped me reach this moment. I talked of the believing, not dreaming, and of the Pygmalion Theory, which was a centerpiece of my coaching.

I wanted to leave people with something I learned late in life.

"Wayne Huizenga told me, one thing he said, 'Jimmy, let me tell you something. I know how hard you work. Don't forget about QTL.' *Quality Time Left*. Think about that. I'm seventy-eight years old and I think about QTL all the time.

"Let me tell you something, folks, the people that you love, like my family right over there—appreciate those people, because there will come a day you're not going to be able to appreciate them be-cause they're not going to be around."

So many people weren't around to hear that speech. Linda Kay had died a few years earlier. Wayne and Marti Huizenga were gone, too. Hubbard Alexander. Joe Brodsky. Joe Avezzano. So many people who played a role in our success.

I still think of QTL all the time.

20

QUESTIONS FOR COLLEGE FOOTBALL

There's not a world of difference between coaching in college and the NFL.

There's a galaxy.

You can't compare them. In college, you're the coach, the general manager, the team president. You answer to a school president, not the team owner. In many cases, you're a bigger name than the school president, too.

Beyond that, if you're in one of the top ten programs in college football, the difference in talent is so vast compared to scheduled opponents that you're going to win ten games just by kicking off. That's never the case in the NFL.

Your coaching goes beyond the field in college, too. You're a mentor, a father figure, a moral compass. These are eighteen- and nineteen-year-olds away from home for the first time and many problems coming across your desk have nothing to do with football. Homesick problems. Girlfriend problems. Academic problems. You spend time not just coaching them but making sure they're growing up. In the pros, they're grown men making a living with one general concern: money. Their money. And making more of it.

Then there's the game itself. I remember when Steve Spurrier went from the University of Florida to Washington in the NFL. He looked at a practice field and wondered if it was the defensive practice field. In college, you have enough players to separate the offense and defense on different fields for much of the practice. In the NFL, you have fifty-three players. Everyone works together.

All that said, I loved my time in college football. The kids. The energy. The traditions. And yes, the winning. Have I mentioned we finished 40-4 in my final four years at the University of Miami?

Yes, college football is a great, rewarding, and exciting game in so many ways—if it's not ruined by two recent changes.

The first is the transfer portal that allows players to change schools like dinner orders at a restaurant. That changes one of the primary roles of a college coach. When I first talked to new Oregon coach Dan Lanning, who was previously at the University of Georgia, he said, "You've got to work as hard recruiting your own players as you do your recruiting class."

That puts a higher premium on getting the right kind of players in your program. If you get someone who's strong-minded, smart, and disciplined they'll stick with you. If you get a weak-minded person who doesn't like the way you coach, it's easy for him to go somewhere else. That gets back to the way I evaluate players: intelligence is a top priority.

Sure, there's a selfish element in a coach not wanting players to transfer. The coach wants the kid to stay in school, grow in his program, and play a big or small role in winning. But this is a situation where the greater good is served as well. The freshman or sophomore perhaps struggling in football or in the broader aspects of college learns to persevere through problems.

If a fifth-year senior wants to leave—if he has earned a degree and wants to play somewhere else to help his pro aspirations—that's another matter. This is about the younger players, the ones who need to grow up in college like we all did. If they're dissatisfied with something, the transfer portal allows them to say, *The hell with this, I'm transferring out.* That doesn't help the player grow up at all. It most likely doesn't help them in football, either. It's too often the easy way out. Is that the lesson we should be teaching?

Here's the other issue of the transfer portal: How does a coach now deal with a player who's a bit of a discipline problem? Do you still come down hard on him? Do you go a little softer knowing he might threaten to transfer? Do you change your teaching habits to temper any frustration he might feel?

That's one unnecessary problem for college coaches.

Here's the other one: the rule permitting players to earn money from third parties off their name, image, or likeness (NIL). You could see this one coming like a dust storm on the horizon. It already has changed college sports in its opening moments. The Texas A&M football program and my University of Miami are out front in helping players through NIL money. Alabama football coach Nick Saban called them out, saying there weren't many regulations and they were "buying players." He was right in some regard. He also didn't like the world changing when he was on top and now finished behind Texas A&M in recruiting. That's where he better change.

Put it this way: if you're a top school and not in the NIL business, you're not going to be a top school anymore. You're not going to get good players. Recruits can say all they want about how they liked the coach or the education at a school, but once you place $200,000 before him, that'll sway his decision. Miami businessman John Ruiz has budgeted as much as $10 million to pay players with NILs and use them to advertise his businesses. I've talked with John. His intentions are 100 percent positive. He wants to help kids and help Miami's programs to return to the elite levels back when he went to school there and I was the coach in the 1980s. I also know if Miami has one John Ruiz, some other schools have three or four. If we had this rule back when I was at Oklahoma State, I know several oilmen who would've stepped up and contributed millions. College sports now becomes a game of who has the richest and most generous alumni. If you don't have the alumni, you're going to be a second-tier program.

All this is good for the kids, people will say. Players have deserved to be paid something for some time. But what's going to happen when that top prospect doesn't pan out in the expected manner? Will these boosters or companies apply pressure or cut off the money at some point? What if a kid doesn't meet academic standards and loses a $100,000-a-year job? Can you see the finger-pointing stories of broken promises and innocent kids—or, in some cases, not-so-innocent kids? Will there be lawsuits? Fans turning on the kid, so money goes to the next high recruit?

That's a constant issue in college sports, too: the top recruit who doesn't develop, while the last player you signed becomes a star. Russell Maryland, remember, was the last player signed to his recruiting class and became the No. 1 pick in the NFL Draft.

The people who should be screaming about the NIL issues are colleges' non-revenue-producing sports. Football and men's basketball are the only sports that typically make money at a school. The other non-revenue sports, including women's sports, generally rely on the money from football and basketball and booster donations to the athletic programs. Now those donations are going to buy players. Where will that money be made up for the other sports?

I know people will say this is just boosters paying money aboveboard that they've been forever paying under the table. I coached at nine colleges. A couple of them had NCAA investigations (none directed at me, by the way). But as a coach at so many schools, you hear some truth and many rumors about illicit money and college football. Players worked the edges on occasion, too. While I was a defensive coach at Oklahoma, for instance, players sold their game tickets—especially

the Texas-Oklahoma tickets—for good money. That was an NCAA violation. I also know of players getting some money from a booster. Not
big money. A hundred dollars. Two hundred. That's also a violation.
So is a free meal—another perk I heard players got from boosters. But
does anyone care too hard about stuff like that? I know I don't. That
might break the letter of the law but not the spirit of college sports. A
meal or a little money isn't going to have some undue influence on
kids to go somewhere or stay for another year.

That said, I never saw widespread violations involving big money.
That might surprise people who see college sports as a sewage system
of corruption and backdoor payments. But there was never a time
in recruiting against a team or coaching against a top program that I
heard another school was offering significant money. I certainly didn't
work that way. I never suggested anything to a recruit about paying
him. I was never asked by one, "What are you going to do for me?"

NIL changes all that. You need boosters to do something for the
kids. Their influence moves directly into the lifeblood of recruiting
now. That means as a coach you're not just asking them to invest in a
new weight room or better lockers to compete. Now you're empower-
ing them to have a hands-on ability to work with and influence the
kids. Are coaches ready for what might happen there? Are kids?

The agents come into play, too. They meet the boosters. The
agents strike deals for players. The agents might not be overly excited
about making relatively small deals for players who might not be
drafted years down the line. But what choice do they have except to
get in on the ground floor with players now?

NIL isn't an issue when it comes down to the actual game and the
coaching inside the team. Competition dictates who plays and who
doesn't. That won't change no matter how much a booster pays one
of them. The good players understand that—they want to win jobs
on the field, too. It's no different coaching in college than the pros in

that regard. There may be obvious jealousies inside the team with a recruit who got paid being surpassed by one who didn't get paid.

"How about me?" that player will start asking. "When do I get my money?"

That's something coaches will have to deal with. But regarding the nuts and bolts of coaching, the daily work at practices and deciding who starts, NIL shouldn't have an effect.

As far as the game itself, it seems like the same handful of programs keep winning. Why is that? Success feeds on itself in the college game. Winning helps recruiting and recruiting helps winning. This isn't just true in today's world of Nick Saban's Alabama meeting Georgia or Ohio State atop the polls most every year.

It was how it was decades ago, too.

I could still be winning at Miami.

21

TODAY'S NFL

P eople ask if my ways would work in today's NFL.

"They're working right now," I say.

That's always met with surprise.

"Look at New England," I say.

Bill Belichick coaches the way I did if you get beyond the surface of our different public personalities. The philosophy of football is the same. Physical. Disciplined. Unforgiving of mistakes and creative in game plans. That always was my way.

The league would make me coach differently today, though, and I wouldn't like some aspects of it. We had physical practices in pads in training camp and preseason and scrimmaged on Wednesday, Thursday, and Friday during the season. We never practiced in shorts. We rarely went in shells—helmets and shoulder pads. If we wore shorts in a practice, I got bored. I wanted physical football. The Middle Drill. Daily scrimmages. That's how your team gets better.

Practicing in pads is how you stay healthier, too. I've talked to many trainers and strength and conditioning coaches about this. I even did a FOX show, incorporating their comments. A half dozen trainers said the lack of contact in practice actually leads to more injuries. Players aren't accustomed to falling. They're not used to protecting themselves. I talked to Jacksonville's strength and conditioning coach Tom Myslinski whom I drafted in Dallas, and he said it takes a couple of weeks for players to get accustomed to game speed due to a lack of physical practices.

Don't tell that to the players union. They want legislated rules against hitting in practice. This, too, favors veteran players, considering a rookie still learning the game and system needs physical conditions to improve. Would I have started a Zach Thomas without seeing him excel in a physical training camp?

But since the rules are the rules, great coaches adjust, just as they always have. The Don Shulas and Tom Landrys could coach in any era of football because they adjusted through the years as rules and ideas shifted. They began in the defense-heavy 1960s, employed physical offenses in the 1970s, and opened up their offenses when the rules favored that in the 1980s.

Here's another necessary adjustment to make in today's game: your coaching staff had better be full of good teachers and systems that are easy to pick up. Most teams keep more rookies because of their minimal salaries and can't afford to have many learning from the sideline. So, you have to teach them. Teams are also typically picking up players off the street during the season and need them ready to play. Again, that demands good teaching. These kinds of roster contortions didn't happen in the 1970s or 1980s, when owners could spend whatever they wanted on payroll and players stayed with teams for full careers.

I would change with the times if coaching today, too. I might not have liked it some days—just as I'm sure many of the coaches today don't like some of the practice limitations or roster demands. But it's about winning.

And I liked to win.

Let's talk analytics.

People act like this is some modern creation, like stats and percentages and odds-on decisions haven't been used by quality coaches for decades. We'll get into that. But let's start in the second quarter of the final game of the 2021–22 regular season. Los Angeles Chargers coach Brandon Staley faced a fourth-and-one at his 18-yard line. He trailed at Las Vegas, 17–14. The playoffs were on the line, raising the stakes of every decision. Staley, a first-year NFL coach, became the proud flag-bearer of analytics, as many saw it, by going for it on fourth down, citing that he wanted to lead that way and demanded his team play that way.

No one was more aggressive than I was as a coach. Fourth downs. Fake punts. Whatever it took if a day called for that. But there has to be a risk-and-reward equation to consider in any decision. You have to measure the situation—the score, the time left, sometimes the weather (not in this case, since it was played in a dome).

Facing fourth-and-one, the Chargers ran up the middle and *lost* 2 yards. Las Vegas got the ball at the Chargers' 16-yard line, couldn't move it, and made a simple field goal. So, Staley gift-wrapped three points to Vegas. Those were important points, too, as the game was tied at the end of regulation. The Chargers lost in overtime.

What was the risk in the call? Exactly what played out. That was the best-case scenario, too, as Las Vegas couldn't move 16 yards against the league's 20th-ranked scoring defense for a touchdown. Still, Staley's decision cost three points, which cost the playoffs in some form—a full season lost due to going for it from your own 18-yard line.

Here's the other side of that decision: What was the reward if Staley had gotten that first down? The Chargers would have had the ball at their 20-yard line. They would still have had, what, a 25 percent chance of scoring from there? We can bump that percentage up a bit because Justin Herbert is a great quarterback with plenty of weapons. Thirty-five percent?

Was the risk of giving Vegas three or seven points worth the reward of the Chargers' chance of scoring?

With the season on the line?

Analytics brings more information. You want all the information you can get. It's what you do with the information that matters. Too many coaches use the idea of analytics as a crutch in making decisions.

Here's a simple version of it: The team that kicks off will usually benefit from the better field position early in the game if you have a quality defense. Why? The return is usually around the 20 on most possessions. Teams are usually conservative on their opening series. If the defense allows only one first down, that means after a punt you'll get to start around the 30-yard line.

In 1993, we went into overtime against the New York Giants on a cool, windy January day in the Meadowlands, on the last regular-season game of the year. The NFC East title and a first-round bye were on the table for us. The Giants won the coin flip in overtime and took the ball. That's the way you always choose, right?

"Would you have taken the ball?" Giants quarterback Phil Simms asked me years later.

"No, we would've kicked off," I said.

All the percentages say to take the ball like the Giants did. But those are numbers collected in a vacuum—in domes, on sunny days, irrespective of the offensive and defensive talents.

We got the wind, had the league's best defense, and forced the Giants to punt. We drove to the Giants' 29-yard line thanks in good part to Emmitt Smith, who played through the game with a separated shoulder. Eddie Murray's field goal won the game for Dallas, 16–13.

You see, decisions can't be made solely on percentages. Sometimes the conditions or the matchups matter. The margin for coaching error is small in the NFL, too. Consider the last seven games of the 2021 season, from divisional playoffs through the Super Bowl. The margins of victory were, in order: 7, 3, 3, 3, 3, 3, and 3 points.

Decisions make or break seasons in those games. And it's not as clear-cut as saying afterward that you followed analytics.

Patrick Mahomes. Josh Allen. Joe Burrow. Justin Herbert. Lamar Jackson. Deshaun Watson.

Those are AFC quarterbacks still in their mid-twenties.

Throw in Russell Wilson, Derek Carr, Ryan Tannehill, and Matt Ryan.

Those are some veteran AFC quarterbacks in 2022.

Twenty years ago, if you had a mediocre quarterback, a great running game, and defense you could win a championship. Baltimore did it with Trent Dilfer at quarterback in the 2000 season. Two years later, Tampa Bay's Brad Johnson beat Oakland's Rich Gannon in the Super Bowl.

Those days are gone.

You need a star quarterback to win in today's game. The second most important player on a roster? In another era, I'd say a dominant pass rusher, or maybe a star receiver.

It's the backup quarterback in today's game.

If you don't have a franchise quarterback and one to hold down the fort if your starter goes down for a stretch, your chances of winning a title are pretty slim. Everything is reversed from when Baltimore and Tampa Bay won about two decades ago. You can get away with a mediocre defense and mediocre running game today if you have a great quarterback and passing game. Look at Cincinnati going to the Super Bowl in 2022 with Joe Burrow.

What has caused this evolution? All the game's rule changes favor the offense. Fans like offense. Owners like money. Why do you think the NBA added the three-point line in pro basketball? Such an emphasis on offense means that if you don't have one of those quarterbacks, you'd better do everything to find one. If you have one, you'd better do everything to hang on to him.

In some manner, it's always been that way in the NFL. Look at the Hall of Fame. Almost every Hall of Fame coach is there with a Hall of Fame quarterback. Go through the years. Paul Brown and Otto Graham. Weeb Ewbank and Joe Namath. Don Shula and Johnny Unitas. Bob Griese and Dan Marino. Bill Walsh and Joe Montana. Jimmy Johnson and Troy Aikman.

So why do teams miss on quarterbacks if it's the most important position? Sometimes it's because teams are so desperate for a quarterback, they take chances on one. Sometimes it's the adjustment from college to the pro game, though the difference between the two is decreasing as the NFL involves more spread offenses. Sometimes the organization fails to put enough talent around him to succeed.

Sometimes, too, the problem in picking a quarterback gets back to the most important quality in rating players: intelligence. The second most important requirement for a quarterback? Accuracy. A good decision maker and accurate thrower can overcome a lot of other questions.

A strong arm, for instance, is down the list of requirements. A lot of great quarterbacks haven't possessed strong arms. Joe Montana. Drew Brees. I don't know how strong an arm Tom Brady had until he worked himself into a Hall of Fame quarterback.

Success in the NFL is determined not by who makes the most great plays, but by who makes the fewest bad plays. I wanted the running back who gained 3 or 4 yards and never fumbled, as opposed to the one with breathtaking runs who often fumbled. I wanted the quarterback who dinked and dunked and didn't take a sack or throw an interception as opposed to one with big throws and big mistakes.

Here's a perfect example: in my next-to-last year at the University of Miami, we went undefeated and won a national title with Steve

Walsh. He didn't have a big arm, was slightly built—but he didn't make mistakes. We had recruited Craig Erickson, a freshman who had a great arm. In my infinite wisdom, I declared it an open competition the following spring. We charted every practice play, every scrimmage pass. It wasn't a contest. Walsh didn't get sacked, threw it away on bad plays, and moved the offense. Erickson, then a sophomore, made some big plays but had too many sacks and interceptions. I later confessed to Steve that I expected him to lose the competition.

"You taught me something," I said.

You see why some quarterbacks win and others don't?

Look at that AFC list. Some of them have won Super Bowls. Others are knocking at the door.

Who's the best? I'll turn to Norv Turner, who has worked out all the draft prospects in recent years. He says Joe Burrow looked the best of them. But you can win with several of them. You always needed a good quarterback to have sustained winning, and in this era, you need a great one.

22

HOME

It's a warm, breezy, wave-slapping morning, and I'm running the SeaVee at 16 mph, trolling three lines in two hundred feet of the Atlantic, a Heineken Light in one hand, a glove on the other, ready to handle the wire line when a wahoo hits and—well, I've got a word for this.

Paradise.

"Another day of hard work," I say to my fishing buddies, Ted Connor, Siegy Scholz, and Denny Nelson.

I look out the back of the boat at our lines in the water—and then the vast sweep of ocean running to the horizon. We're ten miles offshore, accompanied by the blue sky and morning sun. I've found peace here, staring out at the endless ocean with a cooler of beer.

We have fish stories through the years, too. Sixty-pound wahoo. Every line in the water being hit at once. Ted, Siegy, and I took a run to the Cay Sal Bank in Bahamian waters, down near Cuba, when we saw a blip on the radar about five miles away. We decided to head for home, not knowing that blip was a Coast Guard cutter chasing us, probably because we were close to Cuban waters. A few minutes later, a helicopter appeared alongside, fifteen feet off the water. It tracked us for a bit.

"Hey, coach, we didn't know it was you!" the pilot said over the loudspeaker.

They did a routine check of our boat and were nice enough to give a warning about some missing paperwork. I volunteered a few motivational speeches to the U.S. Department of Homeland Security and the Coast Guard in appreciation of their work.

My phone rings on the boat.

"Hey, T.B.," I say. "Whatcha got going?"

Terry Bradshaw wants to talk business. Out here, miles from shore, is my preferred office. I've been part of FOX meetings, regularly done radio interviews, conducted business, making sure everyone knows my one rule on the high seas: if I hang up suddenly, it means a fish is on the line.

Truth is, catching a fish is a bonus. I'm just happy on the water, the sun in my face, living the life I want. Maybe what Troy says is true: my greatest feat was knowing how I wanted to live and leaving the seductive fame and fortune of coaching behind, rather than waking up thirty years later wondering where my life went.

Many mornings, I come out fishing alone on one of my 39-foot SeaVees—one has a diesel engine, the other four 350-horsepower outboards. Each is named *Three Rings*, same as their predecessor, though the narrative on the name changed at one point. When I opened a restaurant and got a boat after my first Super Bowl in Dallas, the name referred to my winning a championship ring as a college player, a college coach, and an NFL coach. After the second Super Bowl title, it was easier to drop the ring as a player from discussion rather than change the signs. I'm all about practicality.

I only put on the rings for a photo or a speech these days. Most of my football stuff is kept in a small workout room that no one really sees, and that rigid lifestyle of a well-known coach is tucked in there with it.

The small-town Islamorada lifestyle is the way I roll now. No pretense. No attitudes. No shoes if you want, either. I first came to the Keys early in my University of Miami days on the boat of a booster, Ron Stone. We stopped at Holiday Isle for a rumrunner. We drank another. I don't remember too much of the rest of that trip other than that I was in love with this place. I came back and learned to scuba dive. That became a passion, especially in the break between the Cowboys and Dolphins. My GPS on the boats became marked with lobster holes and my freezer was full of lobsters—it's always full of fish and lobster, for that matter.

I learned to fish in the Keys, too. I started with a Kmart-style rod. It worked good enough to pull in a ninety-pound yellowfin tuna, though you'll have to excuse my friends if they questioned my weight estimates back then. I once got on the boat radio, all excited, saying I had caught a forty-pound wahoo. Then I recalculated it to thirty pounds. By the time we weighed it: nineteen pounds. Don't all fishermen exaggerate?

Slowly, surely, I improved to the point where I now have a room with a hundred rods and enough tackle to start a fishing store. I don't have the patience for backcountry or sit-on-a-reef fishing. My style resembles my football—always on the move, attacking and, in this case, trolling the waters.

Through the years, I picked spots to make the Keys my home—to be part of this community that Rhonda and I have come to love. In 2008, during the recession, I got a call from a mutual friend about a restaurant needing some help. The question was if I'd become part of it to help its owner, Larry Calvano, succeed. That's how "Jimmy Johnson's Big Chill" started. Sales increased 78 percent the first month.

From Larry to the executive chef, Dominic Congemi, Big Chill became my place. I always needed a place to take my crew. Occasionally I'll throw a small party for a friend's retirement, or some other event full of the food I love—nachos, pizza, fried grouper, or conch. Some craziness might break out. I once had a Corvette with a few thousand miles on it but called up my dealer in Homestead during a party.

"When can you have another one here?" I asked.

"Forty-five minutes," I was told.

I put the names of the twenty people at the party in a hat. The name drawn, I said, would get my barely used Corvette. When the guys from the dealership arrived, they offered people a thousand dollars for the right to buy their names in the hat. No one budged. That's how a friend, Marc Brown, drove away with a Corvette that night.

Another time, I stuffed a box full of cash and taped it up. Same deal. Twenty names in a hat. The last name drawn was a single mother who had just lost her job.

"I'll give you five thousand dollars instead of what's in the box," I said.

She kept the box.

"I'll give you ten thousand," I said.

She stayed with the box. It was the right choice. She began crying when she saw the money inside. I might have cried a little that night, too. I enjoy giving things away, enjoy making people happy—enjoy living this chapter in my life more than the previous, more public ones.

I take my John Deere "Gator," a utility vehicle, down the road to Founders Park in Islamorada to the bayside boat of my friend Denny and his wife, Julie. We'll meet friends for events there. The first responders' barbecue lunch. The nautical flea market, where you not only pick up good supplies but have some laughs. This past winter I saw a fishing rod marked for $100 and asked what they'd really take for it.

"It's two hundred for you, you rich bastard!" the guy said.

It was gone when I returned.

"Someone bought it for seventy-five, you cheap bastard!" he said.

That's my Keys—calling me rich and cheap—always keeping me laughing. I get stopped for autographs, for selfies, or just a few words about my 'Canes and am fine playing that role in public. I really am in small doses. I always did the dog and pony show as a coach for boosters or some Chamber of Commerce meeting, always fulfilled my role as a public name working in a public place. But don't get the wrong idea here.

I didn't like being around people then.

I still don't.

My circle of friends is small. I can be rude at times. I don't see many people. I walk five miles most mornings with Denny. I talk on the phone with Nick Christin and Dave Wannstedt once a week, Norv Turner and Tony Wise—every couple of weeks. Terry, being Terry, calls every three or four days.

Other than Rhonda, I might see two people all week out of football season. That's who I am. I enjoy being alone. I enjoy fishing out on my boat alone. I enjoy puttering around the house alone. It doesn't bother me.

Here's a story: Jerry Jones and his wife, Gene, were nice enough to invite me years after I retired to their anniversary party, a big extravaganza in Cowboys Stadium. I typically pass on those events. Terry didn't expect me to attend his seventieth birthday party on his Oklahoma ranch—even if others were shocked that I didn't go. Curt Menefee was having a destination wedding in Europe, and I offered him and his wife congratulations.

"I won't be going," I told them.

But I went for Jerry and Gene's anniversary, due to our times together. It was a big party. Jerry doesn't do anything halfway. They got up and told a story about how the night after I left Dallas, Jerry was lying in bed, head on his pillow, and Gene said, "Now what the hell have you done? You really screwed things up!"

"I know I have," Jerry said.

Everyone laughed. I sat at a table with multimillionaires, and everyone was drinking and having a good time. I was miserable. I don't like small-talking and having social conversations with people I don't know. I got a drink, found an empty room in the stadium, and sat there until it was about over. Then I got Rhonda and came back to Islamorada, to the life I've constructed in retirement.

I putter around the home with small projects or hop in the boat by myself. There's something to being out on the ocean, alone, just the quiet and the separation. I used to look hard to find silence in the circus—now it's right off my dock. I was alone catching my first blue marlin. I had just dropped the lines in the water when one started singing. I alternately brought in the other lines, drove the boat after the marlin, and—my heart pounding, my arm exhausted—brought in the marlin after an hour-and-forty-five-minute fight. That was a day.

I had a different kind of fishing experience alone and twenty miles offshore in 2015 when I felt some pain in my chest. I called Rhonda.

"I'm having a heart attack," I said.

She wanted a helicopter to come and get me. I shoved the throttles down and sped back. It took nearly forty-five minutes. I never felt like it was the end of the line for me, but that was an anxious ride home. When I got to the dock, an emergency squad was waiting. I was put on a gurney. Rhonda was crying. I was taken to the local hospital, then up to Miami, where a second stent was put in.

Islamorada is where I'll be until my heart gives out—even if it gets broken in other ways, too. When Hurricane Irma hit in 2017, I sat in the FOX television studio at 3:30 a.m. Pacific time watching the news. Photos of the damage were sent to me. I hopped on the plane right then, rather than stay for our show. The storm surge brought six feet of water into our property. Sand blew in from the ocean to block our ground floor. Electric lines were down. Our giant tiki hut where we'd sit after fishing was destroyed. The pool had six feet of sand in it.

When Rhonda and I arrived, we began crying. We were two of the lucky ones, too. The damage was worse south of us. We had the money to rebuild. And we, all of us in the Keys, rebuilt paradise, too.

I've had fun throughout my good life.

But the happiest I've been is living right here.

In May of 2022, nearly three decades after our first Super Bowl, I had some of my old crew down to Islamorada. Dave Wannstedt. Tony Wise. Norv Turner. Butch Davis. Rich Dalrymple. Troy Aikman. We told stories, laughed hard, and enjoyed each other's company in a way we never did while winning those Super Bowls.

"Maybe this is the time we were meant to enjoy our winning," I said at one point.

All my life, I didn't believe in luck. I believed the harder you worked, the luckier you got. But standing there with my crew that weekend I again realized how much good fortune actually played into my success.

I'm older now, hopefully wiser. I've always said everyone carries a bag of rocks through life. Some bags are heavier than others. I was fortunate to be around people who lightened my load in a way I can see now. It started with being born into a solid, hardworking family. We didn't have a lot of money, but we had a lot of love. My parents gave me discipline and determination. Those were tools I needed to achieve. My friends growing up in Port Arthur helped me understand and appreciate people of different financial, racial, and social backgrounds. That helped me deal with people as individuals.

I was fortunate Jerry Jones and I went to college together and developed a friendship that led to our working together decades later in Dallas. My early career rubbed up against smart coaches like Frank Broyles, Chuck Fairbanks, Johnny Majors, and Jackie Sherrill. They opened opportunities for me.

Those opportunities and hard work helped me be successful. People wonder if I needed to work that hard or could have maintained a better balance in life. I look at the successful people from the top football coaches to CEOs of companies. Jerry and Wayne Huizenga are perfect examples. They worked hard and sacrificed. Wayne, as successful as he was, said in his sixties he never played his beloved golf during the week. That's how he worked to achieve at that level. I liked to go in early before anyone else arrived to plan my day and concentrate on specific issues. When I hired Norv Turner, I'd arrive at my normal 5 a.m. and he'd already be there. I came in at 4:30 a.m. the next morning and he still was there. It became a competition.

"Hey," I told him, "we keep beating each other to the office, we're not going to get any sleep. We have to make a pact when we'll arrive."

We laughed about such stories that weekend together. My crew is mostly retired now. My players are now coaches. Mario Cristobal invited me in the spring of 2022 to talk to his University of Miami players. Mario tells stories about me as a coach. They're big stories about how I built his team into champions and small ones about how I made a deal with the devil to keep the afternoon thunderstorms from rolling in off the Everglades until practice was done.

Like my crew, Mario remembers the Pygmalion Effect, too. It was part of every stop in my career. Of course, one of the best examples of the Pygmalion in action was my applying it to a kid who became the first in his family to attend college. Football provided him an opportunity. An education. A broadened path. How could he maximize that chance? What heights could he reach if he were *treated as he could be and should be*?

I believed. I set high expectations.

I Pygmalioned myself.

Now it's Mario's time, his ways, his chase for the next win, just as it is for all those coaches and general managers who visit in the Keys. I talked to Mario's players about what their coach was part of at their age, something we created with our great Miami teams . . .

"Something that started right here in Miami—*swagger*," I said. "People get confused about swagger. Sometimes people look at the old Miami teams and they say swagger was celebrating. No. Swagger is confidence. You're confident that you're going to kick somebody's ass. That's what swagger is.

"We were one of the least penalized teams in the entire country. We didn't taunt. But we were excited. We celebrated. I wanted our guys to be excited, to be enthusiastic. Swagger."

Those teams reflected me.

My best teams always did.

ACKNOWLEDGMENTS

This book was the idea of my good friend Nick Christin and guided from the start by literary agent David Black, who has some swagger of his own. Thanks to Brian Belfiglio's deft editing and Emily Polson's good eye and the team at Simon & Schuster. Finally, and most important, a deep appreciation to all the coaches, players, team officials, and friends through the years who are part of my story.

INDEX